Dancing 'Round the Han

A life-changing book and resources to su
hard-working women to dance to their own tunes
and find balance between work and life

Dedications and Thanks

This book is dedicated to my daughters Catherine and Jennifer, who have yet to experience the dance of juggling work and life; I hope that this will be of use when they do. However, I actually hope that the world of work will have changed in a way that is supportive of their need for balance, their need to play to their strengths as women, and also provides them with an environment in which to release their potential to dance their best life.

This book is also dedicated to my dear friend Ali Dawson – my ALLY, soul-sister and my business partner in ALLY Coaching & Mentoring. Ali is just there, alongside me, there for me on the brilliant days and the dark days. Her unconditional love and support in work and in life make her so special to me. I hope she walks beside me for life; I am so grateful.

I love you all deeply, and always will.

Dancing
'Round the Handbags

A life-changing book and resources to
support hard-working women to dance
to their own tunes and find balance
between work and life

Lynne Copp

Anoma
PRESS

Dancing 'Round the Handbags

*A life-changing book and resources to support hard-working women
to dance to their own tunes and find balance between work and life*

First published in 2012 by

Anoma Press

48 St Vincent Drive, St Albans, Herts, AL1 5SJ, UK

info@anomapress.com

www.anomapress.com

Designed by Michael Inns
Artwork by Karen Gladwell

Printed on acid-free paper from managed forests. This book is printed
on demand, to fulfill orders, so no copies will be remaindered or pulped.

ISBN 978-1-907722-64-6

Contents

Thanks and Acknowledgements

I would like to offer thanks and heartfelt gratitude to all my women-folk who have always been there in the background, listening to me rave on about the book, and encouraging me to 'get it out there' because 'women need this book!' They have also supported me to dance to the right tunes, de-clutter my handbag when needed and have stepped on to that dance floor with me! This book is dedicated to all of those who have danced, have watched me dance and know all the tunes!

They are:

My close friends – Beverley Beasley, Karen Kilworth, Kim Leitch, Laura Campbell, Wendy Frost and Lisa Hurley and finally my dear friend Jo Lynch, who, like Ali, has been a guide, coach, adviser and friend for so many years. Thank you for your encouragement!

Thanks also to my family whose support and love, pushing me to get the book finished, has driven me on to manage my critical voices as well as my time, particularly my husband Kevin, my mum, my mum-in-law and my sisters Claire and Caroline.

Finally, to all the women out there who are part of my network, those who support me, encourage me and keep on nagging me to get the book out there. I would particularly like to mention my network of business Goddesses: Sylvia Baldock and Jacqueline Rogers (Goddesses of The Athena Network), Elaine Yarbrough (Goddess of Gender Communication), Dr Lynda Shaw (Goddess of Neuro-Science), Laurelle Rond (Goddess of Sound), HP Goddesses - Fiona Barnes, Karen Rizzello, Corinne Buivenga, Marian Edwards and Roisin Reilly. Sarah Speake (Goddess of Google), Vicki Cooper (Goddess of IBM), Judith Eastwood (Goddess of BAE Systems), Shirley Horn (Goddess of California – all of it!) and Mariann Harris (Goddess of Birmingham).

My thanks too, to Mindy Gibbins-Klein, my publisher at Anoma Press. We met five years ago at The Professional Speakers Association and she has quietly, patiently and yet assertively badgered and encouraged me to write the book. She has danced alongside until I was ready to hand over the final manuscript. Her patience is her virtue; it's not easy to influence a perfectionist!

Finally, thank you to the creative and energetic source that played the first few notes of this tune to me in a dream in 1994, allowed me to turn up the volume within, catch the rhythm of the beat and compose it into a wonderful book that can help women to dance their best life.

Foreword

The idea for this book danced into my handbag of consciousness in 1994. At that time I had been promoted to Head of Learning & Development and Diversity for HP. The role required relocation to Bristol from Reading. My daughters were two and one, my husband and I had just split, my live-in nanny didn't fancy moving to Bristol and my marital house had been sold at great loss in a recession. I had to find a new home, a new nanny, settle the children, manage the debt, redirect, reorganise and renew everything from furniture to utility bills and, at the same time, wind down my old role in HR whilst developing strategies and team trust in my new. To define the challenges as 'stressful' would not really capture the extent of the exhaustion, worry, guilt, fear, sadness, happiness and terror of that time. My inner resilience and belief that things would get better pulled me through. After a year of two nannies, chicken pox, an ant infestation, two house moves, business transformation strategies aligned with long-term leadership development and a divorce, my body and mind were almost ready to give up the ghost! I remember crawling (literally) up to bed one night and after a cursory tooth clean and wash, collapsed into a well-earned slumber. In my world of balancing two tiny children with a huge, demanding job and the stresses of building a new life, I discovered that my bed and sleep were absolute luxury! I would long for that time when the children were asleep, the dishwasher loaded, the email tamed and the house silent. I loved the feeling of slipping between the cool sheets into my big king-size bed and drifting off into a well-earned coma!

One particular night as I lay in motionless rejuvenation of my body, I had a very strange and yet memorable dream. In it, a tall, slim and unrecognisable figure stood in front of me. 'You are going to write a book, the book is called Dancing 'round the Handbags.' I awoke suddenly, and as I lay there in that dreamy state, I said to myself, 'What a fabulous title for a book!'

I wrote the name of the book on a piece of paper so as not to forget it. It sounded quite strange and I couldn't imagine myself writing about nightclubs and dancing, but maybe I was to write something else? The idea danced in my mind as I ate breakfast and set off to drive the fourteen miles to the office. HP in Bristol used to be a really beautiful site, a real showcase campus, with three state-of-the-art buildings and leisure facilities. It was a great place to work, a little piece of California, nestled in the leafy suburbs of Filton in Bristol. Our neighbours at UWE (University of the West of England) next door were often encouraged to use the campus and its facilities as well as get involved in the engineering innovations that were being developed on site. Creativity and innovation was core to HP and the leadership culture encouraged people to tap into and find time for creative pursuits. People were encouraged to get away from their desk, walk, play squash at one of the on-site courts, attend an aerobics class (which were scheduled throughout the day), play any number of sports, paint, draw, read or run around the trim trail! If it encouraged innovation, well-being and balance, then that was good enough for the HP culture. We worked hard and yet we played hard, and HP's business results and employee engagement soared. As I walked from my car into the building where my L&D team were housed, I bumped into one of our senior managers, a fantastic and well-respected woman who headed up one of our major technological functions. We shared our 'good mornings' and I then said, 'I had the most amazingly vivid dream last night! I was told that I was to write a book!' 'It wasn't called Dancing 'round the Handbags was it?' she interjected. My blood ran cold; I could not believe what I had just heard. 'Yes!' I managed to respond, and she continued, 'Lynne, I had a dream last night that I was going to be asked to contribute to that book and that I should do it, because it was going to be an important book for women.'

Later that day, I was talking to a wonderful and experienced colleague with whom I was working who was based in Colorado. Her name is Elaine Yarbrough and she runs an organisation called The Yarbrough Group. Elaine has over 30 years of experience in gender diversity and facilitation of leadership cultures as they change. She is an amazing role model and ally for women in the workplace. She and I were working together to bring her very successful 'Women and Men Working Together' programme into HP and were scheduled to talk that afternoon. I told her about my dream and about my conversation that morning. 'Wow!' she yelled, in her endearing Texas accent. 'I was flying into Colorado from San Francisco last weekend and was reading the in-flight magazine. There was a line in the article that said "Dancing 'round the handbags". It jumped out at me from the page and I said to myself, "That's the title of Lynne's book isn't it?"'

I don't know how you feel about this or what you think, but I know one thing for sure: I only need three coincidences and I am sitting up and listening! At the end of the day, and as I slipped between the sheets of solace once more, I reflected on the events of those 24 hours and, with mixed emotions of excitement, trepidation and curiosity, I committed to writing this book that you are now holding.

As I finish this last entry for the book, it is now 2011 and those days of exhaustion and just surviving every day seem a faded and ghostly memory. In 1994 I had no idea what the book was going to be about, nor did I have time to write it. In the 16 years that have danced between the message and the publication, I have lived, worked, raised my two beautiful daughters, moved house three times, set up my own business and remarried. I have coached, trained and supported women in their worklife balance and I have watched, learned and developed solutions for businesses large and small. I have gained recognition for my skills and speaking and, through every step of the dance, have choreographed all the best lessons into a book – a very special book. Hindsight is a wonderful thing and, as I look back, I realise now that I could not have written this and begun to compose tunes for future books without living the journey of experience that has allowed this book to now be shared with women and men across the world in a way that absolutely, and with love, encompasses the metaphor of the handbag and the dance. Enjoy it, scribble in it, buy it for your friends and make the changes happen that are so necessary.

Dancing 'round the Handbags® uses the metaphors of the dance and the handbag to support you, the reader, to reflect on your work and life and make the changes necessary for you to achieve balance and what you want. By tapping into the feminine aspects of leadership, influence and communication, it supports you to de-clutter the handbag that is you, and rejoin the dance floor of life, dancing to the tunes that you want to dance to. Dancing 'round the Handbags® has already been life-changing for many of the women who attend the workshops and seminars.

Chapter 1 in the book is The Dance. The Dance is a metaphor for what women do each day: dance to the tunes of others. These are all the day-to-day tunes that either project women towards their purpose and goals or hold them back, creating imbalance, stress and guilt. The multiple roles of mother, wife, boss, friend, daughter, lover, cook and colleague etc. mean that a woman sometimes dances to too many tunes all at once. This often results in rarely having time for herself, soon forgetting her own dreams and doubting her unique potential, her own music.

The handbag in this book is a metaphor for being female and the remaining chapters are different handbag items, each being a metaphor for varying aspects of a woman's work and life. For example, the Mirror chapter explores her image, how she sees herself; the Lipstick explores how women mask stress to show resilience and coping ('putting on a brave face'); and the Diary chapter explores worklife time and priorities.

Dancing 'round the Handbags® is a self-development book, series of workshops and one-to-one coaching aimed at hard-working women. Using the metaphor of the handbag and the dance, it supports you to create clarity about personal direction whilst maintaining balance between your work and life. Beyond that, it is a catalyst to change the way we work and live. Our societies, workplaces and families are out of balance and it is essential that we redress the balance if we are to maintain well-being and create a lasting legacy for the way we want to live. By reviewing your dances and de-cluttering your handbag, you will return to the dance floor of life, to dance to the tunes that you want to dance to.

Oh, there is one more thing about the book that you should know. Throughout the book there is a fictional story that sets the scene for each chapter and puts in context the sorts of things that we have to juggle on a day-to-day basis. I believe that stories are important; they create myths and legends, campfire stories that built nations, communities and cultures as well as entertain and bewitch us with possibility and imagination. In ancient tribes, women passed stories on to new generations and I believe that in our busy and frenetic lives, we are losing the precious time to just sit down, as women, tell stories and talk at our deepest levels, learn from each other and from the wisdom of our elders. The tale in this book is about a character called Karen. Karen is 40 years old; she has a husband called James and two children, Tilly and Josh. Karen also has elderly parents and her dad has dementia. Karen's friend Lucy has just undergone breast cancer treatment and has a baby girl, Annabel, who is 11 months. Karen works for a large general hospital and is a fully-qualified staff nurse who works full-time on the men's ward. James is an IT engineer and works for a large Blue Chip. When not working, Karen takes care of her family, parents and looks after baby Annabel three nights a week when she is on day shift, to allow her friend some rest. Karen is exhausted. She rarely has a moment to herself and, as time goes by, her dreams and goals are being pushed further and further down the list. Karen's life is very similar to so many other women's and illustrates the worklife balance challenges faced day to day. However, Karen is about to meet someone who can really help, and through that help this book can also bring help to you too.

I love stories, and when my daughters were little I loved the bedtime routine of bath time, clean pyjamas and the girls excitedly snuggling down under their covers for a bedtime story before dropping off to sleep. Whilst teatime, homework, hair-washing and the occasional visit of head-lice combs were always exhausting and fractious, the bedtime story was a time anchored with relaxation, imagination and love. Just recently I commented to a friend to savour these moments and enjoy every one, because children very soon bathe themselves, take themselves off to bed and want to read their own books. I cannot remember the last time I read to my girls at bedtime, I don't even remember what that very last story was. If someone had told me 'tonight will be the last bedtime story ever!' I might have filmed it or marked it on a calendar. That magical, enchanting and loving time just fizzled out and blended into all the other memories of tooth-fairy visits, stabilisers being removed from bikes and the fateful Christmas when Father Christmas was no longer real. Therefore I have included this story throughout, so that you too can tap into those days of childhood when your imagination and dreams were formed. As a girl, you, like me, would have read stories and also made a few up in your head. You would have imagined a life that you could live, the house that you would live in, the family, children, friends etc. that you might have. What did you want to be when you grew up? The story in this book will support you to gain clarity about your purpose and direction.

In each chapter you will be encouraged to go to Karen's world and then explore your own. In addition to the book, there are downloadable audio files and other resources, which will support you to implement the lessons from each of the chapters. These are summarised below:

- **The Dance floor Meditation** – *Visit your dance floor and review the dances that you currently dance to.*

- **My Tissues** – *Explore your health and well-being and how you might improve both.*

- **My Diary** – *Look at how you manage your time.*

- **My Lipstick** – *Explore the masks you wear and your authentic self.*

- **My Mirror** – *Here you will take a look at your image – both internal and external.*

- **My Phone** – *The phone is about your communication networks, both social and professional.*

- **My Purse** – *Discover choice and change and how you deal with both.*

- **My Snack** – *Discover your strengths, your development plan and the skills and capabilities you need for the future.*

- **My Keys** – *Symbols of the keys to your heart and the keys to your success. You will discover your needs in terms of the home and your values and beliefs.*

- 🍂 **My Photos** – *In this chapter, you will reflect on your relationships and how they impact your balance and link to your sense of security.*
- 🍂 **My Perfume** – *The perfume relates to your identity, your purpose and your sense of femaleness through spirituality and sense of community.*
- 🍂 **My Pen** – *In the final chapter, you will explore your goals and the vision for your life.*

As I finish this Foreword I want to end with a lesson that I received recently. I received a gift and wise message from my mum. She rarely writes, but she sent me a card and in it she placed the poem that I include at the end of this page, one that many of you will have seen before. Take time to really read it, I did. My mum added a few words of her own in the card, words that resonated at a much deeper level and in fact made the poem much more poignant. Her words are the basis of this book and its deepest lesson. She wrote,

'I don't know whether or not you've ever read this poem; I think it's lovely. I am so proud of you in all you do and ever will do, but do remember your "me-time". Take care, lots of love, mum xxx'

This intuitive gift said: don't be too busy to forget your family, not watch a sunset, have some me-time, and don't be so successful that you have no time to just enjoy what you have now as well as what you can create. Don't be so tired that you forget your mum, your friends and your daughters – your women folk. Take time to listen to your own music and to the notes playing from others that could support you to dance your best life!

As I reflect, I realise that great women surround me and, when all is said and done, it is they who are the best and most important in supporting me to choreograph this dance of life and work. Each has the wisdom to know when to let me dance and when to pull me off the dance floor. Their wisdom has been, and is, key to my personal growth. The women in my life provide wisdom when needed and silence when not. Through the hugs, conversations, tears, tissues, rants, laughter and love, they listen without judgement, empathise without fixing and support with unconditional love. Thank you for being there to support me to dance my best life.

Slow Dance

Have you ever watched kids on a merry-go-round?
Or listened to the rain slapping on the ground?
Ever followed a butterfly's erratic flight?
Or gazed at the sun into the fading night?
You'd better slow down.
Don't dance so fast.
Time is short.
The music won't last.

Do you run through each day on the fly?
When you ask 'How are you?' do you hear the reply?
When the day is done, do you lie in your bed
With the next hundred chores running through your head?
You'd better slow down
Don't dance so fast.
Time is short.
The music won't last.

Ever told your child 'We'll do it tomorrow?'
And in your haste, not see his sorrow?
Ever lost touch, let a good friendship die
Cause you never had time to call and say 'Hi'?
You'd better slow down.
Don't dance so fast.
Time is short.
The music won't last.

When you run so fast to get somewhere
You miss half the fun of getting there.
When you worry and hurry through your day,
It is like an unopened gift... thrown away.
Life is not a race, do take it slower
Hear the music before the song is over.

David L. Weatherford

1 My Dance

I used to have dreams and goals for myself!
Nowadays my life seems to revolve around dancing to the
tunes of others. I have precious little time for myself and find
it very difficult to say 'No!' to colleagues, family and friends.
I dance to many tunes all at once: mother, lover, employee,
friend, daughter, sister, boss, counsellor, cook, cleaner, wife,
and more! The sad thing is that I have danced to the tunes of
others for such a long time that I have almost forgotten my
own music; my dreams, skills and desires feel like they are
drowned out forever. I feel tired, worn out and I hardly even
know what my music is any more...

Balance is our natural state
of being; it is the meeting point
of two complementary opposites
in the dance of life.

The room is dark, the strobe lights pulse, the music starts to play and, in a frenzied surge of enthusiasm, you and your friends migrate on to the dance floor, all keen to dance to your favourite tune. You claim your dance floor territory, squashed into the writhing mass of other willing dancers. The rising crescendo of music whips your body into spontaneous rhythmic movement and, mimicking those around, you conform to the beat. The track soon changes and you find yourself gyrating to a different tune, maybe this time to a different group of onlookers. Very slowly, in the continuous rhythm of the dance, you become oblivious to your surroundings, locked into the world of your own motion. The faces around you become invisible, the dance more subconscious and hypnotised by the demands of the beat, you are in a place where little conscious thought exists, only movement. Movement is key. To stand still would be weird... to stand still would not be an acceptable option. You continue to move, to blend, to become one of the massive spasm of humans entrained in synchronised motion that maintain the heartbeat of the dance. Eventually, the music stops and you snap back into a world without dancing, a real world that has no audible beat. You are tired; it's time to sit the next one out...

Life is a bit like that too. We become hypnotised into a world of 'doing', of moving to the beat of others, dancing to other people's tunes. We give little thought to what, why and how. We dance; from the moment we rise in the morning to the time we drop back into bed at night, exhausted by the dance of life. We have periods that seem to be even more challenging and busy than others. During those times we do so much dancing that we have precious little time to reflect or prepare for the next task. In work we run from meeting to meeting, in life we run from main carer to taxi driver! However, at the end of each day we often feel little sense of achievement, just exhaustion and stress of too much to do.

As women we continue to dance this way with a belief that when the children grow, the husband shares the load, the boss becomes less demanding or the world slows down a little, we will be able to find time for ourselves to dance to our dreams. As the years pass, the dream of running our own business, or gaining a degree, or doing something different becomes a faded memory. Alongside this daily existence of frenetic activity grows the nagging seed of doubt; a sense that you deserve, want, crave a different dance – but HOW? For some, it merely manifests in day-dreaming of a different life, fantasising about what we would do, be or have if we had choice. The sad fact is that many women feel they have no choice but to dance their life this way until its last note plays.

Putting everyone else's requests and needs first is a common dilemma, but if you are going to be effective at looking after your personal resources, workload and time, surely it is important to avoid allocating your time solely on the basis of those who demand it? In a busy day, it is easy to be sucked into the turmoil of other people's priorities for you: 'Mum! Where's my gym kit?', 'Wife! Where is my clean shirt?', 'Employee! Have you done that report yet?'

Instead, it may be better to allocate your time on the basis of those things that deserve it, and that includes time for you. Almost everyone that you encounter will think they have a better idea than you about how you should spend your time and conduct your life. If you keep saying yes to their demands, all that will happen is that you will become even more exhausted and they will continue to demand. By the end of your life, you will have done lots that you cannot remember and achieved little that you dreamed of.

For many elderly women that I have spoken to, there is a real sense of regret, a real sense that they have danced to the tunes of others for such a long time and that their life has passed them by. These women say, 'I wish I could have my time over again, I would do things differently.'

In contrast, some women in the middle of their life (often when their partners or friends are beginning to think about, or actually wind down towards, retirement) notice an orchestra of change warming up inside them. These women ask, 'Is this all that I am? After 30 years of working (in and/or outside the home), working for employers, caring for others; is this all I have to show for it – a sub-standard pension and dishwasher hands?' Suddenly, inside, a new or often a re-mixed song begins its drumbeat of rhythmic passion, becoming louder each day and swelling

to a crescendo as its lyrics chant across the rooftops of opportunity, singing It's my turn'!' These women suddenly lift up their handbags and ignite with a burning desire to do something significant – to dance to their own tune! They leave their employer, set up their own businesses, climb mountains, open cottage industries, study degree courses, set up charities, emigrate and some even leave their home and family to start a completely new life – alone. Whatever the outcome, the fact is that this is more than a midlife crisis; this is a need for them to ignite their suppressed dreams and goals to make a difference, do something significant. In the UK, of all the businesses started by women, 68% are started by women who have had enough of dancing to the tunes of others!

If you are reading this book, you are probably now ready to take time out to explore your own dance – your life, before it's too late. If you are, then use it to make the rest of your life truly significant. Your journey will be unique to you; no one else will dance the way you dance. This book will provide you with choices about your music, choices about how you may want to dance, choices about when to rest and choices about how to dance your best life! Choice is key because you are not being forced to change, or indeed stay the same.

But what is worklife balance and how do you know if you have balance or not?

Balance is our natural state. We seek balance in many ways; too much or too little of one thing or another generally encourages us to seek balance. Balance is the harmony created when two opposing extremes blend. Balance between work and life allows us to experience the natural give and take that creates appropriate choice. If you feel that you have choice to work hard and give of your best, balanced with the choice to go home so that you can engage with family, friends or leisure activity, then you feel in control and are likely to have a better sense of balance. When you feel you have no choice but to work long hours, or care for others too much, or be at everyone's beck and call, then you are more likely to feel a sense of imbalance. Imbalance creates stress and stress directly impacts your well-being, relationships and ultimately your work and life balance.

Consider worklife balance represented by a pair of scales. On one side we have work and on the other we have life. They are not separate, but joined by the pivot that creates balance between both. Sometimes the scales experience increased pressure, or load, on one side or another. Once the pressure is removed, then the scales can naturally fall back into perfect balance. Sometimes this happens in work or in life. For example, workload increases due to a customer deadline and you are forced to work longer and harder for a period of time to meet the need. During this busy time, work becomes the focus and you sacrifice life priorities in order to deliver what is required. Once the project is complete, the pressure is relieved and you can revert to a more balanced environment. Alternatively, one morning you wake to find that your child is sick, your car has broken down or your elderly parent has fallen ill. In those emergency situations, life comes first and so work is sacrificed while you deal with the challenge.

Sometimes, life and work issues are more long-term, e.g. caring for a terminally-ill parent or wishing to work fewer hours while your children are small or taking time out to run for the British Team in the Olympic Games. These are not emergencies, but they are life needs and life always comes first. The most important thing is that in order to achieve balance there should be give and take on both sides; giving to work as required and taking time for life as required. Work and life pressure happens,

alternating like this, and balance occurs when there is give and take and a sense of choice. However, some people feel as if they have no choice, and that is when too much stress is exerted on both sides of the scales.

The scales, just like our work and life, become out of balance for two reasons:

1. Too much load is placed on one side for prolonged periods of time, causing the scales to be permanently tipped one way or the other.

2. Too much pressure is exerted on both sides at once, which creates too much pressure on the pivot and it eventually snaps.

Many people experience the first symptom above, and often report that the scales are tipped towards work. We will explore the reasons and implications of work imbalance later in the chapter. However, some have been known to experience the second, and this is more dangerous in terms of your natural well-being. In general, women experience the second more than men because 86% of caring responsibilities in a family are still carried out by women. Most women hold down at least two full-time jobs – employee and main carer in a family.

Let us consider work and life, and what creates imbalance for women.

What is work?

-   **A source of income** – the money that you need to live the life you have or want to have.

-   **A career** – many people regard work as a career; striving towards a goal, a desired job, your own business, having certain expertise and being well-regarded for the career you have.

-   **A vocation** – for some people, work is more than just an income or a career, it is a vocation, 'who' they are. It expands beyond the traditional vocations of nursing, teaching, etc. and includes any role that defines your identity.

-   **A purpose** – some of the most stressed people in our society are the long-term unemployed because they have no reason to put their feet on the floor in the morning. Having a sense of purpose is key to our well-being and balance.

🦢 **A social environment** – *we meet many friends at work and many people meet their life partner, too. It is a social community and because we are herding animals, that sense of belonging and team collaboration is important.*

What is life?

🦢 **Family** – *what does family mean to you? It could be traditional: partner, children, mother, father, siblings etc. or, for you, family could be your next-door neighbour or your friends – who do you regard as family?*

🦢 **Friends** – *your close friends, chums and acquaintances, your work friends, your relationships and social interactions.*

🦢 **Leisure** – *hobbies, pastimes, holidays, sports, groups, interests, fun and social life.*

🦢 **Learning** – *could be qualifications, art classes, reading books like this! Learning a new language, a new skill or learning more about you.*

🦢 **Self** – *me-time, spiritual development, personal growth, pampering, caring for you, well-being and health. Self comes at the foot of the list because, for most women, that is where it is.*

Flexible working allows organisations and people to ensure that the scales continue to swing from side to side in perfect balance. Sadly, in our working world the demands of work often far outstrip the demands of life. Scales are snapping under the severe stress of long hours, unreasonable targets and the demands of out of date leadership styles.

If the scales of worklife balance are tipped towards work then the most common reasons for that imbalance are:

🦢 Workload

🦢 *Interruptions*

🦢 *Unachievable targets*

🦢 *Management style*

🦢 *Long hours or presenteeism culture*

🦢 *Self - Work addiction*

When the scales are tipped towards life, the most common reasons for imbalance are:

- Childcare issues
- Sick child or relative
- Long-term caring responsibilities
- Emergency
- Hobby, pastime or community commitment
- Self – health, mental health, capability

Imbalance also occurs when the demands of both sides put a woman under so much stress that she literally snaps. In the UK, 80% of all sickness absence is work-related and 46% of that is worklife imbalance.

In my book I'm Glad I Spent More Time at Work I refer to the long-hours culture and the demands that this places on all people, but especially women. We work 44% longer hours in the UK than any of our European Union neighbours and we are 27% less productive. That makes no business sense! Just like the scales that are always tipped to one side, sooner or later there is no time for life as it is all dedicated to the long-hours addiction.

Just because someone works longer does not mean that they are effective, efficient, creative, innovative and productive. In fact, over time, the opposite is true. The long-hours macho culture of measuring commitment by hours worked is an out of date and useless leadership approach. This approach does not suit the female style of leadership and does not suit her life demands either. If promotion, success and better salaries are awarded based on the perceived notion of hard work (i.e. hours of input) then women's future in the world of work does not look good. However, there is a move towards the female leadership style and this is the subject of my next book.

Women in the current business model do not succeed as well as men – fact! On average, only 10% of working women ever reach senior levels; in the USA it is a whopping 11%! Some countries fare better, but in truth there is not a picture of consistency or equality. This is unacceptable;

over 50% of graduates are female (most clutching better grades than their male student friends), and yet the complexity of experiences and cultures literally weeds them out. Of the women that have risen (and well done to them), at what cost have they done so? What have they had to sacrifice – their family, identity or their female leadership style? I know many who have held on to all three and I applaud them, they are true role models. I understand that this is a complex issue, and that there are many facets to explore; however, there is one key statistic above all the others listed below that I would draw your attention to:

76% of senior women (75% of the 11%) have a life partner (husband/ partner) who is in an equally professional role. 75% of men in senior roles (which is 90% of senior managers) have a wife who stays at home. Source: Boston Study of Senior Women

I suspect that it is the same in the UK, and our new study will look at this data. However, is it any wonder that there is little empathy for a female need for flexibility and a different way of working?

Our cultures of long hours, presenteeism and old-fashioned leadership styles demand a traditional approach to work in which women and young employees find it particularly difficult to operate. 86% of caring responsibilities in a family still fall on the woman to do; and caring can take up to 50 hours a week – two full-time jobs! If employers demand that people turn up by 7:00 a.m. and don't leave until 8:00 p.m., then how do children get to school, little ones to nursery? Horses fed? Parents cared for? I know one employee who was taken to task for turning up 15 minutes late every day, even though she was their star performer and had earned that business over £4M in sales. She couldn't get to work any earlier! She had a three-year-old son to drop at nursery before her commute through the city traffic to get to the office for her 8:30 a.m. start. She and her baby had been getting up at 5:30 a.m. every day since she returned from maternity leave. When she dropped him off at 7:30 a.m. (opening time of the nursery), she then had an hour-long commute to work. Her company was measuring her on time (input) rather than contribution (output). She resigned. They lost talent and commitment; she lost her

job, her dignity and her sense of respect for this employer – all because of inflexibility! If employers are inflexible, it leads to the attrition of women, but it also prevents women from applying for jobs and being promoted. Studies show that in the ten years after having a child, only 4% of women ever get promoted. This is partly due to inflexible organisations (how many macho companies call meetings at 8:00 a.m. or 6:00 p.m.?), but it is also to do with women having no more to give; juggling work and family is enough without having the added burden of managing a career. It is no wonder that women cannot break through glass, and indeed concrete, ceilings. In the UK today, 41% of parents spend less than an hour a day with their children! What are we doing to our family structures and communities and future by demonstrating to our young people that they are less important than a meeting or email? In research carried out by The Worklife Company, 94% of employees across all sectors said that they would stay with their employer if they were given more flexibility (there was in fact no gender difference in this study).

When I worked for the Hewlett Packard organisation, our CEO at that time was a man called Lew Platt. He sadly lost his wife when his children were very young. He knew the struggles of bringing up a family and holding down one of the top jobs in the IT sector. However, this man was a fantastic role model for flexible working, working from home, worklife balance and diversity. His children have now grown up and Lew himself sadly passed away a few years ago, but not before he had created a culture of dignity, trust and respect for all the people who worked at HP in those days. Many leaders today could learn the lessons from this great man and those that demand long hours and create no dignity and respect will, one day soon I hope, topple into the abyss of dinosaur bones to which they belong. As Michael Gerber says in his books, 'the fish always rots from the head down' and so leaders everywhere need to wake up to the future of work and the flexibility that is required to create great places to work for women as well as men.

Women juggle roles and tunes for many years, more tunes than the previous generation, and many are hitting the wall – dropping down exhausted, stressed, ill or dead. This is a growing predicament as more women work outside the home. Today in 78% of married couples, both partners work outside the home and one in six of those has children under the age of 16. We are also living in an ageing population where, on average, 26% of women in the workforce have responsibility for elderly or dependent relatives. Women are also delaying having their first child until much later. In the 1950s/1960s, mothers had their first child (on average) somewhere between the age of 18 and 24. Today the average age of a professional woman when she has her first child is around 30. By that age, a woman has established herself in an organisation, she doesn't want to lose her career, and she believes that she can dance to the company tune, the motherhood tune and the eldercare tune all at the same time. Some can and do, by adapting and sacrificing, but many cannot. 49% of mothers do not return to work after giving birth and many cite lack of flexibility from their employer as their main reason.

The world of work must change. We must change it for the sake of our future success as a nation. 68% of female business owners set up their organisations because of their need for both flexibility and a working style that suited their female leadership skills. They said that they had become sick and tired of the inflexibility and incongruent working practices of the companies they were employed by.

It's not all bad; there are some organisations that provide a great working environment for women – in fact, all of their people – but there are still aspects of the female that they are not adopting in their business model. Recent reports show that those banks that have a mix of women and men in senior positions have actually fared better in the financial downturn than their all-male counterparts. Is this coincidence or is there substance in this argument that mixed gender is better for business management teams? I suspect the latter, and seek to prove these aspects in my research and will share much in this book.

What do women need? By the end of this book you will know what you need, and that is the gift I give to you. By raising your self-awareness, you can begin to understand and hear your true internal music and be able to dance to your own tune.

What do you dance to?

Our story ...

Karen couldn't remember the last time she had had a day to herself. It seemed like years ago. It was not that she didn't want to take time for herself, it was just that with the children, the job, the housework, her ageing parents and her friend's breast cancer scare, she just didn't seem to have time. In fact, just recently she had noticed that she hadn't even been to the dentist for a routine check-up in over three years. 'The money just isn't there for such things at the moment,' she told herself as she cancelled each six-monthly appointment. 'Gym shoes and get well presents have to come first!'

Today was different though. Karen had a lunch invitation to her favourite restaurant – from a complete stranger! She had listened to the telephone answering machine message many times over the last few days: 'Hello Karen, it's me! I thought it was time we had lunch; meet me next Monday, 12:30, at that nice restaurant on the beach.' If Karen was honest, each time she had listened to the message, the voice sounded familiar, but she couldn't quite place it. Intrigued, the decision was made – she had to go!

She took the day off work, and as it was a lunch appointment, knew that childcare would not be needed; she could be back in time to pick the children up from school. Coincidently, her elderly parents were going to visit a friend that day and so she knew that they, too, would not need her until the evening. She even decided that the trip to the supermarket could wait and she would do all the ironing on Sunday so that she didn't feel guilty about that as well. After dropping the children off at school, Karen spent time getting ready for her mystery lunch appointment; she even called the restaurant to see if there was a reservation. 'Yes!' said the voice 'it is booked in the name of Karen Emanuel.' Karen replaced the handset, even more confused than before; what kind of person would book a table in the name of their guest, unless they were playing a practical joke? Karen considered the date; it wasn't her birthday, anniversary or even April Fools' Day! She could not fathom it out.

Karen turned up early to the restaurant; she was keen to be there before her lunch partner. It was a beautiful summer's day and as she climbed out of the car she felt the warm summer sun dance on her skin. It felt good, like a warm cuddle. She loved summertime most of all. The sea air floated into her nostrils and she sucked in deep lung-fulls of the fresh salty breeze.

'Breathe in that salty air, it's good for you!' her mother would announce when she was little. Nostalgia washed over her and she was whisked back to the carefree days of childhood when life seemed so simple; playing in the rock pools, chasing crabs, building sandcastles and balmy summer nights camping on the beach with her chums. Summer seemed to last for eons! School holidays were dawn to dusk explorations, imaginations, skinned knees, tree houses, imaginary lands and toffee apples by the shore. The longing to bring it all back engulfed her in waves of desire. How perfect, simple and stress-free her childhood had been; how she longed to feel that peace again.

Karen walked towards the restaurant, its whitewashed walls stark and bright in contrast to the deep aquamarine of the sea beyond. Seagulls swooped and dived in the sky above, their cackling screeches mocking one another's prowess as they hunted for fish in the boiling surf below.

Lobster creels in a twisted tyranny of modern art presented a coiled welcome at the entrance. Advancing sand from the beach clung to their surface, hitching a ride on their surreal perfection.

Karen wandered into the darkness of the interior, her eyes taking a few moments to adjust to the darkness within. The restaurant, cool and cave-like, displayed water features that trickled sparkling droplets of water over pools of lazy Koi Carp. Palms and tropical plants nodded their approval over their internal oasis. 'Can I help you madam?' a voice whispered from behind. Karen jumped from her serenity. 'Oh, I believe that you have a table for Karen Emanuel?' she asked. 'Ah yes!' said the waiter, 'Karen is already here and waiting for you.' 'But …' Karen decided not to try to explain that she was in fact Karen Emanuel. It didn't seem to matter to correct the waiter. He beckoned her into the restaurant. It was empty apart from one person studying a menu at a table at the far end. The restaurant was large. On the left, huge French windows opened on to the white sand beach. The view was perfect and on a summer day like this, the doors would usually be flung wide open and families would wander in and out all day. However, today the doors were closed and both the beach and the restaurant were unusually deserted. The restaurant itself had many tables of differing sizes, neatly scattered around a large dance floor. Karen recalled many happy summer evenings dancing the night away to a variety of Take That, Spice Girls and Michael Jackson! Her memory drifted to the first time she met James; they danced on the beach and when he kissed her during the last slow dance, she knew that they would be together for the rest of their lives. Karen stared at the dance floor, its wooden plinth adorned with tired and dusty old ships' lanterns, fishing nets and other seaside memorabilia.

As Karen walked across the restaurant towards her lunch guest, she started to feel anxious; the woman stood up and turned around to greet her. 'Hello Karen! It is so lovely to see you,' the woman smiled warmly. Karen hesitated, her mind was whirring; every detail of this woman suggested that she was a family member – she had the family squint front tooth, the little mole on her neck, her height and hairline. Most of all, Karen was intrigued by the little silver seal brooch on her jacket! She had one exactly the same. It had been given to her by her granddad on her 10th birthday – it was her Selkey. It had been made especially for her; there were no others like it, but this woman seemed to have one too! Karen could not speak; her mind whirled in a frenzy of confusion, dismay, shock and a thousand questions. She could not move, she stared in disbelief, her eyes searching every part of this woman's being, looking for clues, looking for a wry smile that would admit to this being a joke. James would pop out from behind a palm and they would all have a good laugh at her expense.

'Have we met?' Karen eventually managed to stammer. 'No, not yet, for I am your future self – the person that you want to become,' answered the other woman. *'I beg your pardon?'* frowned Karen *'is this some sort of joke?'*

'No, this is indeed real, I am your fully resourceful self, who you could become if you were to get the balance right and start living your own dreams. Right now, your life is spent doing so many things for other people and spending no time focusing on your own dreams and goals. If you are to become who you are meant to be, then achieving balance is so important. So, with a little help from me, your fully resourceful self, you will be able to explore worklife balance, release your potential and become the woman that we are meant to be! I am here to support you to make the changes that will allow you to,' explained resourceful Karen.

Karen stared in disbelief. *'If this is true and you are the future me, then before we continue, forgive me, but I need some proof. That brooch you are wearing,'* Karen pointed, not taking her eyes off the woman *'where did you get it?'*

'Ah!' sighed future Karen *'this is my Selkey, it was given to us by Grandpa McGregor. He loved to tell us stories about the Selkey; the seal that transformed itself into a mermaid. In the depths of the Northern seas, she could shed the skin of the seal and emerge as a beautiful mermaid. Grandpa's wonderful Scottish accent swept us off to the distant shores of our imagination. Do you remember sitting for hours on the quayside, making seaweed necklaces and convincing yourself that you saw the mermaid in the surf?'* The two women laughed. *'He had the brooch made for our 10th birthday and do you remember the little tartan box that he tied with seaweed?'* Both Karens reminisced as they remembered their mother's disapproval. *'But we knew the sea was important to him and to us; it was the sea that bound our dreams and stories together.'* Karen knew that this woman was telling the truth and whilst she didn't know how she could be here, she knew that she was meant to be. She looked at her intently. She looked fantastic, but more than her physical fitness and toning, she oozed confidence, determination and contentment. Karen certainly wanted to feel that way. Right now, she was so tired, out of balance and her mood was much less than confident.

'Where do we begin?' Karen asked quietly, and then in a more determined tone, 'I cannot see where and how I am going to get time to do all the things that I dream of, I am so busy! I work as a nurse five days a week and the shifts are a killer! My husband works as an engineer, sometimes six days, and always works overtime because we need the money! My daughter is currently at secondary school and I have to juggle bus times for her! My youngest is almost seven and he has all sorts of after-school sports and weekend football, rugby and swimming! Childcare is a nightmare, no one wants to look after a 12-year-old pre-teen and 12-year-old pre-teens only get stroppy if you suggest they need to be looked after anyway! My dad has Alzheimer's and my mum's arthritis means that she can't care for his needs as much as she would like, so I make their main meal every day and take care of their chores and dad's hospital appointments. On top of all that, my dear friend Lucy has been diagnosed with breast cancer and, having just undergone surgery, needs me to help her to look after her baby. When I get back from my hospital shift, I spend all of my time cooking, washing, ironing, cleaning, making up packed lunches, washing up and checking homework! When on earth is there time for me in all of that?!' exclaimed Karen, exhausted by just listing her frenetic responsibilities.

'I know Karen, but if you always do what you always did, you'll always get what you always got!' suggested Tomorrow Karen. The women looked at each other for a long time, both feeling the sheer exhaustion, guilt and pain of trying to juggle work and life. The Tomorrow Karen knew exactly what she was going through; the endless military precision that had to be performed every single day from breakfast manoeuvres to bedtime under-cover stories! The guilt was the worst thing. Oh boy, it ate into every aspect of her life; not being a good enough mother, employee, team player, daughter, wife or friend. Overwhelming feelings of letting people down swept through her like an unrelenting blizzard. Karen felt moist tears rise in her eyes. 'How can I make changes? I feel so useless most of the time!' she choked. 'Other people can do it, why can't I?' Tomorrow

Karen placed a comforting hand on her shoulder. 'You do the best you can, but the fact is Karen, your whole life is struggling and juggling and you know as well as I do that it all feels like a tower of cards that could fall down at any moment! It only needs one dose of chicken pox, one broken-down car or one missed bus to topple your whole life into chaotic mayhem. Well, we are going to fix it! We are going to stop juggling and start balancing our work, life and time for self. And to fix anything in our life, we must start with the current reality!' announced Tomorrow Karen. 'Now, choose something from that sumptuous menu and when we've eaten we will begin.'

The menu choices were indeed sumptuous and, in no time at all, the delicious food was served to their table along with their favourite bottle of wine. As they lay down their cutlery and sat back in their chairs in a gesture of warm satisfaction, Karen was the first to speak. 'That was truly delicious, I love the food here! It certainly beats the food in our hospital canteen!' she joked. Then her face changed. 'Oh, I hope they are coping without me, I feel so bad leaving them to it today while I sit here having a lovely lunch and doing nothing.'

'Karen!' cried Tomorrow Karen 'listen to yourself! We must add guilt to the list of things that you are to work on! For now though, we must look at the tunes that you dance to and the fact that you always put everyone else's needs ahead of your own. Now, let us step on to the dance floor ...'

As Karen turned her head, the lights dimmed and the spherical disco ball in the centre of the floor began to spin gently while extending its beams of light in search of objects on which its phantom glowing tendrils of sparkling light could dance. Karen looked around and, as she did, she began to notice the emergence of many familiar yet ghost-like people move into position, ready to dance. She recognised every one of them: her husband, children, family, friends, colleagues and acquaintances. Their presence filled the space; they mingled, engaged in muffled and incoherent conversation that seemed distant and muted. Every one of them was oblivious to the two Karens, as if the two women were invisible.

Karen watched as a lone figure walked on to the dance floor; a shadow of herself as she was just yesterday. She walked slowly to the centre of the dance floor, her dress, tired from wear, matched her drawn features and wearied smile. The distant sound of the DJ's muffled announcement fills the room and music begins to play, its far-away beat a signal to her phantom self to begin dancing. In an instant, people begin to dance with her. Her children, fighting to be first, vying for attention, scrabbling to be seen and heard, demanding with their 'mummy! mummy! mummy!' cub-like screeches. She shares herself between them. Her husband joins them. He wants her too – to talk, to ask her what she has being doing; he wants to be close to her, to hold her, to have her for just him. The music changes; it's the turn of her parents, then the beat changes again; her friends now. With each new turn and new tune appears a new dance and with it another person demanding her time. Karen continues to dance in rhythm with the beat and the crescendo of demands. Karen tries her best to listen to them all and answer their needs. Her boss, her colleagues, her team all want things from her and try to push in, separating Karen from her family. She deals with them too and dances for a while. Then it's the turn of the banker, the credit card company, the supermarket queue. She dances with them all. She even dances with the overflowing wash basket. Karen sees other people sitting out, people she would like to dance with, but never gets the chance. There is the lady that runs the local Salsa dancing club, the artist that does the watercolour painting courses, the gym owner, the spa manager and, most of all, the tutor that runs the garden design courses – oh how she would love to do garden design for a living! Within her she hears the distant beat of that music, beautifully playing like a whisper of heaven. But soon the louder and demanding beats of everyone else's needs overwhelm this whisper of what could be. Soon the music begins to slow and fade. The people fade into the darkness and, like the disco ball, Karen's head is spinning with the visions that she has just seen. Tomorrow Karen gently asks, 'Did you notice that you appear to be dancing to everyone else's tunes and not your own?'

Learning to balance work, life and time for self is a struggle for most women. However, we don't all have 'future selves' who will show us just how much we dance to the tunes of others. Therefore, Tomorrow Karen and the exercises throughout this book will act as your future self, providing you with the tools, mentoring and coaching to support you to stop juggling and start balancing work and life. You will also learn to turn up the volume on the whisper of who you can become. I encourage you to keep a journal as you work through its content and I also suggest that you share it with other women, grow a co-mentoring and coaching group to support each other and attend the workshops and coaching resources that are available to you.

The Dance floor Exercise

The Dance floor is a tool has been designed for you to use throughout the book. We will explore each facet of the Dance floor and, by reflection and exercises, redress the balance in your life and work, take charge of your direction and goals, and begin to take action towards dancing your best life! The Dance floor is a bit like a wheel of life, but has different headings and sections based on the content of your handbag. These reflect the chapters of the book and will provide you with the resources and personal development you need.

Remember, the life that you want will not just land in your lap; it requires that you dream, plan and take action. You will begin by reflecting on your current reality; what is life and work like right now? In other words, what is your starting point? Of course, life has a habit of changing overnight, so you may want to use this tool regularly to see where you are and make decisions for the future. You, as a member of the Dancing 'round the Handbags sisterhood, can download blank copies of the Dance floor for your own use.

Once completed, you will begin to reflect on how it could be. This will form the basis of your goals and desires. Moving on from that stage, you will reflect on what needs to start, continue and stop happening in order for you to achieve the goals that you have set.

I have included some tips on goal setting to support you to write them or compile them in a way that suits you and your style and these are covered in the My Pen chapter. Have fun with this tool and be true to your true self!

Dance your Best Life!

When you decide to do this exercise, make sure that you have enough uninterrupted time to be able to give it the level of concentration and attention that it will need.

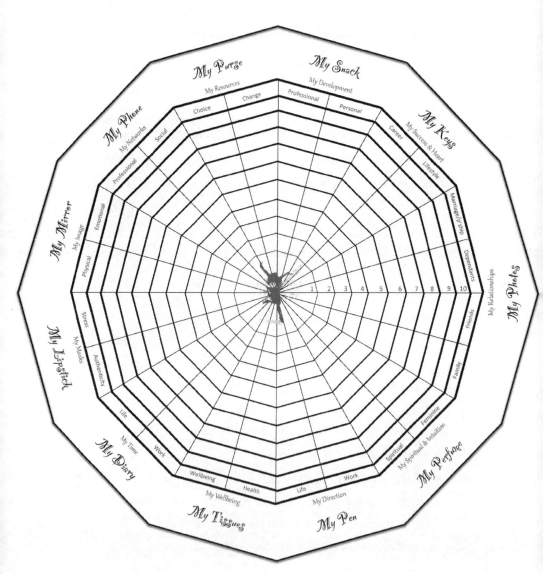

As you look at the Dance floor, you will notice that there are 11 headings around the outer circumference. These headings relate to different chapters in the book and, once scored, should provide you with some level of priority about which dances you need to balance first. The 24 headings that appear inside this outer group are the main aspects of work and life balance that you will measure and usually the dances that we dance to. Each of these aspects is described on the following pages and provides guidance for you to score your current reality. You can download a full-size and colour version of this tool from the website: **www.dancingroundthehandbags.com** – I encourage you to do this as you will use it time and again as your work and life begin to change and you create the life that you desire. You will need to visit the member area, where you will find loads of tools and resources to help you.

Do not try to score it without reading the descriptions and having them to hand, as many of the headings may not be what you first think. Score each element where 1 is 'poor' (out of balance) to 10 which is 'fabulous' (perfect balance). Take your time to truly reflect on each aspect and score it AS IT ACTUALLY IS and not how you would like it to be. For each, ask yourself 'do I have a sense of balance and contentment with this aspect of my life?'

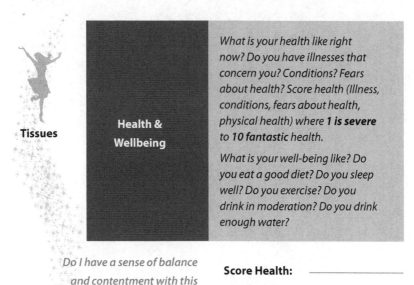

Tissues

Health & Wellbeing

*What is your health like right now? Do you have illnesses that concern you? Conditions? Fears about health? Score health (Illness, conditions, fears about health, physical health) where **1 is severe** to **10 fantastic** health.*

What is your well-being like? Do you eat a good diet? Do you sleep well? Do you exercise? Do you drink in moderation? Do you drink enough water?

Do I have a sense of balance and contentment with this aspect of my life?

Score Health: _____

Score Well-being: _____

Diary

Time and Workload – Professional and Life	***Work - Time dedicated to work*** - meetings, workload, demands, prioritising, hours, planning time, quality time? ***Life - Time dedicated to life*** - Relationships, caring, self, Chores – housework, caring tasks for others, tasks, life management etc.

Do I have a sense of balance and contentment with this aspect of my life?

Score Work Time: _____

Score Life Time: _____

Lipstick

Masks – Stress & Authenticity	***Stress & pressure levels*** - physical and emotional responses to stress, worry, guilt, shame etc. What is your stress like right now? ***Public Self*** – Authenticity, living to your true values; being who you truly are. What is your score for public self?

Do I have a sense of balance and contentment with this aspect of my life?

Score Stress: _____

Score Authenticity: _____

Mirror

Image – Physical & Emotional

Image - *Dress, hair, shape, grooming, dress for personal brand. What is your image like? Do you dress and groom to the standard expected by your authentic self? Score 1 for poor and 10 for living the brand*

Emotional - *Confidence - sense of self-belief, 'can do', self-esteem, assertiveness, worth and sense of deserving. Score 1 if you feel worthless, hopeless, useless, helpless, weak and don't deserve happiness. Or up to 10 which is high confidence, self-belief and worthiness.*

Do I have a sense of balance and contentment with this aspect of my life?

Score Physical Image: _____

Score Emotional Image: _____

Phone

Networks – Social & Professional

Social - *Community, social, recreation, leisure, sport etc.*

Professional - *Colleagues past and present, customers, suppliers, work groups, committees etc.*

Do I have a sense of balance and contentment with this aspect of my life?

Score Social Network: _____

Score Professional Network: _____

Purse

Resources – Choice & Change

Choice – *Choice creates balance and creates options to live the life you want. Having no choice creates oppression, depression and despair. Do you have the financial and personal resources to make choices about your life and work?*

Change – *Change is about risk-taking and ability to make the changes that you need to live your best life. Do you have the risk-taking ability to make the changes required? Are you satisfied with your ability and willingness to make change happen?*

Do I have a sense of balance and contentment with this aspect of my life?

Score Choice: _____

Score Change: _____

Snack

Personal Development – Professional and Personal

Professional – *Career qualifications, skills development, business coaching, mentoring, professional bodies etc.*

Personal – *Life Coaching, counselling, skills development, personal development, groups and activities, fun.*

Do I have a sense of balance and contentment with this aspect of my life?

Score Personal development: _____

Score Emotional Image: _____

Keys

Success and Heart

Keys to Success - *Career direction, stepping stones, mentoring, growth. Are you doing what you love, and love what you do? Are you satisfied? Score 1 if you have no sense of career direction, personal development or personal growth.*

Keys to your heart - *Lifestyle you desire, home, material wealth, possessions etc.*

Do I have a sense of balance and contentment with this aspect of my life?

Score Keys to my Success: _____

Score Keys to my Heart: _____

This section is about our significant life relationships – Partner, dependants, family and friends. For each, it is important to score them in terms of your sense of balance and satisfaction.

Marriage/Partner/Significant other – are you in one and happy, out of one and unhappy, out of one and happy, in one and unhappy?

Dependants - Children, dependant care, pets, people or animals dependent on you for their day-to-day care or survival. What is your sense of balance and contentment with this group?

Family - Whom you regard as family - parents, siblings, aunts, uncles, grandparents etc.

Friends - Close friends, chums, acquaintances

Photographs

Relationships – Marriage/ Partnership, dependents, family & friends

Do I have a sense of balance and contentment with this aspect of my life?

Score Marriage/Partnership: _____

Score Dependants: _____

Score Family: _____

Score Friends: _____

Feminine - 'Femininism' - sense of being female, female intuition, sexuality, sensuality, nurture, importance of relationships etc.

Spiritual - Religion, spiritual, meditation, me-time, 6th sense, etc.

Perfume

Sensing Self – Spiritual and Feminine

Do I have a sense of balance and contentment with this aspect of my life?

Score Feminine: _____

Score Spiritual: _____

Pen

Goals – Professional and Life

Professional - Where will you be in your career in 5 or 10 years? What are your goals for role, company, team, etc.?

Life - What are your life goals? At the end of your life, as you look back, what will you leave as your legacy?

Do I have a sense of balance and contentment with this aspect of my life?

Score Life Goals: _____

Score Professional Goals: _____

You now have a picture of your current reality in relation to work and life. If you have done this exercise properly, like everyone else you will see that you have highs, lows and aspects of your life that are scored somewhere around the middle. That's normal! There is no right and wrong answer; no one is a perfect 10! Also, life has a habit of throwing things at us that suddenly put a high scoring aspect into the low scoring areas.

There is also no right area to focus on first. You may find that focusing on a high-scoring area will actually have a positive impact on a low-scoring area. This is because your dances flow across all aspects and create a cause and effect impact. For example, if you have scored low in your partnership box, this may be 'caused' by working too many hours, or by focusing too much on family.

On the **page 28** you will see a table. Transfer all of your scores on to the table, and then for each, complete the questions in the heading columns as follows:

1. *Is it a challenge? In other words, is this a problem area in your life right now? Remember, it is not a problem unless it is a problem! Write a Yes or No in this column for each of the categories. Highlight where you have marked Yes – these are your priority areas. You don't need to work on the No's for now, but be aware that cause and effect mentioned above can have an impact and you may need to come back to some of the No areas.*

2. *What is the current reality? What is it like now? How do you feel about this current situation? Be specific and clear.*

3. *What is the cause? How did it get like that?*

4. *What needs to change? For this, we will use the mnemonic* **BAG***:*

    B **Bin** *- What do I need to stop doing/having or need to give up or de-clutter from my life?*

    A **Add to** *- What do I currently have or do that I need to add to, continue to do or improve?*

    G **Get** *- what do I need to get, or start doing, believing or attracting into my life/work that I don't have at the moment?*

This table can also be downloaded from the

website: www.dancingroundthehandbags.com

by registering your unique book number when visiting the member pages.

	Score	Is this a Challenge?	What is the Current Reality?	What is the Cause?	What needs to Change? BAG!
My Health					
My Well-being					
My Stress					
My Authenticity					
My Emotional Image					
My Physical Image					
My Career					
My Lifestyle					
My Choices					

	Score	Is this a Challenge?	What is the Current Reality?	What is the Cause?	What needs to Change? BAG!
My Change					
My Marriage/ Partnership					
My Dependants					
My Family					
My Friends					
My Social Network					
My Professional Network					
My Work Time					
My Life Time					

	Score	Is this a Challenge?	What is the Current Reality?	What is the Cause?	What needs to Change? BAG!
My Personal Development					
My Professional Development					
My Feminine Self					
My Spiritual Self					
My Professional Goals					
My Life Goals					

> We all dance to the tunes of others due to our internal programming and our external circumstances. To create balance we must look within as well as around us. The Mirror and Lipstick chapters will help with this.
>
> You are not alone; other women juggle too. Take time to realise what you do achieve and begin to keep a gratitude diary. Every day, write at least one thing in your diary that you are proud of doing that day. After a month, read it; it'll make you feel good!
>
> Reward yourself! Buy a piggy bank (I have one that has 'Handbag Fund' engraved on the front). Every day, think of something that you have done well, or are proud of achieving, and drop a pound in the bank. When it comes to your birthday, buy yourself a present!
>
> It'll take time to change a lifetime of habit, so be generous to yourself and positive about the changes you can make over time. It is always good to look back, so keep a journal!

TIP

BAG - My Action Plan

BAG stands for **B**in, **A**dd and **G**et

B	What will I **Bin** that no longer serves my life or goals and prevents me from dancing my best life?	
A	What am I already doing, being or having that I could **Add** to or improve in order to dance my best life?	
G	What will I **Get** that will serve me well and help me to dance my best life?	

Dance your Best Life!

2 My Tissues

Introduction

Your tissues represent your health – without that, you have neither work nor life. Your health and well-being underpins your ability to do well in both. In this chapter we will explore your physical well-being in relation to worklife balance, in the Lipstick chapter we will explore emotional stress and the Mirror chapter will explore your psychological well-being.

Allow me to first of all say that I am not a doctor, not a health specialist, not a nutritionist and certainly not an athlete! However, I do understand that as women we have ups and downs in terms of our health – never mind our dress size! I also know that there is a myriad of good advice, poor advice and downright dangerous advice out there for all of us to read or watch. There are more diet scams, 'perfect weight' charts, 'ideal body shape' influences and a multi-billion pound image industry which tells you that you are not good enough the way you are! I intend to provide you with some ideas that will help you to look at your health in relation to work and life balance. I have worked with some excellent individuals who know more than I do and I will share their experience too, given in the spirit of improving your energy, your well-being and building your resilience under stress.

You are amazing!

You are, in simple terms, a vibration of millions of cells, molecules and electrons, all held together in chemical harmony. If we were to drop you in a test tube and have a good look at you, we would see that you were exactly that – a chemical soup! When this body that is you has the right chemical ingredients, in the right proportions, it works well and serves you well. On days like that, you feel on top of the world; you have loads of energy, you can think straight, your mood is good, you can concentrate and have plenty in reserve should you need it. But do you feel like that every single day? I suspect not. We live in a world where we are bombarded with stimuli that create a less than optimum environment for our wonderful bodies. External stresses like pollution, chemicals and toxins 'act on us' and fatty, processed and bad food and drinks that we ingest, that 'act in us'.

Top athletes understand that in order to warm up, deliver peak performance and warm down effectively, they must nourish their bodies with foods that will provide peak performance and avoid those which add nothing or detract from their full potential. Like an athlete, you may live a lifestyle that demands peak performance throughout the day – at work, looking after the family and taking care of a home. It is easy in our frenetic world to take the easy option when it comes to our diets, hydration, exercise and rest.

Our story ...

As usual, Karen was first to rise. She always managed to wake just a few minutes before the alarm clock, and switched it off before it woke the whole family. It was 4:00 a.m. She didn't mind getting up this early on her day shift during the summer, but during the winter it was a nightmare. Karen pulled back the covers, releasing her body to the early morning chill; the temptation to snuggle back down under the cosy duvet beckoned, but she resisted and quickly, before she changed her mind, wandered through to the bathroom. It was still dark and she didn't *switch the bedroom light on so as not to disturb James. Running the gauntlet of discarded clothes, furniture and pets was always a challenge, never mind when she was still half asleep! On her safe arrival in the bathroom she gently flicked on the light. Her starched uniform hung in stand-to-attention readiness on the door peg and her shoes and underwear formed a neat pile under the mirror as if ready for military inspection. Karen always laid everything out the night before; it saved scrambling around searching for the one lost shoe in the morning when there just wasn't time or patience. Karen allowed the warm water of the shower to wake her up, then dried and quickly scrambled into her clothes, slipping on her shoes whilst briskly taming her hair into the clutches of a hair clip and tucking it under her nurse's cap. It was 4:30; she squeaked through to the kitchen, her rubber-soled shoes audibly marking her passage, and in a flurry of activity, boiled the kettle, made her breakfast, laid the table for the family, made the children's packed lunches, packed Josh's PE kit (again), signed Tilly's maths homework and wrote her a note to skip swimming 'she must be the only girl to have a period every time there is a swimming class' she murmured under her breath as she licked the envelope and poked it into Tilly's rucksack with a wry grin. Then she fed the ever-hungry cat and dog, topped up the hamster's seed, fed the fish and took something out of the freezer for supper. She ate her toast while putting on her coat, wrote a cheque for the milkman and stuffed it in an empty bottle with one hand while she tugged the front door closed with her left foot. Phew! And it was only 5:00 a.m.*

The commute to work was easy at this time of day, and in the summer that meant a walk across the Common instead of driving. The sun was just poking its head above the rooftops of the local school which lay slumbering, peacefully silhouetted against the blue-green of the morning sky. Rabbits bounded about in the morning dew as she approached, some nibbling and munching on the cool wet grass, a final snack before descending into the relative safety of their burrows for the day. Karen rarely saw anyone at this time of the morning, but now and again there was a dog walker – who either couldn't sleep or had an early start for work too – or maybe the local paper boy who, in his keenness to own the latest computer game or mobile phone, decided that earning money on a paper round was a good idea. Karen noticed that these teenagers began their new-found role with all gusto and enthusiasm in the spring, but as the long chilly mornings of autumn began to turn to winter, their commitment waned and their desire to get out of bed meant that sightings of them cycling across the Common with their newspaper bag flopping behind slowly froze to zero in line with the weather! Today, the Common was all hers. It all too soon gave way to civilisation once more, and on the opposite side of a usually busy road the hospital rose like a fortress of granite and glass in front of her. Karen watched as the morning sun danced across the windows as if searching to see what had happened during the night: a baby born, an old person passed away, a new dressing attached and a nurse on night shift ready to hand over duties to the day staff. Karen ambled across the road. 'If anything dramatic was going to happen to a patient's health, it usually did so in the middle of the night' she observed to herself as she drifted off into her own thoughts once more. Unconsciously, she climbed into the lift, pressed the button and allowed the unquestioning metal carrier to meander its sleepy and creaky ascent up to the fourth floor. The doors pulled back like theatrical curtains and the sign in front of her on the stark white walls announced 'Men's General Ward' in tall blue letters. Karen was met with a cacophony of noise, which snapped her back into the moment. As she approached the ward, she saw that the curtains were being pulled around a bed, doctors and nurses were running frantically to and fro, defibrillators like large slumbering beetles were being hurtled towards a patient in cardiac arrest. Karen whisked off her coat; the day had indeed begun in earnest. By 11:00 a.m. the man in Bed 3 had been stabilised and moved to intensive care. The bed sat serene and empty, remade in sharp lines of perfect order, all evidence of trauma gone, standing to attention in its crisp, clinical whiteness for a new patient to be delivered.

It was lunchtime and Karen left her station clutching a pile of papers and other admin tasks that she could complete over lunch. The canteen was the usual bustle of staff trying to fit in a well-earned break in an otherwise hectic day. The choices of food were less than inspiring and the heat lamps had done their best to genetically modify every tray of hot food into the same bubbling, over-cooked mass of splodge. The sandwiches sat in neat rows of white bleached bread filled with what looked like a cold version of the overcooked splodge, the odd lettuce leaf gasping its escape to freedom from the clamped bread. There was always the option of the fruit bowl, provided in an attempt to offer a 'healthy option', but it usually contained all the leftover fruit that nobody really wanted to eat: crumbly sour green apples and the odd black and bruised banana. Karen plumped for a sandwich and a chocolate bar ('for energy' she told herself). She huddled over a cup of lukewarm coffee and, while she ate her sandwich, she also ploughed through the forms, reports and emails that she had brought for company.

By 2:00 p.m. the ward was buzzing, surgery was over for the day and the next round of drugs, dressings and temperature checks had been completed. Outside the ward, the usual throng of expectant visitors hovered in anticipation of their loved ones' recovery or deterioration. With the shift handover completed, Karen fought her way through the morbid bunch of voyeuristic visitors, and once again pressed the lift button that watched the closing of the curtains on another episode of 'Men's General Ward' for the day. The silence of her descending cocoon was comforting, a sanctuary from both work and life. Then, suddenly, she was hurtled once again into the reality of the reception hall where members of the public milled around waiting for news or outpatient appointments, or emerged from the hospital shop clasping a pink balloon and a matching teddy bear to welcome the new arrival. Karen fought her way through the heaving throng and into the fresh air, snatching a big deep breath as she charged headlong over to the bus stop.

She jumped on to the first bus into town, which would give her just enough time to whisk round the supermarket, go to the bank and be at the school gates to collect Josh at 3:15. Josh was full of conversation about his day and chattered continuously all the way back to the house. He ran straight upstairs to get changed out of his school clothes while Karen went into the kitchen to put away the shopping. The kitchen was a pigsty! The remains of breakfast lay dead on the table: crusts of toast slain by hungry children were discarded on plates, dried cereal clung to the side of bowls, and the unsuspecting carton of milk, which had been left out all day in the warmth of the summer heat, was doing its best to incubate as many bacteria as it could. Karen poured the wasted milk away and began to clear up the battlefield that had been breakfast. She prepared supper, she took Josh to football practice, she picked Tilly up from her piano lesson, they ate supper, the children bathed, James came home late, she made his supper, he watched TV while she cleared away the dishes, did the ironing, laid out her clean uniform and at 10:00 p.m. decided that it was time to collapse into bed once more. She was tired, her legs ached and her ankles throbbed their tune of exhaustion. A nice soak in the bath would have been good but there was no chance of that tonight as she was too tired and, in any case, Tilly would have used all the hot water! 'Why do such skinny teenagers need so much water?' she mumbled to herself as she spat out the foaming surge of toothpaste from her mouth. 'Because they can!' sighed a voice from behind her. Karen yelped with fright and she whisked round to see Tomorrow Karen sitting behind her. 'Where the hell did you come from?' squawked Karen like some rabid dog spewing foam, her heart beating with fright. The future-Karen's eyes twinkled with humour, but she continued without answering, 'You have had a very busy day, and they are all like that, aren't they Karen?' 'Yes,' replied Karen, spitting the final remnants of mouthwash down the sink and drying her hands. She turned to face the other Karen. 'Yes, they are all busy, as you well know! And I am aching with tiredness every night. I spend the whole day on my feet and it feels like my legs are going to drop off! James has the opposite problem; he sits down all day and then sits down in front of the TV all evening; his legs must be atrophied!' They both laughed. The two women went through to the bedroom. The light was dim and Karen always burned a nice scented candle to make the room feel cosy, relaxing and inviting at bedtime. The children were asleep and from the noises emanating from the lounge, James had nodded off too! The two women sat on the bed like schoolgirls on a stay-over; they sat up perched against the soft pillows, the duvet covering them snugly. Between them was Karen's handbag and she fumbled inside to look for a tissue. Tomorrow Karen was the first to speak. 'Do you remember when we met at the restaurant and we observed all of those people on the dance floor?' Karen nodded; how could she forget? 'Today, you have been dancing to many of those tunes and are worn out as a result. Therefore, we must now begin the work of looking at you and your life in more detail and make some changes – fast! We will use your handbag as our classroom, and every item within it will become an aspect of you and of your life,' explained Tomorrow Karen.

'I am not sure that I understand,' replied Karen.

'Your handbag will become a metaphor for you. When you go out dancing, you would normally dance around your handbag – true?' Karen nodded. 'Well, in this lesson, we will metaphorically stop the music and the dance of life for a while, take you off the dance floor, open up the handbag and relate each item to a different part of you! Take for example that packet of tissues; let's assume that relates to your health and physical well-being! Your lipstick will be something else, your purse something else.'

'I see! So my phone could be about who I talk to?'

'Got it!' smiled resourceful Karen. 'By using each item in your handbag, we will explore what you need to do to gain better balance in your life and start living your own dreams. In other words, dancing to your own

music! Tonight, we will begin with your tissues because your health is the most important as it underpins everything else.'

'I think I am quite healthy!' announced Karen. 'I never get colds or anything!'

'Being vertical and cold-free doesn't mean you are healthy, does it?' asked Tomorrow Karen rhetorically. 'So, shall we explore your health?'

Tomorrow Karen looked down at Karen's handbag and Karen mirrored her stare as well. All of a sudden, Karen felt drowsy, the room began to spin and Karen had the weirdest feeling of spinning down and down and down and down and … thud! Karen looked around. 'Where on earth am I?' she asked. 'You are inside your own handbag!' confirmed Tomorrow Karen. In disbelief, Karen pulled herself to her feet. The blue satin lining streaked upwards in shards like the cobalt shimmer of the Northern Lights. High above, she could see the faint glimmer of the candlelight and her bedroom beyond. This was truly surreal and, in many ways, she knew she must be dreaming and that she would wake up in the morning and delight in the story, but it all seemed so real at this moment.

'Let's find that pack of tissues!' hailed Tomorrow Karen. The two women began to look around. There was her purse, its large green surface shining like the sides of a giant locomotive. It stood proud and fixed in its position, which was almost the full length of her bag; she had always meant to get a smaller purse but she did love the emerald green of this one. To the right was her mobile phone, erect and tall like a building silhouetted against the deep blue sky of lining behind. Her lipstick lay propped at a jaunty angle in front of it, making it look like a tunnel entrance to the mobile phone building and there, tucked beneath in its neat cellophane wrapper, was the packet of tissues. The two women rolled the lipstick to one side and gently freed the packet of tissues.

'The tissues are a representation of your health and well-being from a physical perspective. That includes your well-being, your nutrition, your rest and your exercise!' informed Tomorrow Karen.

Karen was intrigued but said nothing. She was still bemused by how she had got here in the first place and how this whole metaphor was going to help her to regain balance; but Tomorrow Karen had continued and it was time to listen…

'Look at the packaging first of all, look at what is written on the back,' Tomorrow Karen instructed. She turned over the giant pack and there on the back, in place of the normal 'ingredients' or 'contents', was a written account of Karen's health and well-being. Under 'contents' it defined her nutritional intake over the last week and it didn't make for good reading! It defined her exercise regime (or lack of it), and even though she slept reasonably well, it was more a two-ply rough sleep than a three-ply soft and comforting sleep. The barcode said it all… it defined the long-term cost of all this lack of well-being; eventually, it would cost a lot with little return.

Karen flopped down on to the packet and, sitting with her head in her hands, announced 'Time I started looking after me a little better!'

'Yes!' agreed Tomorrow Karen 'and that has to begin with a good night's sleep!

Your Well-being

There are many aspects to well-being and health, but just because you can put your feet on the floor in the morning and get yourself out of bed does not mean that you have optimal well-being. Well-being is impacted by a number of things, and in the well-being wheel shown right, I suggest that each of these has a great impact on our well-being.

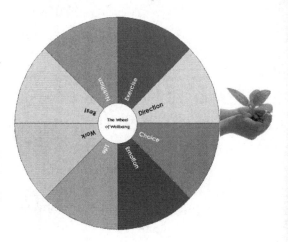

Direction

Having a sense of direction or goals provides us with a sense of purpose. Having something to strive towards has an impact on our motivation, mood and sense of purpose. These will be explored in detail in the My Perfume and My Pen chapters.

Choice

At a society level we have a great amount of choice; in a democracy we have choice about who runs our country, we have choice about our beliefs, where we live and how we raise our families. There are many countries that do not afford that choice to their people. These people are oppressed and unable to live freely. Choice affords freedom to live authentically and appropriately. We also have the ability to make micro-choices in our day-to-day lives, but again there are those who do not feel they have these choices due to some kind of lack in their life. Whether it is lack of money to move out of an abusive marriage, or lack of choice of jobs in their location, or lack of confidence to change career, perception of 'lack of choice' impacts our well-being.

Emotions

We are emotional beings and our emotions, because they are linked with our physical self, directly influence our health. Thoughts drive mood, mood drives emotion, emotion drives behaviour and physical outcomes – what we think about we bring about! When you feel happy, on top of the world and joyous, do you feel healthier and more alive, or sicker and more drained? Managing our emotions intelligently and being aware of all of our emotions helps to improve health. Emotional well-being is often measured by happiness, sense of vibrancy, energy and motivation. We will address this topic in more detail in the Perfume, Mirror and Lipstick chapters. However, in relation to emotional well-being, if we want to increase a sense of well-being in our communities, spreading happiness is important. For example, many people suggest that if they were wealthy, they would be happy. Whilst having an excess of wealth would be good, it does not create well-being in and of itself. It must be combined with emotional well-being, which comes as a result of emotional happiness.

- *Happy people are healthier.*
- *Happy people cope better with illness and live longer.*
- *Happy people are more productive and 'can-do'.*
- *Happy people are much more positive – in their language, outlook and mood.*
- *Happy people are more persistent at solving problems – they become challenges and opportunities, not problems.*
- *Happy people are more giving – they give more to others and giving rather than receiving creates well-being.*

Work and life should be in balance for us to ensure well-being. In today's busy world, we tend to define ourselves by what we do for a living; in previous centuries we were more likely to be known by our family or clan. Work and being able to work provides a sense of self-worth, which positively impacts well-being. However, there is a direct correlation between working too many hours and lack of well-being; figures from UCL research suggest that by working more than 11 hours a day, we increase the risk of heart disease and cancer by 67%.

Begin by trying the following quiz to assess your sense of well-being in relation to work:

	True	False	Don't Know
I see my workplace as somewhere that I enjoy going to			
My workplace has a clear sense of purpose and meaning			
I fully understand and buy into my workplace vision			
I have a real sense of belonging at work			
I see myself contributing to my full potential at work			
I feel supported and encouraged at work			

Continued ▶

	True	False	Don't Know
My differences and uniqueness are accepted and encouraged at work			
My manager develops my potential at work			
I am proud of the work I do			
I am proud of the organisation that I work for			

Life – this is the most important of all the aspects and has the biggest bearing on national well-being, social well-being and communities. Our sense of well-being at this level is linked to democracy and freedom and has a strong link with Human Rights. For example, when the Berlin Wall was pulled down in 2000, the population's well-being improved as a result of perceived access to better public services, political freedom and improved living standards. Therefore, living in good neighbourhoods, with good public services, perceived safety and a sense of belonging is key to our well-being.

*What are **the 3 best things** about living in my area/community?*

_____

_____

_____

*What are **the 3 best things** about living in this country?*

_____

_____

_____

*What are **the 3 things** that could be improved that would give me a better sense of wellbeing now, and in my future in this community/country?*

_____

_____

_____

*What **one thing** could I do for me, that would improve my wellbeing in this environment, now and in future?*

_____

The NEF Centre for wellbeing (http://www.neweconomics.org/programmes/well-being) state:

'Social relationships are critical to our well-being. Survey research has found that well-being is increased by life goals associated with family, friends, social and political life and decreased by goals associated with career success and material gains. Governments can shape policies in ways that encourage citizens to spend more time with families and friends and less time in the workplace. For example, employment policy that actively promotes flexible working and reduces the burdens of commuting, alongside policies aimed at strengthening local involvement, would enable people to spend more time at home and in their communities to build supportive and lasting relationships.'

Visit the New Economics Foundation to find out more about their work in relation to social and life well-being. They have a fantastic number of resources, questionnaires and tests that you can use and resource from them to support you and your organisation.

Each of the aspects of the well-being wheel has a real impact on our health, whether it is lifestyle, mental or physical. In this chapter, we will specifically explore exercise, nutrition and rest. The objective is to provide you with ways that you, through focusing on your well-being, can bring a sense of wellness and health and therefore balance.

Your Nutrition

Women are often referred to as the 'gatherer and nurturer' and apparently the reason why we carry handbags is due to our instinctive need to gather! I like that very much and accept it whole-heartedly; I now have an excuse for buying beautiful handbags!

Your need to gather, to store, to nurture, to feed is an important part of the female instinct as it is for animals and birds and other creatures. For humans, eating is more than just survival; it is also a social gathering. Women often tell me that they hate to eat alone. Sometimes travelling

45

businesswomen would rather order food to be brought to their hotel room than have to eat alone in a restaurant. Therefore the nourishment that you bring to yourself and your family also feeds your need to build community, love, growth and development for yourself and others; this is what builds well-being. For many women, eating is a time of ultimate gathering, bringing the family or friends together around the table, to talk, to eat and to celebrate the food as well as the company. In many ways it is the combination of both that creates well-being. Many families have lost the ability to share family mealtimes because of the frenetic lifestyles that they lead. One delegate on a workshop told me 'We needed the space in our small house, so we decided to rip out the kitchen and change it into a bedroom as we never used the kitchen anyway!' I find this story sad, and whilst I respect her need for more space, I question whether she has not only lost a kitchen, but indeed lost the heart of her family community? Our need for speed and convenience has resulted in many family gatherings being reduced to burgers and the X-box or TV box. In some of these environments, families no longer communicate, children don't know their extended families and lying on the dinner table is not a steaming shepherd's pie or apple tart, but the discarded plastic carton of some salt- or sugar-riddled toxic waste of ping-ping food propped up against a bottle of fizzy blue chemical drink. Mum and dad, if they are there, are often disengaged and in their own world of TV Soap surrealism. One friend told me that, one evening, he suddenly noticed that his sons were face-down in their computers, his wife was mesmerised by TV and he was email weeding for the tenth hour that day! He called a family meeting immediately in which they changed their lives forever. Two years on, this family now works hard but also plays hard. He said, 'We decided to run our family like a business – you have to! If you were running a real business, everyone would work hard to make it work! Everyone would have their role and there would be teamwork.' In this family, his wife is Finance Director, he is CEO and his sons own entertainment. Every Friday night, they meet in the gym at their local sports hall, they exercise together, they moan about all the stresses of the week to get it off their chests and exercise it out, then they go out for supper together and into their weekend, stress free! 'At Christmas, we have a big strategy meeting and plan what we want to do that year, where we want to go on holiday, what we want to do for fun, what we want to achieve and then we pin it on the fridge to remind us that we have fun together, love each other and support each other to achieve our goals. I love my family and I care enough to not lose what is so precious. I would never go back to that silent world of separateness.'

Above my breakfast bar at home, I have painted a mural and written in calligraphy above the mural are the words 'A house is no home unless it has food and fire for the mind as well as the body'. As I ponder on these words for a moment, food for the mind and fire for the mind come from a sense of passion, belonging, values and filling the mind with that which grows it in a positive way from being part of a family group. Is it any wonder that we have problems with knife crime and gun crime in our society when some children have been fed violence on computer games since they were young and chemical mayhem into their bodies? Over 41% of our families spend less than an hour a day with each other; how can you pass on values, respect, dignity and integrity in such short bursts of time? What are employers doing to the future of our country and its generations when they deprive fathers and mothers from going home to be with their family? Well-being and health begins with the connectedness of family and community. As women, we owe it to our society to start feeding our minds and bodies with those things that will nurture, not destroy our social communities, of which family life is at its core.

What is your sense of nurturing and gathering for others? Try this quick quiz:

Your Nurturing & Gathering

	Strongly Agree	Agree	Disagree	Strongly Disagree
I enjoy creating a nice home for my family to enjoy				
I like to browse around market stalls or supermarkets picking out nice fruit, veg, produce				
I love to find a bargain, a cost-saving, an opportunity to get more for my money				
Sitting around chatting with the family, laughing, spending time together makes me feel good				
I love it when my fridge or cupboards are full of yummy things to eat				
I really look forward to a girls' night in or out with friends				
I often buy myself a little treat if I am shopping for others				
I enjoy family get-togethers like birthdays, weddings and Christmas (or other religious festivals)				
At work, if I have the right team around me I know we can achieve great things				
I enjoy browsing magazines for ideas for image or home				

If you ticked Disagree or Strongly Disagree to any of the above, explore what would need to happen for at least two of these to be added to your life right now. For example, if you live alone or don't have family to feed on a regular basis, why not have a dinner party for a few close friends, go out to get all the ingredients, find nice candles, visit some farm shops or delis that are off the beaten track, send invitations and prepare your home for a lovely evening? If you don't have the space, find somewhere you can go! Then answer the questions again. Or think about your behaviour around certain times of the year, like Christmas or Eid. Do you gather gifts, food, special things? How does it make you feel? I love the excitement of getting home and laying out all my purchases and Christmas presents on the table. Sorting them into a what's-whose pile, littering the floor with garlands, paper, tags and bows and standing back to appreciate the gathering that I have done. I gather to give, as most women do.

The Food we Eat

It used to be that we ate what we gathered and that was based on seasonality as well as availability. Therefore, variety and quality is key to our human dietary needs. In today's busy world, we have access to the most amazing foods and seasonality doesn't seem to come into it any more – I seem to be able to buy strawberries as well as Brussels sprouts for Christmas lunch!

Dietary advice can often be confusing. Not a week goes by without us being told that another foodstuff is not good for us, or to forget everything that we learned last week. If we were to place our faith in fad diets, then we would soon grow very confused about what the actual truth is! In basic terms, we should stick to what is good for us – which has always been good for the chemical balance of our bodies. Simply, that means good fats, good hydration, good protein, good carbohydrates and good dietary fibre.

So what is the right thing, and what if you don't have the cash or the access to good local produce? What if you can't cook (or don't want to cook) or haven't the time? Or, what if you have a family that 'won't eat' the healthy options? Here are some simple, common sense tips that balance your body, your mind and your worklife balance:

1. Start with good intentions; be the first to make the change yourself. That is VERY important – you must walk the talk with your own eating habits. You will have more energy when you do!

2. Stop buying certain things – I stopped buying fizzy drinks, crisps, chips, biscuits and cakes. My husband complained for a while that there was 'nothing to eat', even though the fruit bowl was overflowing! The children didn't notice that I hadn't bought these things. Addiction to sugar (carbs) is the big thing to reduce cravings for in your family, and when you do you will notice a big difference in their energy levels.

3. Look at the labels – you will be surprised how much salt and sugar are in foods! For example, one small bag of certain brands of crisps has more salt that an adult needs for a week – what is a bag a day doing to our children's health?

4. Use sugars sparingly – as little as possible and, like other foods, avoid refined sugars if you can. Avoid chemical sweeteners – try natural sweeteners or reducing the need for sugar. Cut out refined sugar of all kinds for a month and measure how your energy changes.

5. Bake and cook with your children – tasting as you cook is a good way to excite their palate to new things.

6. Add vegetables to things – I used to blend spinach, carrots, cabbage, Brussels etc. and add them to my 'spag bol' or other meaty dishes. The children never noticed but their growing bodies were grateful.

7. Increase fish in the diet. I am lucky, my family love seafood, especially shellfish, and we do not suffer from intolerances or allergies. I make sure that I cook fish at least three times during the week. This could be in salads for lunch, evening meals or soups. Oily fish is high on the agenda. If you don't like fish, try fish-oil supplements.

8. Drink loads of water! Buy a big jug, add some slices of orange or lemon or cucumber and leave it out for the family to drink. Reduce fizzy drinks and sugary drinks.

9. Eat a varied diet which covers all the main food groups.

10. Eat when you are hungry. Don't become a human dustbin, stop when you have had enough to eat.

11. *If you over-indulge, enjoy it and then take it easy for a few days.*

12. *Keep active – regular and frequent exercise, which doesn't have to be the gym! Exercise is also a positive way of reducing stress.*

13. *Drink alcohol in moderation – learn from the French – restrict wine-drinking to when you sit down to eat and stop when you finish eating! That doesn't mean drinking the whole bottle quicker! A glass of wine with dinner won't hurt but try to restrict it to weekends if you can, or have a couple of days with no alcohol at all. Know the facts about alcohol and the female body.*

14. *Maintain a healthy weight – you know what that is for you. The best way to lose weight is to eat good food and reduce portion size – buy a smaller plate!*

15. *Choose a diet low in salt, sugar, saturated fat and cholesterol – Patrick Holford's book Optimum Nutrition Made Easy is a good source.*

When eating fruit, eat it with yoghurt or a handful of sunflower seeds or nuts; the added protein slows the metabolising effect of the fruit and therefore reduces the sugar high making it last longer.

16. *Choose a diet with plenty of fruit and vegetables – greens like broccoli are high in vitamin C and zinc, which is good for your immune system.*

17. *Always sit down to eat. Eat slowly and chew your food well; your digestion begins in your mouth.*

18. *Don't expect miracles when dieting and try to avoid fad diets.*

19. *Make your dietary changes slowly and ensure they become a way of life.*

20. *For further information, speak to Kim Ingleby at Energised Performance. Kim works with us and our clients to create optimum health in the workplace. She also works one-to-one with clients on nutrition, exercise and emotional well-being. Above is one of Kim's favourite tips!*

I am not an angel and I don't expect to be one either. I love good food, but I do say no to processed foods for my family.

Nutrition Quiz

	True	False	Don't Know
I drink at least 1.5 litres of water a day			
I avoid too much caffeine and fizzy drinks			
I eat oily fish three times a week (or take good fish-oil supplements)			
I choose whole foods – whole grains, beans, nuts, seeds, fresh fruit and veg			
I eat at least five servings a day of whole grains such as rice, rye, quinoa, wholewheat or oats as cereals, breads, pasta or pulses			
I eat at least five servings of dark green, leafy and root veg like watercress, carrots, sweet potato, broccoli, Brussels sprouts, spinach, green beans, peppers – either raw or lightly cooked			
I eat three or more servings a day of fresh fruit – blues, reds, oranges, greens and yellows – rainbow fruits			
I eat at least two portions of fresh protein a day – fresh meat, fish, cheese, Tofu, egg etc.			
I avoid refined, white and sugary foods, processed foods and additives			
I avoid fried, burnt and charred food, hydrogenated fats and animal fats			

Observations about nutrition

Action plan for nutrition

Source: Energised Performance

Your Rest & Relaxation

It is a known fact that sleep deprivation can cause serious mental health issues and it is not good for your body either! During sleep, both the physical as well as the psychological aspects of well-being are healed, rejuvenated and rested. If you drove your car without maintaining it, without adding the right fuel and without taking care of it in other ways, it would soon come to a standstill. Your body is just the same. It is important that it is given rest and fuelled in a way that maintains your health.

Experts say that an eight-hour sleep is optimum. This makes sense when you consider that the brain processes four hours of physical repair and four hours of psychological while we sleep.

	Always	Often	Sometimes	Seldom	Never
Do you sleep well?					
Do you wake in the night?					
Do you need a nature break in the night?					
Do you build rest periods into your day?					
Can you get off to sleep easily?					
Do you wake up just as tired as when you went to bed?					
Do you have broken sleep due to others or noise levels?					
Do you fall asleep at other times of day?					
Do you have a medical condition related to sleep?					
How else do you rest?					

Below and opposite is a tool that you can use to plot your own body clock rhythms. Over a week, look at your wake/sleep patterns, eating patterns, working patterns etc. Begin to become aware of your body – when it feels energetic, lethargic, creative, analytical etc. By plotting your rhythms, you will begin to notice when are good times for you to do certain things and therefore create more balance and effective patterns. I have included an example of a general one based on the work of others who have studied the mind-body rhythms in relation to food, activity and rest/exercise (Eat, Move & Be Healthy – Chek 2003, and Patrick Holford, Optimum Nutrition for the Mind).

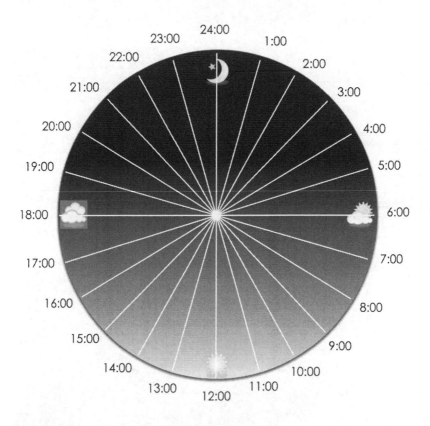

Source: Originally adapted from studies carried out by Patrick Holford as part of Optimal Nutrition and used as a basis for further studies carried out by The Worklife Company into worklife balance and 'great place to work' flexible working and ergo-hours practices in organisations.

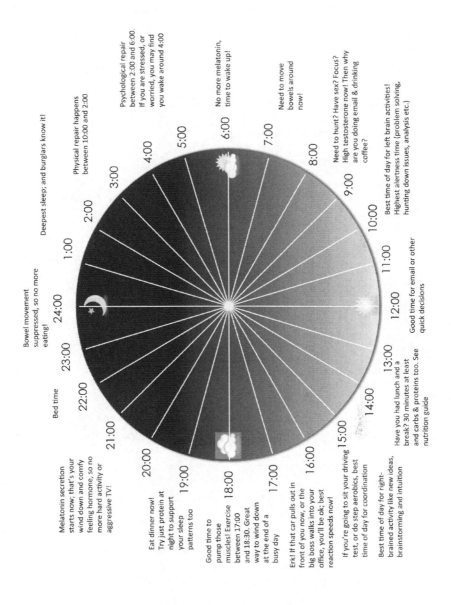

Deepest sleep; and burglars know it!

Physical repair happens between 10:00 and 2:00

Psychological repair between 2:00 and 6:00. If you are stressed, or worried, you may find you wake around 4:00

No more melatonin, time to wake up!

Need to move bowels around now!

Need to hunt? Have sex? Focus? High testosterone now! Then why are you doing email & drinking coffee?

Best time of day for left brain activities! Highest alertness time (problem solving, hunting down issues, analysis etc.)

Good time for email or other quick decisions

Have you had lunch and a break? 30 minutes at least and carbs & proteins too. See nutrition guide

Best time of day for right-brained activity like new ideas, brainstorming and intuition

If you're going to sit your driving test, or do step aerobics, best time of day for coordination

Erk! If that car pulls out in front of you now, or the big boss walks into your office, you'll be ok; best reaction speeds now!

Good time to pump those muscles! Exercise between 17:00 and 18:30. Great way to wind down at the end of a busy day

Eat dinner now! Try just protein at night to support your sleep patterns too

Melatonin secretion starts now; that's your wind down and comfy feeling hormone, so no more hard activity or aggressive TV!

Bed time

Bowel movement suppressed, so no more eating!

1:00
2:00
3:00
4:00
5:00
6:00
7:00
8:00
9:00
10:00
11:00
12:00
13:00
14:00
15:00
16:00
17:00
18:00
19:00
20:00
21:00
22:00
23:00
24:00

Well-being at Work – Tips that promote balance

- *Introduce a well-being suggestion scheme.*

- *Communicate a sense of pride in the workplace.*

- *Schedule time in the diary for 'kicking the leaves'.*

- *Create quiet space for people to rest – train them how to power nap.*

- *Use positive language.*

- *Use colour to enhance well-being.*

- *Use the power of aroma to enhance well-being.*

- *Introduce Yoga, Tai Chi and meditation at the end of the day.*

- *Understand body clocks and introduce ergo-hours flexibility.*

- *Build gender, race, ethnicity, faith etc. networks and support groups.*

- *Introduce chat time in the morning to enhance management and employee communication.*

- *Play to people's strengths.*

- *Build a shared vision.*

- *Hire for attitude and behaviour.*

- *Enhance the environment with natural shapes and plants.*

- *Use pictures and images to enhance mood and growth.*

- *Change performance management systems to reflect strengths, behaviours and potential.*

- *Focus on health and well-being, not sickness and absence.*

- *Focus on physical, emotional and social well-being.*

- *Emotional well-being is key to physical well-being – begin with that – try laughter and fun workshops and focus on happiness and optimism.*

Exercise

Exercise improves mood, reduces depression, releases stress and improves overall well-being. However, we have become desk-bound, especially home-based workers who tend to work longer hours and exercise less than their workplace colleagues. Therefore, it is essential to book time into the day to flex your muscles!

	True	False	Don't Know
I avoid exercise if I can			
I make sure that I exercise for at least 15 minutes a day			
I ensure that my exercise includes weight-bearing and aerobic exercise			
I have been without regular exercise in the last five years			
I suffer from aches and pains after physical work like decorating or gardening			
Strenuous exercise makes me feel out of breath or dizzy			
I understand the benefits of exercise for my mind as well as my body			
I enjoy exercise			

Observations about exercise

Action plan for excercise

What exercise do you enjoy or would you enjoy? Tick all those that would be of interest and look at ways to include them into your schedule:

Running/Jogging		Cycling	
Walking		Water sports	
Gym		Diving	
Swimming		Canoeing	
Dancing		Skating/Skiing	
Sex		Gardening	
Hill climbing/ rambling		Housework	
Ball sports		Other:	

For many women with young children, or demanding schedules, it seems impossible to fit exercise into the week. However, it is essential if you are to stay healthy for your family. Why not try one of the following tips?

1. *Trade – ask a friend to baby-sit while you go for a swim, and do something for her in return. I have two friends who trade chores; one hates and the other loves ironing, one hates and the other loves gardening. So, they each trade two hours a week to the other, doing chores that each loves and escaping from chores that they don't!*

2. *Dance when the kids are asleep! Put on your music, your headphones and dance for an hour. It will make you feel fab while listening to your favourite music.*

3. *Go for a walk with the children too! Switch off the TV and the computer and get out in the air! I have one colleague who cannot keep pets due to allergies and the children have always wanted a dog. So she put an ad in her local newsagent offering to dog-walk children-friendly animals. She and the children now spend an hour a day walking neighbours' dogs and it has become popular with others in her village too.*

4. *Organise a weekly friends' and kids' Clean up our Neighbourhood campaign. This is a great community project for the kids to get involved in and it gets mums, dads and children motivated too.*

5. A 'walking bus' – in Birmingham, the 'walking bus' is a concept that encourages children and parents to walk to school instead of going in the car (which is not good for the environment, congestion and tempers!). It starts off in one location and, as they walk, people tag on and it grows until they have a walking bus.

6. Cycle to work – if you can, get your bike out and cycle. One company could not afford to fund city centre parking for their staff but introduced a Bike Purchase Scheme which was highly subsidised. Over 70% of staff took them up on the offer and bought a bike. Now, staff are healthier, attendance is higher and the company more profitable too!

7. Lunchtime leg stretch – get away from the desk and the office for 20 minutes' brisk walk every day. One nursery school staggered lunch-break times and introduced a power-walk from one end of the street to the other. The total walk was one mile; outbound was uphill and back to the office was downhill. The staff loved it and many good ideas for introducing other ideas were discussed while they walked.

Exercise does not have to include pink Lycra and sweaty gyms! Be creative and make it fun.

My Well-being Plan

My Current situation

Well-being Area	Rating	Very Poor	Poor	Good	Excellent
Nutrition					
Rest					
Exercise					
Emotion					
Sense of work					
Sense of life/community/society					

HINTS

Think about your well-being in terms of the Wellbeing Wheel – which area causes most stress or imbalance?

Complete the exercises and be honest with your answers.

Don't beat yourself up – small steps!

TIPS

Think of well-being as 100% the best you can be, not just 'illness free'.

Put together a plan that will help you to create well-being for life – not just for this week or month!

Develop mental well-being – surround yourself with positive people who make you feel good!

Fill in the starting point exercise above.

Read as much as you can from Patrick Holford and apply his nutritional methods where you can – you'll be amazed at your energy levels!

It'll take time to change a lifetime of habit, so be generous to yourself and positive about the changes you can make over time. It is always good to look back, so keep a journal!

Have fun, be happy!

BAG - My Action Plan

BAG stands for Bin, Add and Get

B	What will I **Bin** that no longer serves my life or goals and prevents me from dancing my best life?	_____ _____
A	What am I already doing, being or having that I could **Add** to or improve in order to dance my best life?	_____ _____
G	What will I **Get** that will serve me well and help me to dance my best life?	_____ _____

Dance your Best Life!

$\mathcal{3}$ My Diary

> 'Your time is limited, so don't waste it living someone else's life.
> Don't be trapped by dogma - which is living with the results of other
> people's thinking. Don't let the noise of others' opinions drown out
> your own inner voice; and most importantly, have the courage to
> follow your heart and intuition. They somehow already know what
> you truly want to become. Everything else is secondary.'
>
> **Steve Jobs, Founder & Chairman Apple Corporation**

This chapter, My Diary, is about time; time for work and time for life, time taken from you by others and time willingly given to others. As women, we often find it difficult to say that little two-letter word – NO! Therefore we will explore the ability to manage our time, say yes when appropriate and that little word when it means that we could be dancing to a tune that is not ours. I bought a birthday card for a friend recently and it announced on the front 'She could speak five languages fluently, but couldn't say No! in any of them!' Time is precious and often in short supply, but even if I were to top up your day with a bit more, you are likely to dance to the wrong tune. However, I cannot add time to your day; you have exactly 24 hours, or 1,440 minutes. Consider this...

You have just won an amazing prize in a dance contest; every day for the rest of your life £86,400 will be put in your account every single day at midnight. The rules of the contest demand that you spend every single penny, every single day. You cannot save any money and leftover unspent money will be deleted from your account. You are not able to transfer it somewhere else or invest it in anything but spending. The harshest rule of all is that it can stop without warning at any time and the account closed.

If this were true, what would you do? Would you buy everything that you wanted, not just for you but for the people you cared for? Would you focus on spending every penny and use it in ways that you saw fit? Are there things that would be a priority? Are there things that you would do for fun or frippery?

The fact is we each receive 86,400 seconds every day at midnight into our bank account of life. Instead of a banknote, it is a beating note that plays in the background of our life music. We cannot hold on to notes for tomorrow, or keep some from yesterday, which means that we cannot save time; we can only spend it. We also don't know when the seconds will run out, so every second counts towards dancing our best life. Enjoy every note of your life, because time dances by so quickly.

Work Time

We spend over a third of our lives in the workplace, therefore work should be a fantastic place to be! Have you noticed that time moves much quicker when you are motivated and much slower when you are bored?

If the scales of worklife balance tipped towards work then the most common reasons for that imbalance are:

- *Workload*
- *Interruptions*
- *Unachievable targets*
- *Management style*
- *Long hours or presenteeism culture*
- *Self - Work addiction*

If they tipped towards life, the most common reasons for imbalance are:

- *Childcare issues*
- *Sick child or relative*
- *Long-term caring responsibilities*
- *Emergency*
- *Hobby, pastime or community commitment*
- *Self – health, mental health, capability*

Imbalance also occurs when the demands of both sides put a woman under so much stress that she literally snaps under the strain. In the UK, 80% of all sickness absence is work-related and 46% of that is worklife imbalance.

Key Facts

Around 68% of women with dependent children and 73% of women without children work outside of the home and 38% of those work part time. One in six working women has children under 16 and the average age of a woman when she gives birth to her first child is 30. The age of the child impacts the number of women in work. Of working-age women with children aged under five, 57% were in employment, 71% of those whose youngest child was aged five to ten and 78% whose youngest child was aged 11 to 15. 86% of the caring responsibilities in a family are still carried out by women and 26% of those have childcare as well as elder/dependant care responsibilities.

Recent data suggests that in the ten years after returning to work after having had children, only 4% of women have been promoted in line with male peers.

Stress-related illness, chronic fatigue and ME are higher in women than in men due to the multiple roles and responsibilities placed on women in our society. 80% of women believe that they have worklife imbalance compared with 4% of men.

Many factors impact people's ability to manage work and life and the reasons for advancement and growth are many and complex; however, time plays a big part in many decisions. Many women spend 40 hours

a week just doing a job and 50 hours a week caring. If you spend 49 hours a week asleep, that's 139 hours; there are only 168 hours in a week, that leaves 29 hours for everything else – where's the time for career development?

Our story ...

Karen was exhausted. The kind of exhausted that makes every bone, muscle and cell ache; even her head felt like it was throbbing. It was Sunday night and thank goodness tomorrow was the start of her late shift. Karen coiled the cable of the steam-snorting iron around its base and put it on the draining board to cool. She folded up the ironing table, her back groaning 'enough' in the spasms of muscle tension. It was 10 o'clock and she had been on her feet most of the day, cleaning the house, doing washing, looking after the children, making meals, clearing up, cooking for her parents and finally doing the ironing. All that was left was packing Josh's gym kit and a final dishwasher load. James was away on business, so there was no one to help. Karen poured herself a large glass of wine and ascended the stairs with a copy of this month's Oprah magazine. She was soon snuggling down between clean sheets, her mag in one hand and her glass on the bedside table. It felt so good to be in bed. The cover of Oprah magazine shone back its promises of life improvement, with the gorgeous face of its host – manicured, coiffured and self-assured – on the front. Karen wondered if Oprah really knew what it was like to juggle work and life. Sure, she had an entourage of writers, but what Karen would do to swap places with her for just a month! She began to consider what Oprah's life must be like and pondered whether she dragged herself off to bed aching from all the housework chores! She decided probably not, and wondered what stress a woman like Oprah really had. As she considered this, she was distracted by an advertisement for an article 'Your Not-to-Do-List' on the front cover. Karen had plenty of 'To-Do' lists, but no 'Not-to-Do-Lists'! She flicked to the article, a thing she rarely did, preferring to first of all skim the whole magazine cover to cover and then go back to specific articles that she wanted to read. This one caught her eye and she proceeded to read through the tips, like not getting upset with teenage daughters when they hate you, to one that stood out the most, 'Don't stay in a job you hate'. The author went on to suggest that doing a job you hate lowers self-esteem and can actually take more time than doing something that you love!

'She is right you know!' whispered a voice to Karen's left. She jumped, almost splashing her prized glass of Sauvignon all over the duvet! 'There's only one thing worse than being frightened to death, and that is someone reading over your shoulder in bed!' the two women laughed, 'at least it is sort of over my own shoulder.' Tomorrow Karen suggested, continuing without pausing, 'When you are not happy doing something, or don't want to do something, you can drag it out! Think about jobs that you despise, do you relish them or do you put them off for as long as possible?'

Karen agreed; doing the ironing was always the last job that she did and it always seemed to take longer than anything else!

'In contrast, when we enjoy doing something it doesn't even seem like a chore at all. Why does time seem to slow down when we are bored, unhappy or stressed?' asked Tomorrow Karen.

'Yes, and why is it that the weekend is over so soon and the whole week seems to stretch in front like a dark, uphill tunnel?'

'What takes up your time at work and at home?'

'Other people and their demands! Menial tasks, chores and interruptions! Also, I suppose I tend to take on too much and have trouble saying no to anyone...' reflected Karen.

'Then let's look at your diary, we are going to look at work and life time, and how we can free you up to begin to focus on what you would truly like to do, rather than have to do!' Tomorrow Karen announced.

Karen laid her magazine to one side, opened her handbag, and waited for the now familiar sinking and spinning feeling as she descended into her own handbag. She stood small in front of her diary, its heather-coloured tartan cover stood tall against the side of her bag like a tall screen. She pulled back the cover to reveal giant pages neatly divided by shiny purple sleeves separating the calendar from address book and notes. Karen pulled the pages apart, scrutinising the scribbled meetings, appointments, reminders and brightly highlighted to-do items. Karen had never really succumbed to the iPhone's structured and synchronised calendar tool, and although she used it, she still preferred the tactile feel of thumbing through pages, the joy of removing a year and replacing it with a new one and the ability to scribble extra things on a page that were not appointments but were important, like 'pick up milk!' or 'mum's birthday present'. The 'always connected' world of her teenage daughter was still not quite her and instead of texting or Facebooking, still liked the joy of the little yellow post-it note and the good old phone!

'Although I seem to be busy, I know that I do even more than this in a day!' justified Karen. 'I am interrupted lots, the nature of nursing is very reactive, but it's not just the patients who interrupt!'

'Interruptions are a big thief of time, and take us away from what is important. We react because we think they are urgent and therefore, based on the advice of a wonderful man called Stephen Covey, we must learn the skills of prioritising those things that are important and those that are urgent.'

'And how does Mr Covey suggest I do that?' asked Karen.

With that, the two women sat down and began to look at all the tasks, projects, appointments, to-do's and goals noted in Karen's diary and began to sort them out with the help of a few spare post-it notes in the back of Karen's large tartan diary.

Karen soon had four piles of post-its: things she had to do, things others wanted her to do, things she dreamed of doing and things she should do. Once the four piles were complete, Tomorrow Karen asked her to sort them into two piles: the things that had to be done right now and those that could wait a while. Once the two piles had been sorted, the final separation was to sort each of those two piles into two more: those that were really important and those that were not. Karen now had four piles: important but not urgent, not important and not urgent, urgent and important, and urgent and not important.

'These correlate precisely with Stephen Covey's Prioritisation Matrix,' explained Tomorrow Karen, and proceeded to stick the notes on to a makeshift model.

'Too much of your time is spent in Quadrant 3, which is urgent, but not important,' noted Tomorrow Karen 'and we need to move you towards working more in Quadrants 2 and 1.'

'That means being disciplined with my diary, interruptions, chores and everything else that I could potentially get involved in, so that I can spend more time in those areas that are more important to me. Especially those things that I dream about, that don't have a deadline, like finding a new job!' confirmed Karen.

The two women continued to sort through Karen's priorities, discuss plans and de-clutter her diary of all the things that were not important. By the end of their time together, Karen's diary for both work and life was much more organised – and a little slimmer!

The Prioritisation Matrix

Repeat the exercise that Karen completed in the story above by writing down as many things as you can on pieces of paper, cards or sticky-notes, under the four headings:

1. *Things you have to do*
2. *Things others want you to do*
3. *Things you dream of doing*
4. *Things you should do*

Now sort all of these into two separate piles – those that are urgent (you must do them right now/today) and those that are not urgent (you can do them at some point in the future).

Now sort each of the two piles into another two piles – those that are important and those that are not important. Important is defined as those things that add to your dance of life; those that don't are not important.

You should now have four piles of cards/sticky notes with different tasks detailed on each. Now, adapted from Stephen Covey's famous prioritisation matrix from 7 Habits of Highly Successful People, I have developed a Dance Prioritisation matrix that provides you with a clear picture of all the tunes that you dance to and which ones need to be stopped, danced by others, scheduled by you and danced by you now.

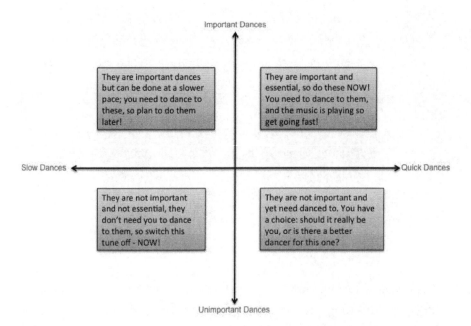

First of all look at all Quadrant 4 items. Remove them from the model and put them straight in the bin. Remove any from your calendar, and if they are not appointments then find ways of saying no to them. Further on in this chapter, we will discuss how to say no.

Now look at Quadrant 3 items. These are the time-wasters because they are not important! These often include things that are demanded or imposed by others. This quadrant needs one of four things to happen to its content, which means you have a choice:

1. *Bin it*

2. *Delegate it*

3. *File it – if it moves up the importance scale, then it will get done, otherwise it won't. File it for a period of time, review it and either delegate it or bin it*

4. *Do it if it is your boss's boss asking, but make sure that something else drops off your list of priorities; don't try to achieve it all!*

That leaves just two quadrants for your attention, both of which are high in importance. As you begin to work on those things that truly matter to you – the needs of your family, or the true needs of the business that you work for – then much of what you do will fall into Quadrant 2. Your objective is to reduce the number of urgent things that require only your attention.

Time and The Thief of Time

In his book The Heart of Success, How to make it in business without losing in life, my dear friend Rob Parsons talks about time and he does the maths for us to provide us with an indication of just how precious time is. I have recalculated the numbers and added a few of my own to put things in a bit of perspective for you. In essence, how you spend your time and how others spend your time for you, is key to your worklife balance:

- *If you have 1,440 minutes in a day, then you have around 9,890 working days until you retire (from graduation to retirement based on current legislation).*

- *If you have given birth today, you have 6,570 days with your child until they are 18 and, in most instances, no longer need day-to-day care from you.*

- *If your child is ten, then you have only 2,920 left.*

- *You will spend 974 of those asleep and 1,856 working.*

- *Without adding up the times spent washing, eating and attending appointments, you actually have 90 days to influence your child –*

approximately three months. Is it any wonder that there are problems in our societies?

🐾 *In addition, if 86% of caring responsibilities for your ten-year-old are yours, then 'time for self' equates to an actual 12.5 days over the next eight years and yet women feel 'guilty' taking time for themselves!*

Even taking a half-day of the 12.5 days would be a challenge to some because life has become a constant dance to other people's tunes. For many women, dancing to the tunes of others has become their way of life. There is no time left for them to dance to their own tune. They have forgotten what it is like to have time for self! How many unread books are on your shelves? How many cancelled hair appointments?

Let us therefore look at time and begin to make you much more in tune with your time – remember every note of your life counts!

Below is a table of typical activities that we participate in on a day-to-day basis. Begin by ticking all of those that are currently relevant to your day; there are some blank lines for you to add your own. Then in the right-hand column, tick all of those that you would like to do in a typical day but never have the chance – add your own here too. There will, of course, be duplicates in both lists.

Actual Time	Tick	Time Spent	Ideal Time	Tick	Time Spent
Sleeping			_____		
Meetings			_____		
Email			_____		
Phone calls (work)			_____		
Doing the job you're hired to do			_____		
Cooking			_____		
Commuting					

Actual Time	Tick	Time Spent	Ideal Time	Tick	Time Spent
Spending time with husband/partner			_____		
Spending time with children/ dependants			_____		
Spending time with family (face to face or phone)			_____		
Spending time with friends			_____		
TV			_____		
Computer (leisure)			_____		
Housework			_____		
Other chores			_____		
Exercise			_____		
_____			_____		
_____			_____		
_____			_____		
_____			_____		
_____			_____		

Now guess the number of hours (or minutes) you spend doing each activity in a day on the left-hand table. Assuming that you had to work, how many hours and minutes would you like to spend doing things on your ideal day? Write these guesses in the relevant column. Transfer each of these times on to the relevant blank pie charts as shown in the example on the following page.

Example **Actual Time**

Time

Example **Ideal Time**

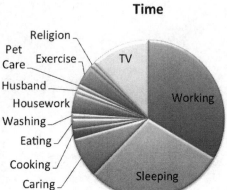

Time

Actual Time

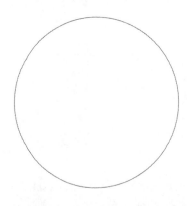

Ideal Time

What are the differences between each of the pie charts?
List them below:

_____
_____
_____
_____
_____
_____
_____
_____

What needs to change in order for you to move towards your ideal day?

What must you BAG? (Complete the BAG Action plan)

BAG - My Action Plan

BAG stands for Bin, Add and Get

B	What will I **Bin** that no longer serves my life or goals and prevents me from dancing my best life?	_____ _____
A	What am I already doing, being or having that I could **Add** to or improve in order to dance my best life?	_____ _____
G	What will I **Get** that will serve me well and help me to dance my best life?	_____ _____

Instead of a guess, you may wish to actually measure how you spend your time and what takes up your time. If so, set aside a typical week in your diary (not one that is holiday or a particularly busy work period) to complete a time log. This can be as detailed as you would like it to be. Some people programme their watch to beep at regular intervals in order to journal each period of time. It is entirely up to you how detailed you want to be; the more detailed, the more data you have from which to make effective decisions. Copy the form so that you have one for every day of the week and then just circle the relevant day. You can also download this form from the website by registering your unique code.

Day of Week (circle) **M   T   W   T   F   S   S**

Date:___/___/

Time	Activity	Comments
9:00 – 9:45	Email weeding	
9:45 – 10:00	Coffee and loo	
10:00 – 11:15	Team meeting	
11:20 – 11:30	Voicemail & email	
11:30 – 13:00	Customer visit	
13:00 – 14:20	Customer lunch	
_____		
_____		
_____		

Was this day (tick) ☐ Typical ☐ More Busy ☐ Less Busy

Total Time Table

Look back over your week and add up the total time you spend doing all the activities that you get involved in. Write them in the table below. Some dances you will want to continue to be a part of your diary but some need to be removed. From the data, you can begin to collect information about what takes up your time. Identify those things that add to your goals and those that prevent you achieving them. Against each activity, highlight those that add value to your life – the dances that you want to dance to – and those that do not. Refer to your prioritisation table earlier in the chapter and plot all of these on to the quadrant.

Then, on the BAG Plan decide those things that you will stop doing, start doing and continue to do that you are already doing. Remember, if you always do what you always did, you'll always get what you always got!

Activity	S	M	T	W	T	F	S
Example -- Email	0	2hrs	2hrs	4 hrs	3 hrs	1 hr	0
Washing	40mins	20mins	20mins	20mins	20mins	20mins	20mins
Housework	4 hrs	1 hr	1 hr	2 hrs	1 hr	1 hr	0

The Thief of Time

Before giving you further tips on how to spend and manage your diary, I must introduce you to the thief of time! She is invisible to you but dances swiftly and deftly through your day, causing delays and feeding your procrastination. She will steal time from your diary and time from your life in many naughty and destructive ways. To know her, and to see her for what she is, takes away her power over you and removes her from your dance of life. You must decide if you want her gone, her name is 'Not Now!'

She has been dancing with me for seventeen years and preventing me from bringing this book to your life. I nearly saw her once when my dear friend Wendy said, 'There are thousands of women out there who need this book and you need to get it finished!' I almost saw her then, as she found loads of other things for me to do rather than write and finish my book. She has found endless excuses for me to do other things rather than sit down and work! 'Not Now' has had me cleaning up my kitchen, surfing the internet, phoning a few contacts and even tidying out my shoe drawers. She will do anything to distract me from being the success that I want to be, sabotaging my time and whispering to me, 'Not now, you are not in the right mood!' or 'Not now, you have to prepare a meal for friends,' or 'Not now, you have to do your expenses.' I nearly didn't get this book to print because of 'Not Now'! When I first spoke to my publisher, she said, 'When can you have the manuscript completed, Lynne?' I replied, 'Well, if I set aside a few hours a day in my schedule, then maybe I could have it to you in six months.' 'No!' she yelled back at me 'I need to have it at the printers in two months, and that's edited! You have exactly five weeks to get it finished, Lynne – this IS your schedule, clear everything else out!' When I put the phone down, I realised that I could finish this book in five weeks; I was already three-quarters of the way through it and five weeks was not long to write the last three chapters! I realised that 'Not Now' was dragging out time for me, and making me procrastinate. When my publisher snapped me into reality with a deadline, 'Not Now' was exposed, I saw her for what she was. You see, as soon as you recognise the time-wasters and time thieves in your life, you can immediately eradicate their power over you. Facing 'Not Now' and seeing her for what she was liberated me from her whisper. I began to stop listening to myself and started talking to myself! Every day I sat down at my Mac and got on with the job of writing. As you are now reading Dancing 'round the Handbags, I was obviously successful in my quest to eliminate 'Not Now' from my life. To think that I might not have published Dancing 'round the Handbags in favour of a clean kitchen!

Exercise – Time Wasters and Time Thieves

On the table below, write down the top ten **time-wasters** or **time thieves** in your life:

After each statement, tick whether they are self-imposed or imposed by others. Prioritise each of them in relation to which are the most likely to prevent you achieving your goals and then choose which five from the list you will eliminate first and this week. Once you have chosen, write your BAG actions in the table below:

Time Waster	Self Imposed	Imposed by Others
1.		
2.		
3.		
4.		
5.		
6.		
7.		
8.		
9.		
10.		

Getting to No! You

Part of the dance is learning the ability to say no. That's a tough call! Some of us have been used to saying Yes to everything for a very long time!

Women often say things like...

> *I say Yes to people all the time! My family, my friends, my colleagues all know that I am just a girl that can't say No! I end up hosting every party, going to lunch when I have deadlines, giving in to pressure from my kids for new clothes, the list goes on! Once I have said Yes I immediately regret it and then spend the next few hours beating myself up for not being strong enough to say No! I end up being exhausted and worn out by the extra things I take on, and I end up with no time left to just relax!*

Putting everyone else's requests and needs first is a common dilemma for women. If you are going to be effective at looking after your personal resources, workload and time, it is important to stay away from allocating your time solely on the basis of those who demand it. Instead, it may be better to allocate your time on the basis of those who deserve it. This is not cruel; it is essential that we set limits and expectations on the amount of time we spend on each task and each person. Therefore, one of the most important words in your vocabulary needs to be the word No!

Almost everyone that you encounter will think they have a better idea about how you should spend your time than you do! If you keep on saying Yes to their demands, what will happen? You become exhausted and they will continue to take up your time! This behaviour is likely to keep you from accomplishing your own goals and ambitions.

No is sometimes difficult to say because you may have been taught differently, to say Yes, to please, to serve, to avoid blame, punishment or being perceived in the workplace as 'not a team player'. There is nothing wrong with saying Yes some of the time, but saying Yes every time is really not the best use of your precious time.

Lynn Battle's 'How to say No and mean it' – suggests that there are six ways to say No. It is not until we can say No assertively and with resolve that our Yes means Yes, and our No means No. Saying Yes when you would rather say No can lead to increased stress and tension – look at the Lipstick chapter for more details about stress.

Some of my coaching clients have told me that they cannot say No because they feel as though they are letting the other person down. I explain that they are confusing the rejection of a request with the rejection of the person making the request.

In reality, you will conclude that people are happier to accept an honest No rather than be faced with indecision and a refusal later on, or a Yes when you meant No. This can lead to frustration and resentment on both sides because you are not being authentic and assertive and the other person knows you're not! This can become harmful to the trust in your relationship.

So, how do we say **No** and mean it? Simple. Practise. Here are the six different ways that Lynn suggests:

The **direct No**

When someone asks you to do something that you do not want to do, just say 'No'. No apologising, just be direct and succinct. For instance, if someone is asking you to join them for lunch, you simply say, 'No, no thank you, not today.'

The **reflecting No**

Here you acknowledge the content and feeling of the request and then you add the assertive refusal at the end: 'I know you want to talk to me about organising the annual department lunch, but I can't do lunch today.'

The **reasoned No**

This technique involves giving a brief and genuine reason for the refusal without opening up further negotiation: 'I can't have lunch with you because I have a report that needs to be finished by tomorrow.'

The **rain check No**

This is a way of saying No to the specific request without giving a definite No. It is a prelude to negotiation. It's not a rejection of the request but only use it if you genuinely want to meet the request: 'I can't have lunch with you today, but I could make it some time next week.'

The **enquiring No**

This is a way of opening up the request to see if this is something you want to do: 'I can't have lunch with you today, but is there anything else you want to talk to me about, other than the office Christmas lunch?'

The **broken record**

This technique can be used an awful lot – in all sorts of situations. Repeat the simple statement of refusal again and again. No explanation, just repeat it over and over. It is necessary to use this with particularly persistent requests:

> 'No, I can't have lunch with you.'
>
> 'Oh, please, it won't take long.'
>
> 'No, I can't have lunch with you.'
>
> 'Oh, go on, I'll pay.'
>
> 'No, I can't have lunch with you.'

And so on.

Practising how to say No helps you to dance to your own tune and gives you greater control over your time and your life. So review these six options and even if you think they haven't sunk in, next time you feel a grudging Yes coming on you'll be surprised at how easily one of these options pops up to save the day.

What if it's my Boss?

'I feel as if I'm drowning at work and at home.' These were a client's first words, but to be honest she didn't need to enunciate them; her body language and the mounting pile of tissues told the tale. Her feelings of not coping are of course familiar to many of us at different stages in our lives and not exclusive to women. Many people work in a performance-driven culture that demands more for less, year on year. In this culture, workload continually increases and employees do not feel that it is appropriate or safe to say No to extra tasks or work. Many fear losing their jobs as a consequence of not saying Yes all of the time.

We are all capable of juggling but, from time to time, events, work demands, health issues, family responsibilities and must-do jobs can just overwhelm us. Therefore I am going to add a seventh to the list above:

Don't Say No say Wo!

When your boss next asks, 'Can you take on this extra project?' instead of saying Yes or No say 'Wo!' Wo! is a word we use with horses and it means 'stop', 'hold on there!' Of course, you want to look positive to your boss and not come across as uncommitted to the company's success and so Wo! provides you with a win-win solution that role-models good practice to your boss and conveys that you are a human being, not a human-doing. This is how it would be used in conversation:

> **Boss:** *'Would you please take on this extra target and complete it by the end of the week?'*
>
> *Employee:* *'Wo! I am happy to take on this extra target for you and of course will do it by the end of the week, but what drops off the bottom of the my to-do list in favour of this priority?'*

By saying Wo! you are slowing down the music, taking stock of the extra workload, and involving your boss in the decision-making about what tune you will drop in favour of this.

I have used Wo! for many years, and it works! If Wo! doesn't work, find another non-word, like Um or Er or Mmm!

If you are a leader or manager in your business, take time to focus employees on the right thing and that sometimes means stopping doing things.

Delegating Effectively at Work

This is one of the skills that can make or break your success as a manager or leader.

The delegation quiz

	True	False
I can delegate easily		
I seem to work longer hours than others in my team		
I often do things for others in my workplace that they could do for themselves		
I often do things for others in my family that they could do for themselves		
I seem to have a backlog of work building up		
It is hard to meet deadlines		
I feel guilty asking people to do things that I could just get on with		
By the time I've explained it, I could have it done!		
It is my place to do it all		
If a job is worth doing well, it is worth doing myself		
My team are already overworked, I can't give them any more to do		
I don't trust anyone to do my work to my standard		
I don't trust anyone to do my housework to my standard		
I hate letting go of tasks I enjoy doing		
Someone else might do it better than me and then my job security would be jeopardised		
Employees always think that I am passing on the unpleasant tasks		
I don't want results to suffer		

Delegation is not easy and yet is one of the most important aspects of any manager's job. When you delegate you deliberately choose to hand over responsibility for a task to someone else. The word 'responsibility' when used in this context implies that the person involved is empowered to do the job properly. Accountability still rests with you – you are accountable for everything that goes on in your department or even in your family.

Three Tips for Delegation

1. *Delegate the right task*

2. *Choose the right person for the task*

3. *Communicate the right information*

Some questions before deciding what to delegate and to whom

- *What is a decision in your work area that you have to make all the time?*

- *What is a task in your work area that would provide good experience for one of your team?*

- *Have you have got someone in your group who, no matter what you give them to do, always does a good job?*

- *What are you most likely to do when you have something important that you want to delegate? Do you always delegate to the same person?*

- *Do you consider it part of your job to develop the people you manage?*

- *How often do you only delegate the tasks that you don't want to do yourself?*

On a separate piece of paper, create a list of tasks you could delegate. Write down the names of three people in your team that you feel comfortable delegating to.

1. _____

2. _____

3. _____

Who has been overlooked when you have delegated to these three in the past?

Why bother to delegate?

- It allows you to focus on the aspects of your job where your strengths and experience are best utilised; properly carried out, delegation improves morale as well as motivation and engagement.

- Delegation helps to train and develop employees and helps with planning your successor.

Things to delegate

- Routine jobs.

- Necessity tasks that have to be done should be delegated, leaving the discretionary ones to you.

- Pet projects – the temptation is not to delegate what you enjoy doing the most.

- Development opportunities for others – what skills, competencies and behaviours do staff members need to develop? How can you provide them with the opportunity to do so?

Things not to delegate

- Duties or tasks that depend on your position as the team leader/ manager and not on your skills.

- Tasks or duties that relate to organisation or policy decisions.

- Personnel matters or confidential matters – maintaining confidence is vital and under no circumstances should such matters be delegated.

- Crises – good managers should not let crises occur; proper planning and anticipation will avoid crisis situations. However, where they do occur they should be retained by you unless you do not have the skills to complete the task successfully.

Use a form like the one below to decide what to delegate and to whom:

TASK	OWNER	TRAINING	DEADLINE
What am I going to delegate?	To Whom?	What training or coaching is this person going to need to do this task?	When will I delegate and when does the task need to be completed by?

Time Tips

- *Prioritise the key tasks that you want to accomplish.*

- *Delegate some tasks to others – developmental ones!*

- *Deal with your mail and email the first time you handle it – don't push piles round your desk or stockpile!*

- *If you are working on a deadline, put an extended absence greeting on email or voicemail to let people know and set the expectation of when you will get back to them. If you work in an open-plan area, set up a 'red flag' system – if the red flag is up, no interruptions; if the red flag is down, come on in!*

- *Work on tasks that require your analytical skills in the morning and creative skills in the afternoon.*

- *Set deadlines for yourself and others, make your own public.*

- *Do not spend more time on a job than it deserves.*

- *Do the jobs you don't enjoy in between those that you do.*

- *Schedule meetings with yourself in your diary – these are QRT meetings. Of course, in your diary they look important and they are! QRT stands for Quality Recovery Time. Athletes know what this is, it is rest time to plan and prepare for the next training session or performance. An athlete warms up, performs, warms down and then has QRT. Like her, you would also do well to build in periods of QRT into your day or week. Without it, you may well end up running from meeting to meeting, and deadline to deadline, in a frenzy of expectation that you will deliver your personal best each time. Unless you build in QRT, you may soon become worn-out and sick. QRT provides quiet times for preparation, planning, reading and thinking. Book at least 20 minutes every couple of hours where you can reflect on the previous two hours and prepare for the next. Find a meeting room or sit in your car or somewhere else that you won't be interrupted. When I need QRT, I tend to work from home.*

- *Clear your desk of anything you are not currently working on. Your brain is unconsciously distracted by everything on your desk even if you are not looking at it. Therefore, in-trays, unpaid bills, coffee cups in varying stages of decay, family photographs and that unopened bar of chocolate are all distractions from the task in hand.*

- *Bin as much paper as possible. Don't hang on to things on your desk; file it, bin it, action it or pass it on!*

- *Highlight important parts of documents and reports so that you don't have to read the whole thing again.*

- *Let people know how much time you can give them and manage your boundaries accordingly.*

- *If you receive an unwanted interruption, stand up and remain standing throughout. If you can't get them to leave, leave yourself. Remember, if you have a big jar of cakes or sweets on your desk and a chair strategically placed to welcome visitors, you are unconsciously crying out to be interrupted! The cakes and sweets are nice but leave them by the water-cooler or coffee area.*

- *Set up a decompression chamber – at the end of the day, spend a few minutes clearing your desk and then find a place or do an activity that allows you to wind down from your day before going home. Some companies set aside areas where employees can meet at the end of the day, share their day, their gripes and stories and then leave the office and all of it behind. Some people prefer to exercise, listen to music in the car or go for a walk – anything as long as it is not work and not quite home.*

- *It allows the brain time to wind down and switch off and you can walk through your front door ready for family time.*

- *Don't do email first thing, leave it until just before lunch, when you will whiz through it to get it out of the way much quicker than you would first thing. Why? Because you are hungry and your brain forces you to be decisive!*

- *Remember: you cannot SAVE time, you can only SPEND it!*

Delegating at Home

Same rules as above really! Note of warning: if you are a mum, we do tend to do things for our family and the more you do, the more they'll allow you to! Run your family like a ballet; everyone has his or her own part and it needs everyone to dance in a choreographed way for it to be a beautiful performance!

Involving children in chores and responsibilities from a young age is a good thing. Of course, we are not talking about Victorian child labour like chimney sweeping! It is appropriate for children to begin to learn responsibility for helping others. My friend has a chart in the kitchen that defines all the chores and every Sunday they all sign up for the ones they commit to do that week. Each day they tick the chart to say the chore is done. Chores include feeding the cat, making the beds, dusting, loading and unloading the dishwasher and emptying the bins. It means that the children contribute to the home and the weekly change means that the job doesn't get too boring.

BAG - My Action Plan

BAG stands for **B**in, **A**dd and **G**et

B	What will I **Bin** that no longer serves my life or goals and prevents me from dancing my best life?	_____ _____
A	What am I already doing, being or having that I could **Add** to or improve in order to dance my best life?	_____ _____
G	What will I **Get** that will serve me well and help me to dance my best life?	_____ _____

4 My Lipstick

The lipstick is a metaphor for the masks that you wear to put on a brave face, or to show a public face. This chapter deals with two things:

🍂 **Stress Resilience** – *your ability to cope with stress and pressure, the masks you wear to protect you and disguise your stress.*

🍂 **Authenticity** – *the masks that challenge self-confidence, self-belief and esteem. The lipstick, or public persona, can sometimes mask the person that we really are, and it includes a number of masks that we have evolved due to circumstances, social expectation, stress and conditioning. This chapter explores how the public persona creates an illusion of who we really are; we will explore the seduction of the mask and why women use masks.*

What is a mask? Masks can be two things:

1. *A means of protection*

2. *A disguise*

The protecting mask provides a protective cover or shield from hazards, external dangers and threats. These masks ensure our safety and well-being in certain situations and form our resilience to stress.

The disguising mask covers the true identity/feelings or needs of the person beneath. They can be used to create intrigue as well as change character. This kind of mask allows us to become someone or something that we are not – it can build or reduce self-confidence.

The Protecting Mask

What is Emotional and Psychological Stress?

HSE Definition: 'Stress is a reaction people have when excessive pressure or demands are placed upon them, and arises when an individual believes they are unable to cope.'

Stress Explained

Stress is our perception of a situation or an event that can be in the present, past or future. It might also be real or imagined, repetitive or a single incident.

The way we physiologically and emotionally deal with the situation, the behaviour that we resort to in order to deal with the situation and our response. In summary, stress is a response made by people to demands made upon them!

Symptoms of Stress

Brainstorm your stress symptoms under the following headings:

- *Physical symptoms*
- *Emotional symptoms*

Examples are shown in the table below:

Physical	Emotional
Headache	Irritable
Indigestion	Guilt
Aching muscles	Weepy

Harmful levels of stress are most likely to occur when:

- *The pressures continue to pile up or are prolonged*
- *People feel trapped or unable to exert control over the demands placed on them*
- *People are confused by conflicting demands*

Possible Causes of Stress

Brainstorm a list of potential causes of stress from your work or life:

Stressor	Cause

Fight and Flight Response

Stress comes from two main areas:

- **Big Life Events** – *these flare up, we deal with them and get back to normal*
- **Day-to-Day Hassles** – *these are the little stresses that build up and cause prolonged and cumulative stress-related outcomes*

Big Life Events

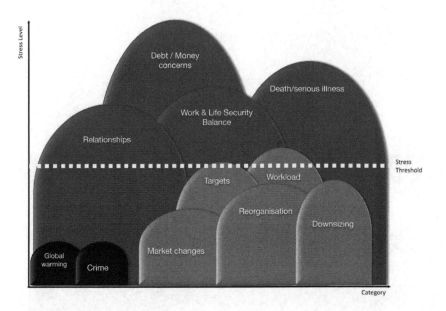

In the diagram above, the dotted line is our stress threshold and there are those stressors like global warming, referred to as macro stressors that, whilst important, do not usually affect us on a day-to-day basis. For example, in recent times crime rates may have dropped but the fear of crime has risen.

These only become major stressors if they impact us directly and in the present. For example, terrorism or natural disaster may be a background fear for many people, but until it comes to the foreground and is threatening our survival now, then it generally does not tip us over our stress threshold.

The cumulative effect of lots of workplace change, plus life issues such as sick relatives or debt, can cause our metaphorical scales to snap. Experts say that it is the life issues, the ones closest to us (micro) that impact us most.

Research by Lazarus and Folkman (1984) at the University of California indicated that it was the daily hassles rather than the major life events that affect us more. It suggests that because very big and stressful life events do not happen every day, it is the cumulative effect of the little dances and hassles that cause more negative impact. The day-to-day continuous little things like inconsiderate driving, time pressures, office politics, queues and trying to get the children off to school in the morning, cause us the most stress because they create a drip, drip, drip of stress that can diminish our well-being.

Small stressors like these can easily be managed by reframing them, or in other words, by looking at them differently. Stress only occurs because of how we perceive something. For example, being in a queue or traffic jam on a motorway is a hassle for some, whilst for others it is an opportunity to sit back, enjoy the radio and have some me-time. Take the example below – the woman sees a lovely flower and has a desire to smell its perfume. However, her brain solicits memories and decisions based on her beliefs about flowers; these are her filters. Then she creates an internal representation of the flower because she remembered that the last time she sniffed one of these flowers, it caused a bad reaction. She therefore has an emotional response to the flower, which drives a psychological reaction, 'Oh no! I am going to be ill!' and this results in her physical reaction to find tablets to prevent the problem (fight or flight).

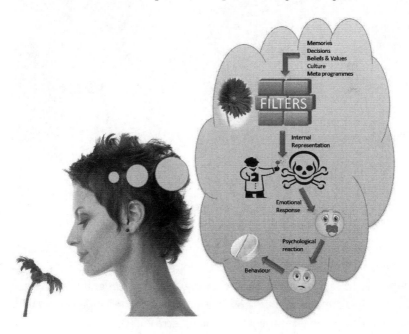

We all have programmes running in our head, and they are not a problem unless they become self-limiting and prevent us from achieving success. These internal filters are built as a result of our responses to events or stimuli and our decisions about them, which are based on our values and belief systems, underpinned by our cultures. Reframing helps the brain to not react in usual ways but to find alternative ways of perceiving the stressor.

List all the little things that are hassles for you on the right-hand side of this table, and then on the left, reframe them into other ways of thinking about them:

Stressor/Hassle	Reframe
I hate being stuck in this traffic jam! I am going to be late for work and goodness knows what is holding everything up!	Well at least I have some me-time to think or relax. There is nothing I can do about the jam, so I may as well use it constructively by doing nothing and just being!

Our minds and bodies are part of the same system, so our thoughts and feelings are linked and so, therefore, are our outcomes. What we think about, we bring about is often so true in terms of stress and pressure. Therefore, by reframing our thoughts and expectations about an event, we may also change its outcome for us in terms of well-being.

Dealing With and Managing Stress

Relaxation and Breathing Techniques

Our breathing is a good indicator of how stressed we are. When we are in control, our breathing is rhythmic and relaxed, but when we are stressed it becomes erratic, shallow or irregular. Gaining more control over our breathing gives us more control over our stress. Regular and conscious practice is very important. Start with 15 minutes once or twice a day for two weeks. Keep a log and monitor your responses.

The Breath Counting Technique

STEP 1. Find a quiet place. Concentrate and focus on your breathing. Lie down or sit comfortably. Any place will do.

STEP 2. Focus on your breathing. Feel the air being inhaled through your nose and exhaled through your mouth. Count mentally to four as you breathe in, then hold for four and breathe out for four. Note when the air feels warm and when it feels cool. Allow your breathing to be natural and relaxed. You might like to try breathing in through your mouth and out through your nose. Choose whichever is the most comfortable for you.

STEP 3. Continue to breathe regularly. Allow the sense of calmness and ready composure to spread through your body as you breathe out. Visualise the clean new air radiating through you in healing waves. Give your incoming clean and fresh breath a colour. Then, as you hold for four, imagine that colour filtering through every cell in your body. Help it to be brighter and more vibrant in those areas of your body that feel particularly stressed. Then, to a count of four, blow away all the stress, tension and anxieties. Watch as they leave you, floating down to earth where they disappear into the ground like raindrops to begin their cleansing journey. Feel balanced and in control. Practise until you feel this effect.

Use this exercise both as a preventative measure and as a procedure for gaining control of a stress reaction. Everybody finds it difficult to stay focused. If you find yourself focusing on something other than your breathing simply let it go and focus again on your breathing. This gets easier with practice. Make concentrating on your breathing your chosen or preferred thought. You can achieve this lovely, peaceful, calm feeling anywhere and as often as you like.

The Walking Breathing Technique

You can practise this technique while walking anywhere.

STEP 1. Walk a bit more slowly than usual and concentrate on your breathing. Notice the detail of your in and out breaths.

STEP 2. Notice how many steps you take with each breath. Do not try to control your breathing, just be aware of how your body is responding.

STEP 3. Now see if you can synchronise in and out breaths with your feet hitting the ground. It doesn't matter how many steps you take in between.

STEP 4. Work out your own personal breathing and walking rhythm. If your mind wanders, gently return it to the task in hand.

If you perform these exercises on a regular basis, you will begin to notice where in your body you hold tension and stress. You can then focus on those areas by breathing and relaxing into them and thereby removing potential discomfort.

Ten ways of cutting down stress at work

1. *Create conditions where employees have maximum control over their working lives, for example by sharing as much information as possible or by encouraging teams to manage themselves.*

2. *Offer learning opportunities for all staff, including some time that can be used for personal development.*

3. *Ensure that every employee thinks about their goals for the week ahead a week before and their goals for tomorrow the day before or early on the day in question.*

4. *Establish a culture where it is expected that individuals will ask for help throughout the day if they are unable to prioritise their own workload.*

5. *Create flexible work arrangements for as many staff as possible.*

6. *Encourage employees to take physical exercise, learn yoga, autogenic training, meditation, sitting posture, regular breathing*

and other useful techniques, by laying on sessions before and after the working day or in the lunch break.

7. *Encourage people to take breaks by taking them yourself.*

8. *Encourage everyone to share their one favourite stress-buster and display these as posters or on your intranet.*

9. *Tell jokes, encourage laughter and actively seek to find the funny side in all that goes on at work.*

10. *Create a worklife decompression chamber. Spend the last hour of the day on the least stressful things, for example making some nice telephone calls, thinking about the next day, or tidying up. Give yourself a few minutes of quiet reflection before you return through your front door at home by stopping the car a few miles away, listening to music in the car, train, or bus, stopping to look at a view if you are walking, and actively switch off your work mind before you re-join your personal world. Never walk in your own front door on a call to a colleague!*

BAG - My Action Plan
BAG stands for Bin, Add and Get

B	What will I **Bin** that no longer serves my life or goals and prevents me from dancing my best life?	_____ _____
A	What am I already doing, being or having that I could **Add** to or improve in order to dance my best life?	_____ _____
G	What will I **Get** that will serve me well and help me to dance my best life?	_____ _____

The Masks Women Wear

The second part of the Lipstick chapter focuses on our coping mechanisms and in particular the masks that we often wear to put on a brave face or hide our true feelings.

The Three Parts of Self

There are three parts to you: there is your authentic self (the true you!), there is your critical self (the one that can hold you back) and there is your public self (the one that other people see). The public self wears masks.

The public self is the visible you, the part of you that is 'on show' to others. It is the mask that you wear and is made up of years of influence, belief systems and experience. When you look in your mirror, this is the person you see looking back at you. It is the visible outer person and includes your 'visible' personality, the personality that is public, that is shown to others. For example, imagine in your mind right now an image of your best friend. You know what she looks like and can probably describe that image quite clearly. Now describe her personality, how she behaves in front of others, her humour, her style and maybe some of her beliefs. That is the public persona, the public self. Are you just your physical self and your personality, or is there more? Are there other parts of you that you don't share/can't share? To understand your public self a bit more, ask yourself the following questions:

1. *If you were a handbag, what would you look like, be made of, colour, material etc.?*

2. *What do you like people to notice about you first?*

3. *If you were introducing yourself, what three things would you tell people?*

4. *What aspects of your personality do you like people to notice first?*

5. *What item of clothing or accessory do you have that sums up your personality?*

6. *If someone were presenting an award to you, what would you like it to be presented for?*

Sometimes we wear masks of conformity to society norms; beliefs that we 'should' behave, live or communicate in a certain way. These 'shoulds' build our internal belief systems, for example, 'I should do all the housework', 'I should be a perfect mum', 'I should be fully qualified', 'I should be thin' etc.

The Disguising Mask

The masks are manifestations of the public self and have their roots in the critical voice. The masks we wear disguise our authentic self.

If you are like most women, you will wear a few masks during particular phases of your life. The masks of disguise can also be interchangeable and therefore more than one mask can be worn at any one time.

They are there to disguise our feelings of guilt, imperfection and sense of duty.

- **The Mask of Perfection** – *the underlying fear is imperfection, which sets some irrational expectations and makes us try to keep up with others' expectations of who we should be. This mask hides our feelings of guilt and shame of not being perfect or good enough; an over-active conscience that creates a tug of war between work and life.*

- **The Mask of Duty** – *linked to shoulds and delivering a schedule of frenetic activity, workload and burden. This underlies our feelings of pleasing others and never feeling as though we can say No to the demands of others. Sometimes in the workplace this can be seen as role confusion – a woman wears the mask of being male in order to fit into a male-dominated culture*

- **The Mask of Coping** – *a cover for underlying stress – putting on a brave face! This mask hides the feelings of stress from trying to cope with everything alone and resisting asking for help. Sometimes this can be linked to perfectionism (only I am good enough to do it) and prevents us from delegating or seeking assistance. It can also be linked to fears related to losing control, fear of failure or, indeed, fear of success.*

Our story ...

As Karen waved her son off to school, she felt a rising surge of guilt and fear. Josh had wanted to walk to school with his friends, and without parents, for such a long time but Karen wasn't ready to let go – until today. The first day back after the Easter break. Josh ran off in a flurry of excitement to catch up with his friends Harry, Nathan, Abi and Emily. The five children skipped off to school, backpacks bouncing with delight as they exchanged the latest collectibles and chocolate biscuits while silently enjoying their new-found independence. Karen watched as they disappeared out of sight, praying that they would be safe and that no weirdo would snatch her innocent lamb. As she closed the door, tears of guilt and regret burst their emotional banks and she sank down into Josh's chair at the kitchen table as if trying to feel his presence. She sobbed uncontrollably.

'Karen,' said a voice, it was the Tomorrow Karen 'he'll be OK you know!'
she comforted. 'I know,' said Karen, aware that the new woman in her life
had just re-appeared from nowhere. 'I just feel so guilty; no, frightened!
My imagination runs riot!' she sniffed. 'James says that I am silly and
over-protective of Tilly and Josh! But he doesn't understand! He just gets
up, showers, shaves and shoves off!' She snorted. 'I put on such a brave
face, but I am scared stiff inside! What if something happens to them?'
she wailed.

'Come on,' beckoned Tomorrow Karen 'let's make a nice cup of tea and
we'll sit in your conservatory for a while!' Karen did as she was told and
within a few minutes the two women were sitting in the conservatory
staring into the garden and sipping tea.

It was early spring, and the persistent rain fell in drops that appeared
determined to penetrate every inch of soil to deliver life-giving moisture
to all the plants. Karen imagines that every raindrop is eager to feed and
encourage every living thing in her garden to burst forth and be the best
it can be. As she ponders, she realises that not one thing in her garden
will grow to become the same as the next; instead it will just be the best
it can be in the circumstances in which it grows – the best grass, the best
tree, the best rose, even the best weed. They may fight for survival round
a stone, an old flowerpot, or Josh's discarded bike, but the fact is that they
will fight to survive, to show off their own unique beauty.

'Doesn't it make you think that we are all a bit like those plants?' said
Tomorrow Karen, interrupting the silence and snapping the younger
woman out of her daydream.

'Yes, in a way,' she nodded, not daring to question the mind-reading!
'If you look at all those plants, they all want to grow, they all want to
develop. It made me think of me and my children in that context too;
how we each grow and develop to be tall, small, large, skinny, black,
white, able-bodied or disabled; all unique.' She continued, 'And before
you say it, I understand that it is important to recognise that we cannot
hold back growth – like Josh this morning, going to school is part of his,
but I feel so responsible and guilty!'

'As we grow, our rain is our personal development; the experiences
that land in our garden of life providing us with the ability to grow into
whatever and whomever we are meant to be. We all have our own
reactions to that rain and other people cannot own our development and
growth; our reaction to that rain is our choice, it's about how we react to
the world around us. Some will grow strong and confident, some will not.
However, unlike the garden plants we can remove some of the barriers
to our personal growth by understanding how our attitude to personal
development impacts our world, how our belief system can hold us back
and how our self-esteem can be impacted by these beliefs. In this chapter
we are going to explore your emotional well-being, which includes your
sense of self worth, your emotional stress and the masks you wear. You
wear masks to show a public face to the world, so today we are going to
explore the next item in your handbag – your lipstick. Some of these masks
hold you back and prevent you from being fantastic.'

Tomorrow Karen reached down and lifted the handbag on to the table
between the two women. The empty teacups were set aside and, as
before, both women stared intently at the handbag in front of them.
Its floppy black handles, draped over the front like arms in emotional
defence, hiding the fastener and protecting the front pockets from
scrutiny, flopped down to the side like arms, exposing the contents of
the bag. The silver buckles reflected the rolling clouds above and, in their
hypnotic drift, drew the eyes of the women into the contents of the bag.

'There's my lipstick,' announced Karen, reaching in and pulling out a
silver bullet-shaped tube. 'In fact, my favourite one, Peach Sorbet!' she
said as she pulled off the lid and twisted its base to expose the peach-
coloured waxy remains of her favourite make-up. 'I must buy another
one of these soon!' she announced as she quickly replaced the cap and
slid it back into her bag, as if protecting the final remnants from over-use
or loss.

As Karen stared at her bag she began to feel drowsy. Her eyelids felt
heavy as she drifted downwards into the well of her unconscious mind.
She began to spin around and around and around her handbag, viewing

every side as she encircled it in some mad dance with an invisible partner who would not allow her to stop. The bag appeared to grow larger and larger as she shrank to a fraction of her normal size. She closed her eyes; the spinning, as soon as it had started, stopped. There she was, sitting astride the lipstick like a child on some abstract hobby horse, inside her very own handbag once more. Karen tried to focus, she still felt slightly dizzy as if she had just been on a fairground ride that had suddenly stopped. This time, Karen didn't try to reason why or how she came to be the size of her roller-ball pen or for that matter how she had arrived safely inside her own bag; she just proceeded to look around. She could clearly see all the objects in her bag. To her right was her purse, looming like a tall skyscraper against the side of the bag, its vertical lines, corners and angles towering above Karen's head in architectural grandeur against the blue satin sky of lining inside the bag. Tucked underneath the purse, like stark steps, were a few neatly-folded tissues and, like some crass corporate-commissioned sculpture, a ball of golden foil left over from a sneaky bar of chocolate eaten (instead of lunch) during a recent shift at the hospital, sat poised outside of the building-like purse.

'I see you have landed on the lipstick!' chuckled Tomorrow Karen as she appeared from behind the screen-like cover of her diary. 'The lipstick is about the masks you wear to cover up your stress and your authentic self. All of your hours of conditioning and living the way you "think you should" can create a public self! In fact, lots of public selves that mask the real and authentic you!' she explained. 'Therefore, we are going to look at those masks and wipe away some of the masks that stress…'

'What kind of masks do you mean?' asked Karen.

'Well, what mask did you wear this morning with Josh?'

'I had to show I could cope! Otherwise I would have been a crying wreck in front of him. So I suppose I wore a mask then? I suppose I wore a mask when I said Yes to lunch with a colleague that I don't like any more?'

'Yes, these are masks and coping is one of the tightest!'

The Mask of Perfection

Guilt is something that we learn when we are very young. We learn it because it is our parents' and teachers' way of providing us with a conscience. Having a conscience is important, as it is the cornerstone of civilised behaviour and emotional intelligence; we are able to understand the impact of our behaviour on others. Guilt is something that we feel as a result of other people's words and gestures, or our own internal voice. Guilt is rooted in control; it is a way for the person in authority to command obedience and respect. It is used so often by parents to inflict a sort of punishment, 'You will make daddy so unhappy if...' We suddenly feel bad about what we have 'not' done even though our initial intention was not to hurt. The child develops a sense of guilt through the words spoken to them; we would never know how to feel guilty unless someone helped us to feel this emotion. From the words used, we are made to feel guilt, which in turn leads to emotions linked to feelings of regret, shame and unworthiness. Feeling unworthy, or not good enough, feeds our critical voice, self-esteem and self-confidence, which in turn can paralyse us into taking less risk, make us into people pleasers and riddle us with worry.

Emotions like guilt often manifest in the solar plexus area or stomach area of our bodies. The sayings like 'I feel sick to my stomach with guilt' or 'worry guts' demonstrate the emotion of guilt in its physical manifestation. It can also make us feel breathless and prolonged worry and stress brought on by guilt may result in chest and tummy complaints like indigestion, IBS and other symptoms.

In relation to worklife balance, guilt is a major challenge that women in the workplace face. To see how it affects us, let's visit Karen at work. She is just about to leave the hospital at the end of a nightshift as she has to get back home before her husband leaves for work...

Our story ...

Having children to get to school, packed lunches to make and catching up on the ironing before her next shift, Karen knew that she had to get out on time today. It had been a tough night. Two new admissions – one attempted suicide and one elderly gentleman suffering from acute angina – meant that Karen had no time for anything routine like paperwork and bedpans! As it turned out, the old man had just passed away and Karen had stayed a bit longer to inform his family. She was exhausted. She did what she could to prepare the next shift but now she really had to go. James would be looking at his watch, itching to get out of the door. The traffic would already be building up and the kids would be hollering at each other across the breakfast table, both claiming ownership of the free toy in the cereal box!

Karen had worked so hard all night, skipped every break and had cut through raft-loads of duties like a chef fan-chopping carrots. She had run from job to job in a frenzy of effort that she hoped conveyed to others around her a clear message that said 'Look at me, I work so hard and I am so dedicated so please don't give me a hard time when I need to go home!' Karen is nervous that no one has noticed the hard work; they have only noticed that she is eager to go.

Karen rises from her nursing station and pulls on her coat of guilt. This coat has two badges on it: one states 'I feel guilty leaving my colleagues behind to carry on working.' The other states 'I feel guilty not being there for my family.' Once she has done up the buttons to make sure the guilt coat doesn't fall off, she pulls on her hat of shame which also has two badges, one that states 'I am not a good team player or a good mother!' and another that states 'I am all alone in these feelings of shame; other women get it right, why can't I?' She pulls it down tight over her ears to muffle the ensuing comments and then begins to run the gauntlet of ward politics. First there is Shelley-the-DINKY (double income no kids yet) whose ambition in life is to run the hospital single-handedly and prove to the world that you can have it all. Shelley flicks a disapproving glance at Karen as she picks up the blood pressure monitor and stomps off down the ward, her heels like heavy summer rain pounding on a bus shelter. Her disapproval is merged with insincere pity and a look that roars into Karen's ears, 'Shame you'll never make it like me.' Then in a flick of her monitor and swivel of her hips, she is lost in patronising conversation with the elderly gentleman in Bed 9.

Then Karen meets Madge's glare; a scary troll that has neither empathy nor sympathy for today's working mother. It is at least 30 years since her family were young but she was a good mother and of course stayed at home when they were young. She stares from above her spectacles, neck muscles twitching disapproval from beneath her starched uniform and equally starched attitude. She fidgets in her seat; a gesture that simultaneously convulses into a heaving sigh as she raises her lizard-like glare towards the clock. This is the signal for Henry and Seb (the student doctors) to launch into their hyena-like cackles and snarls. 'B****y part timers!' they yell across the ward in fits of hysterical, shoulder-convulsing laughter. If that's not enough, finally there is Matron. She stretches her neck above the shell-like security of her desk in the corner office, her pallid tortoise gaze searching for the cause of the noise. She wants a quiet life, she wants to meet her targets and then go home for breakfast. She wants no hassle; she just wants the job done. She doesn't know how to deal with these behaviours or how to deal with Karen leaving on time; it wasn't covered in the 'Managing People for Results' course that she attended. Her desperate work-torn eyes say 'I don't know what to say!' and Karen suddenly feels guilty for her too.

Finally Karen bursts through the glass front door of the hospital and back into the driving rain for the second time today. Her heart is racing, her mind is buzzing and the tightness in her stomach is nothing compared to the heaviness of her coat of guilt and the pressure of the shame hat on her head. The day is not yet over, her other full-time guilt job is about to begin…

So what can you do if you wear the mask of guilt?

Exercise – Dealing with Guilt and Shame

Forgiveness stems from understanding, acceptance and compassion, but it doesn't necessarily mean approval. You may not approve of your ex-husband running off with another woman, but you can learn to forgive him and yourself. Feeling guilty for not being a better wife cannot change the things in the past that we regret; they have happened and cannot be reversed. We cannot live our life walking backwards always staring at past events. We must recognise our past mistakes, learn from them, forgive ourselves and then be willing to turn around and face the future. Doors close during our life, but if we constantly stare at closed doors we will never notice the new doors that have opened up to us!

Five Point Exercise for Guilt Stain Removal!

1. *Examine why you feel guilty and the purpose of your guilt from your perspective – list them.*

2. *Step into the shoes of the other party who was involved and talk to yourself from their perspective – what would they really say to you? Make sure it is from their perspective.*

3. *Step into your shoes again and respond to the other party from your perspective.*

4. *Step into the shoes of your future self and, from that position, give advice to yourself.*

5. *Finally, step back into your own shoes and, from that first position, really forgive yourself and, if necessary, the other person who was involved. Choose what you want to do in the future to prevent things being repeated.*

Finally, imagine that you are packing up the mask of guilt and placing it in a box. I now want you to imagine that you are holding this box in front of you and watch it as it shrinks smaller and smaller. It so small now, much too small to wear and it would only clutter up your handbag if you

were to drop it in there so, in your imagination, drop it into a dustbin where it will be taken away for recycling. You are no longer carrying the heavy weight of the mask with you. You feel lighter, more energetic and free to move in any direction that you want. Feel free to walk forward knowing that you have let go of your mask of guilt.

The Mask of Duty

The mask of duty means that you should:

- Be the perfect ten
- Be the perfect mother
- Be a hard worker
- Be home on time
- Be happy
- Be the perfect employee/business woman
- Be the perfect housewife
- Be the perfect cook
- Be the perfect lover
- Be the perfect daughter
- Be …

Fill in your own below:

_____

_____

_____

_____

_____

_____

When I was in my early 30s my children were young. My eldest was born just after my 30th birthday and my youngest just after my 31st! My husband and I separated when my youngest was just a few months old.

My eldest was about to start nursery when my employers decided to relocate me to another region about 100 miles away. I sold the house, I had no new home to go to straight away and a nanny who had been my rock for two years refused to go with us! These were challenging times to say the least! I remember one day dragging myself into the office having had about two hours sleep, I was exhausted, my business suit had the evidence of new baby on it and I was close to tears with the guilt I felt about not being a good mum, or a good employee. At that time I had a PA, a wonderful Irish lady – a real mother figure for everyone in the team. She was always there when we needed her and she was the most intuitive person I have ever met. She spoke to everyone as her equal, from the most senior Vice-President to the cleaner. She said that they all deserved respect, an ear, a shoulder to cry on and the odd 'bringing down to earth' (that only she could do). That day she must have noticed that I was not myself. She wandered over to my office and, in the pretence of sorting out my desk, she said something to me in her lovely Dublin accent that I have never forgotten and, in that moment, she released me from the perfection tug of war. She said, 'Lynne, can I ask you, was your mother perfect?' 'No, indeed not!' I replied.

'Mmm, that's what I thought you'd say. You see, sweetheart, no mother is perfect, they only do the best they can in the circumstances – they're not able to do any more than that. If I were to ask you to go outside now and pick me up a perfect pebble, could you do it?'

'No,' I answered.

'Correct!' she acknowledged 'and neither can you find me a perfect mother or a perfect employee; any person in this world, whatever their role, can only do the best they can with what they've got!'

In that moment I was released from my guilt as well as my need for perfection. I said, 'You're right! My mum wasn't perfect but she was still my mum, I loved her and still do! If I can create the best I can for my children then that's good enough for me, because they won't be comparing me. It is me who is setting a standard of perfection that I cannot achieve; I can only be good enough.'

At the time of publishing this book, my daughters are 19 and 18 and regularly announce that I am the best mum in the world and they love me for all the love and encouragement I have given them. To be told that I am loved and to be able to give love is the best part of being a parent. What more could I want? To be told that I keep a perfect house or a perfect garden or that I am the best cook? No thank you, when all is said and done those things are irrelevant. What children want and remember is not perfection, but the love and encouragement they are given. If you are still tempted by the perfect house, ask yourself this: what did you clean on the 23rd of September last year? Can you remember? Try the 3rd of April, or the 14th of January this year? Then ask yourself: what did you do on your child's 1st birthday or on their first day at school, prize-giving or religious festival? I bet you remember those. Consider this …

If your child has been born recently, you can expect to have 6,552 days until they are 18 and no longer need you for their day-to-day pastoral care. If your child is ten you have 2,912 days left. You will spend 1,092 of those asleep and if you work outside the home, 1,213 days at work, which means that you have 607 days with your children – just over a year and a half. In the UK right now, over 41% of parents spend less than one hour a day with their children. Let go of your guilt and enjoy every possible, squeezable moment with your children; they and the health of our future society need you to do this. Perfect is a trap; set yourself free!

From the exercise above, transfer all your 'perfects' into the right-hand column of the table below (see example) and in the left-hand table, write the words 'I could'. Read them out loud.

I could	Be a perfect mother

'I should be a perfect mother' means that you have no choice; 'I could' allows choice.

Worklife balance occurs when people feel that they have a choice. Remember, when people feel that they have no choice but to work long hours, achieve high targets, etc., then imbalance occurs. We all have some levels of choice, what will you let go of today?

The Mask of Duty

The mask of duty is closely related to guilt and perfection, but it dictates how we should spend our time and often relates to giving ourselves to everyone else. Having a 'sense of duty' is not a problem unless it turns into one – it can feel like a heavy mask and often results in burden.

The duty of:

- *Visiting or calling parents at certain times*
- *The duty of cooking, cleaning and other domestic chores on a specific day or time*
- *The duty of organising birthdays, holidays, entertainment etc.*
- *The duty of sex, intimacy, relationships*
- *The duty of …*

Complete your own duties in the left column below:

These duties are often protection against threat, which can lead to guilt or shame. 'It's best to just visit my mum every Sunday, rather than have the stress of her complaining if I don't'. In the right-hand column, write down the consequences of not doing the duty and, once again, reflect on the choices that you do have. Sometimes we feel that we have no choice but to fulfil our duties; however, by creating choice and asking yourself 'what's the worst thing that can happen if I don't do it?' you will be amazed at how much you can let go of.

Many women wear the mask of 'got to be seen to cope'. They believe that they want it all and can do it all … reality is often different. Asking for help, not doing it all yourself, and admitting you cannot 'do it' or 'have it all' is, in the long run, a strength. The mask of coping or pretending that you are coping with all that life is throwing at you is generally not sustainable, even for the most resilient among us. The exercise above relating to shoulds can be expanded to include the 'only I can'…

Only I can…	Who else could help me?
Look after my baby	
Do my housework	
Do my job properly	

I recall a time when my children were very tiny – four and three. I had just moved into my new house in Marlborough, was trying to get the girls settled into nursery, hire a new nanny, have time for my personal relationship, deal with family situations and a full-on demanding role as Head of Marketing Communications for HP's computer organisation. I was practically on my knees, but felt that 'I could do it all!' The problem was that the knees were beginning to buckle under this already overloaded donkey! Then I had my first wake-up call. I had been working incredibly hard on a project that included the sponsorship and support of one of the James Bond movies. Product placement was key and I had worked tirelessly with our head of product marketing to ensure that HP's products were used and visible in the film. The project, although it sounds trivial now, was exciting at the time and I was keen to make it a marketing success. The night of the premiere came and it was a splendid event – all very elegant and awe-inspiring. After the show, we all gathered for dinner at one of London's top restaurants. I remember sitting opposite our Director of Marketing and whilst sipping a glass of red wine, felt utterly exhausted and unable to fully enjoy the event. I was actually shaking with tiredness. He gently took the glass from my hand, and extending his index finger, sunk it into my glass of Fleurie! 'My finger,' he proceeded to explain 'is you, Lynne! The glass of wine is HP.' Then, with a tug, he quickly removed his finger and looked back into the glass from where it had been plunged. 'Oh look!' he announced 'NO HOLE! The fact is, Lynne, that if you were to drop dead tomorrow because of stress, there would be no hole in HP, the slack would be taken up and the job would get done. However, I suspect that there would be a big hole in the glass that was filled with your family. Don't ever be so successful that you deprive them of the most important thing in their life – you.' This man gave me a very defining lesson that night and helped me to see that no amount of thousands of pounds of salary and bonuses and successful marketing campaigns could ever be as important as my family. I thank him for that lesson. I was trying to cope with it all and I almost paid a very high price.

Over the next month, I would like to ask you to focus on those things that you can let go of, or ask for help with.

What will I let go of this week?	What do I plan to let go of this month?
Who can help me?	Who can help me?

Role confusion

In business, I come across many women who have become what I refer to as 'adapted females'. That means that they wear the mask of a man and, in some cases, have become more masculine than their male counterparts. By becoming too male in their approach, these women have forgotten their natural female style. The men don't like them because they are scary women to be with and the women don't like them because they tend to be poor allies. They see other women as soft, a threat, competition or of no use to them. In the end they become isolated from both genders, leaving them with feelings of alienation, loneliness and betrayal.

I have coached many women in this position and have supported them to drop the mask and re-connect with their natural leadership skills, freeing them to be authentic and liberating them to build relationships with their women colleagues and become supported by their male ones.

Your Authentic Self

The authentic self is the real you, the core you, the you that is the shining diamond of potential that was born into this world to be the best it could be – not better than others, just the best you could be. It is your potential, your truth, your self. Here are some questions that you might ask yourself to get in touch with the authentic self:

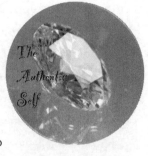
The Authentic Self

114

1. *How do you dance when no one is looking?*
2. *If you could be anything at all in the whole world, what would you be?*
3. *Name a person alive or dead that you truly admire and state why.*
4. *If the other two parts of self were chipped away, who would you be?*

Michelangelo was once asked how he carved such beautiful and perfect angels from stone. He considered the question and responded,

"It is easy, I see the angel trapped inside the stone and I chip away until she is free!"

Your job is to chip away to find the authentic you. In the final section of this chapter we will work on the authentic self and, in the final chapter, you will do this work in more detail to set goals for your future, true self. However, in this chapter we explore who this authentic self is. I often hear women say that they do not like to be alone with their own thoughts, and some even do not like to be alone at all. Being alone, or taking time to think, to explore and to be can be a very frightening prospect for some, so they fill their life with constant 'doing' in order to avoid just 'being'. Being alone with your thoughts can begin to open up many doors – doors that you would rather remain tightly closed!

On my office wall, I have an extract from Nelson Mandela's famous speech, which is recorded in Marianne Williamson's book A Course in Miracles. It reads, 'It is our light, not our darkness that frightens us most'. I believe he is right. We fear success more than we fear failure. To really succeed would send our critical voice into a tirade of insults and self-limiting sayings that would keep us in our comfort zone. To release that light would be amazing, and yet frightening, because we would not be conforming to the norm. We learn to conform, to fit in, to be one of the rest, not one of the best. As women, we are taught not to boast, not to get ideas above our station, not to take up too much space in the world, and all of these cover our true authentic shining spirit.

Authentic Self Exercise

What seven things will you do in the next week to build your authentic self-worth?

1.	
2.	
3.	
4.	
5.	
6.	
7.	

Exercise for Removing and De-cluttering Masks

Find a quiet space where you will not be interrupted for at least 30 minutes. Listen to the guided exercise in the 'The Lipstick' of the website, and then in your notebook write as much as you can about what happened, what you saw, felt, heard or imagined. Keep on writing until you have captured all details. Then identify the key things that you have learned and will take forward. Then complete the BAG exercise below.

BAG - My Action Plan
BAG stands for Bin, Add and Get

B	What will I **Bin** that no longer serves my life or goals and prevents me from dancing my best life?	
A	What am I already doing, being or having that I could **Add** to or improve in order to dance my best life?	
G	What will I **Get** that will serve me well and help me to dance my best life?	

Dance your Best Life!

5 My Mirror

The Woman in the Mirror

When you get what you want in your struggle for self

And the world makes you queen for a day,

Just go to the mirror and look at yourself,

And see what that woman has to say.

For it isn't your father or mother or husband

Whose judgement upon you must pass.

The person whose verdict counts most in your life,

Is the one staring back from the glass.

She's the person to please, never mind all the rest

For she's with you right up to the end.

And you've passed your most dangerous, difficult test

If the woman in the glass is your friend.

You may fool the whole world down the pathway of life,

And get pats on your back as you pass.

But your final reward will be heartache and tears

If you've cheated the woman in the glass.

Author unknown

Introduction

As a new-born child, you may well have been showered (and sometimes drenched) in the rain of good wishes, hopes and love from everyone around as they wished you a happy, successful and healthy life. No one would have wanted bad things to come your way but instead they would have wanted you to dance your best life. In reality, life has its challenges – good and bad. As a result, by adulthood the effects of these experiences manifest in your beliefs about life and in the ways that you behave, conduct yourself with others and regard yourself. Most of all, by looking around at others on the dance floor of life, you compare yourself with them – often negatively.

The mirror is therefore about two things:

1. **Your Emotional Image** – *how you see yourself, your self-esteem, self-confidence and those behaviours that support and hinder your growth.*

2. **Your Physical Image** – *the image that you portray to others in your personal brand; it can fuel your public self and often masks the true authentic you. What is your personal brand and are you loyal to it?*

In this chapter we will explore your image and sense of the authentic you. De-clutter those things that prevent you from growing in confidence, conviction and with a real sense of being worthy of happiness. In relation to our handbags, this chapter is the mirror. We are about to hold up a mirror and look at the whole physical you.

By the end of this chapter of reflection, you will have discarded the images that no longer make you look and feel good about yourself – and you may have even bought a new mirror that reflects a new and fantastic you!

Our story ...

Karen felt like crying; nothing fitted her properly. She looked like a whale in everything she tried on – fat, frumpy and almost forty! When did she suddenly go up a size in her clothes and why did she look so ugly in everything? What would people think when she walked into James's office Christmas party looking like a lump of lard?

Karen slumped down on the bed miserably. She wouldn't go, she would give an excuse: tummy upset, flu, tonsillitis, kids' Nativity performance. She would let James go himself; after all, it was his work colleagues, not hers, and what would she talk about all night anyway? As for dancing – no way! She couldn't possibly parade her blubber on the dance floor in front of James's boss! Not only would that kill any chance of promotion, but his wife is a perfect size 10!

'Why am I so fat and ugly?' snarled Karen, staring at her hips and stomach and wondering what it had been that had caused the shape-shifting. She didn't think that she over-ate, but she was partial to the odd bar of Green & Black's chocolate; she had cut down on wine, and was walking to work every day! She resolved that it had all 'headed south' before her 40th birthday! She had read about it, but honestly she didn't expect it to rain down on her hips in one season – and just before the Christmas parties!

'You can't let me go alone! You're definitely coming with me!' announced James. 'I am not going by myself! Why wouldn't you come?'

'Because I'm fat!' hissed Karen.

James stared at her, not knowing what to say for the best and, fearing his usual capability of getting it wrong anyway, merely pleaded, 'Karen, I love you!' Sadly, the emphasis was placed on the word 'I' and Karen immediately picked up on this, believing that only he loved her and the rest of the world didn't.

'You love me, only you? You mean you love me even though I am fat and loathsome with a backside like a battleship and jowls!' she announced, then repeated 'JOWLS! I look like my mother. What you really mean is that you would like me to be a few pounds lighter, but just can't say it! I can't possibly go looking like this, what will your boss's wife think of me?!'

James was too confused, perplexed and frightened to respond, he just stared, not knowing what to say. Of course, that was the confirmation that Karen needed; she was indeed loathsome, and she sank into the pillow and began crying uncontrollably.

James took this as his cue to depart and, whisking up his son, disappeared off to the local sports centre, via the supermarket for flowers to apologise for something that he had obviously said but he didn't yet know, and that would be explained later when Karen felt less prone to meltdown.

'Karen, Karen …' a voice consoled, a hand gently stroked her shoulder. Karen lifted her head and wiped her eyes. The light from the window shone behind the older woman, giving her an almost iridescent aura.

It was time for today's handbag lesson, and Karen had a feeling that she knew which item they were going to explore and she didn't like the prospect. Silently, she lifted her handbag on to the bed between the two women. Its silver chain handles flopped either side of the navy leather bag, prising open the top and making the contents just visible. Karen reached forward as if to open it wider, but the old lady stopped her. 'Karen, as you know, your bag is a symbol of you and each item inside relates to a different aspect of your personality. Today we will explore your image, how you see yourself, your sense of self-worth and esteem and your physical image too.' Karen snorted as the older women concluded, 'Yes, it is not a very positive image at all.' She continued, 'Your handbag will help us to achieve our lesso … and we will search for the answer in the mirror.'

The two women gazed down at the handbag on the bed in front of them, and Karen suddenly felt strange. The room began to spin; the images around her grew strangely large and blurred. She closed her eyes, but the spinning felt more intense. She tried hard to focus, she was spinning around and around her handbag, viewing it from every angle and watching as it appeared to be growing larger and larger, closer and closer. She tried to look away from the handbag and into the room, but everything appeared hazy, like surreal spectres of reality fading into the distance. She spun down and down towards the open top of the bag, suddenly knowing that it was not getting larger, but that she was in fact getting smaller. Downwards she spun into the handbag, down, down, down, and thud she landed at the bottom. She sat there, slowly trying to come to her senses. 'I know I wanted to be smaller, but this is not what I meant!' she joked as she wobbled to her feet.

Appearing from behind her purse, Tomorrow Karen smiled at her comment and continued, 'Look for your mirror!' she instructed as she disappeared round the side of the mobile phone.

'It is over there!' pointed Karen 'in that pocket! I always keep it there to protect it from breaking!' she announced, catching up with the other woman, both now facing the zipped inner pocket nesting the mirror. Using the lipstick to stand on, the two women climbed up to the pocket and proceeded to lift out the compact mirror (which was now the size of them) and then carefully positioned it on the soft floor of the handbag, safely propped up against the diary.

'There! That should do it!' said Karen. 'Now what?'

'Take a few steps back, look into your mirror and tell me what you see,' encouraged Tomorrow Karen.

'I see me,' said Karen 'a woman in an old pair of jeans with a big bottom and saggy boobs!' she mocked in self-loathing tones.

'Look again and tell me what you really see,' Tomorrow Karen scolded warmly.

Karen looked back into the mirror and whilst she still saw herself, she also noticed that the surface had begun to change. Her image faded into a swirling fog-like mass and, as she tried to focus, she saw emerging a critical, self-deprecating woman who constantly criticised and complained; a twisted and vicious woman who could not see the good in herself; a hard, cruel, nasty and painfully negative person. Karen did not like her at all. She turned to her older self. 'That is your critical self, Karen. Look and listen.' Karen turned back to the image in the mirror and for the next few minutes listened and watched as her critical self voiced and displayed and relived all of Karen's failings. As Karen watched she felt herself become more and more down and disheartened by this horrible person's attitude. 'This person is a part of me and she talks to me like this all the time, doesn't she? This is how I talk to myself isn't it? Why am I so cruel and nasty to myself? Why do I worry about everything? I always think so badly of myself and others too!'

'What is the purpose of the critical you?' challenged Tomorrow Karen, ignoring her questions for now.

'It is definitely depressing me and I want her to stop it! Her constant negativity is overpowering and I suppose that I end up believing what she says. If I do, then I suppose she holds me back, stops me from taking risks and making changes?' Karen answered.

'Exactly! Earlier, for example, she told you that you were fat and loathsome, and that you couldn't possibly go to James's party.' Karen remembered it only too well, and that this critical voice was not only being cruel about her shape, but was limiting her life as well. Tomorrow Karen continued, 'Your critical self is self-limiting, but its intention is good.'

'How can that be?' asked Karen. 'What is so good about the tirade of insults and negativity that this person displays?'

'Your critical self, whilst negative and focused on your past mistakes, is actually keen to keep you safe! By reliving past traumas with you, or past

failures, it is trying to keep you safe from doing that again,' explained Tomorrow Karen.

'I see, it looks back into my past and uses those experiences to stop me from making the same mistakes again? It keeps me in my comfort zone!'

'Indeed, and in some instances that is a good thing! However, it can also become too dominant and hold us back from dancing our BEST life!'

'How do I deal with this critical self and stop it from holding me back on things that I should do?' asked Karen

'Recognising it is doing so is the first step. By recognising that it is your critical self speaking, you can immediately begin to take away its power over you. The next thing is to recognise whose voice it really is and to really listen to the context of the words so that you can change.'

'I don't understand!' said Karen. The older women continued…

'Nathaniel Brandon once said that Self Esteem is the integrated sum of SELF CONFIDENCE and SELF RESPECT; it is the CONVICTION that you are COMPETENT to deal with life's challenges and that you are WORTHY of happiness. Simply put, self-esteem is about the way that you talk to yourself. It is made up of all those things that were said to us as a youngster, and our belief about ourselves as a result. For example, if you were always told that you were clumsy, what will you believe as an adult? Sometimes parents, guardians and teachers don't mean to hurt us, but they create our self-limiting belief patterns.' Karen thought about this as she looked back into the mirror. All of her life this self-limiting belief stood close to her shoulder ensuring that it had a very negative effect on her life. It stopped her from being happy, from being herself – from just being! Her voice always said 'In Case'; as a child being fearful of playing on the big slide in case she hurt herself or talking to the older kids at school in case they bullied her. She saw the teenager afraid to go out at night in case she was attacked, and fearful to drop history at school even though she wanted to do biology in case her father got angry. As a young

adult fearful to put herself forward for promotion at work in case she was laughed at and, most of all, frightened to tell her boyfriend James that she loved him in case he left her. It was time for 'in case' to be evicted from her life; no longer would she dance to this tune. 'In case' came from her mother, it was her voice: 'Wear a coat in case you get cold, take an umbrella in case it rains! Pack a first aid kit in case you cut yourself on holiday!' The list of 'in cases' was huge and created so much self-limiting baggage. Karen recognised that her mother's intentions were good, but it was holding her back as an adult. She knew that 'in case' was holding her back from parties (in case James's boss's wife laughed at her) from promotions (in case she couldn't do the job) and from life in general (in case she failed!).

'It is time to de-clutter 'in-case' from your bag and your life. 'In case' stops you from taking risks and it forces you to carry extra baggage around in your suitcase of life. This manifests in your real life too. How many times have you packed for holiday and taken things 'in case' you may need them? Look around this handbag; how many things are in here 'in case' you need them? By letting go, you not only lighten your handbag, but you lighten your life!' laughed Tomorrow Karen. 'Look back in the mirror, how would you look if you were being the best that you could be?'

Karen stared into the mirror, its dark but smouldering surface began to change once more. Bright sparkling lights flashed across its surface. Colours began to emerge, bright, shimmering light manifesting images of the true Karen, the authentic Karen, the Karen that was free of fear, free of self-limiting belief; the Karen that had been hidden in the dark for all these years! This Karen was truly alive, she was living her life authentically – she was dancing her best life! She was also standing right next to her.

The Three Parts of Self continued

In this chapter we will explore the critical self in the most detail. As you read, ensure that you have your journal and a pen as you may discover some things about you which you will be able to relate to the guided imagery that you will complete as part of the exercises. Like Karen, you will go inside your handbag, find your mirror and face up to your critical self.

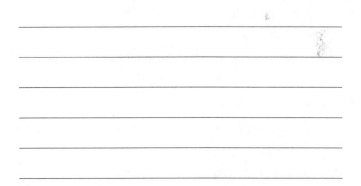

The critical self is that part of you that is self-limiting, critical and sometimes even cruel. It relives past mistakes and can often hold you back. Its intention is to keep you in your comfort zone, keep you safe. Let us begin to explore the critical self by asking you to participate in an exercise. In the space below, write down your answer to the following task:

Your Task: **Describe Your Body**

_____

_____

_____

_____

_____

This question was asked as part of a piece of attribution theory research carried out in the USA. Attribution theory suggests that women and men attribute their success or failure in opposite ways. Women tend to attribute their success to some external cause that supported them, and men to their own internal abilities. The opposite being true for failures:

women blamed themselves and men some external cause. In the exercise above, the answers from women were a catalogue of internal or perceived faults, with 'fat' being the number one answer.

The critical self is that part of you that is never happy whatever you do! It is made up of many years of conditioning and sometimes well-intentioned lessons that, whilst appropriate as a child, can hold you back as an adult. It is that little voice inside that limits you and fuels your negativity and guilt. It sits behind the public self and is a muddy layer of negativity, fear, worry and criticism. It may be a voice that tells you not to get ideas above your station, or a voice that tells you that girls should not show anger, apply for big jobs or even be happy.

The critical voice is not all bad! It is also there to protect us, to stop us from putting ourselves in dangerous or risky situations. It is also there to reflect those things that we should face up to and change. To understand your critical self, ask yourself these questions:

- *What names do you call yourself when you do something wrong?*
- *If someone were presenting negative feedback to you, what would you not like them to say about you?*
- *What secrets do you have that you have not told anyone about and why?*
- *What are your least favourite aspects of you and what do you say about them internally or to others?*
- *On days when you feel good, do you feel thinner? On days when you feel bad or down, do you feel fatter?*
- *What do you feel guilt or regret about?*
- *What do you hate people to notice about you when they are first introduced to you?*
- *If you were invited to a reunion of old friends, colleagues or school chums what would you not want them to find out about you, or what would you focus on changing?*

It is often a voice that calls you names and is often more rude to you than you would ever be to anyone else!

Like Clara's story …

I am left-handed and as a child found it difficult to coordinate in
a right-handed environment. Often I would knock things over or
spill things without meaning to. My mother and teachers would
scream at me 'You clumsy idiot! Why can't you pay attention to
what you are doing?' For years I believed I was not only clumsy but
an idiot that could not pay attention. The reality formed itself in my
behaviour – I was always daydreaming and not paying attention
in class and of course I failed a lot of exams because I was fulfilling
my belief that I was an idiot! Nowadays, I am working on my
critical voice and keeping it at bay, but it is not easy and sometimes
if I drop something, I hear my mother's voice scream in my head!
I have worked hard though and having recently qualified as an
Occupational Therapist, I can now help other children to cope with
dyspraxia and other coordination issues – an idiot I am not!

By identifying your critical voice, you are on your way to letting it go and
releasing yourself from self-limiting beliefs.

> "Self Esteem is the integrated sum of
> Self Confidence and Self Respect; it
> is the conviction that you are competent
> to deal with life's challenges, and that
> you are worthy of happiness."
>
> Nathaniel Brandon

You weren't born with a critical voice, you grew one! After all, how
many babies do you know that lie in their cradle worrying about how
the neighbours will react to the noise they are making? Critical voices
are developed from many years of conditioning communication, which
eventually creates our self-esteem. In addition to the definition above,
self-esteem can be simply defined as 'the way that you talk to yourself'

and is determined by your self-image, 'who you think you are' which is validated from:

- *How people treated you, experiences and messages that you received as a child.*

- *Your own conclusions and beliefs about these messages.*

Some of the messages that you heard were not intended to hurt, but nonetheless they stuck like glue and, for women, they are often more about what we 'didn't hear' than what we 'did hear'. For example, Jane was brought up in a loving home with lots of encouragement and support – especially from her dad. Jane had two older sisters – Elizabeth and Harriet. Their dad loved to introduce them to new friends like this: 'These are my three daughters; Elizabeth has the brains, Harriet has the looks and Jane is the sporty one!' Like most good dads, John just wanted to give credit to each of his daughters' strengths, thereby setting them apart. However, John unintentionally had the opposite effect. He did not know that his three daughters would interpret his compliments with a negative critical voice. What these girls didn't hear was actually what they heard:

Elizabeth – intelligent, but ugly and can't do sport.

Harriet – good-looking but stupid and incapable of sport.

Jane – sporty but ugly and stupid.

Often, women will tend to look for what they don't have rather than what they do and will blame internally for their 'lack'. For example, women see themselves as larger than they actually are and measure themselves on smallness. Women start worrying if they cannot get into their tiniest jeans; men don't start worrying until they can't fit into their car or through their front door! Women set an unrealistic standard based on a multibillion-pound advertising industry that says the only acceptable image is wafer-thin. We are bombarded with thinness and set ourselves unrealistic standards based on our mode of viewing ourselves – not as small as...

Women often view themselves as ornaments (where the measure is attractiveness) whilst men view themselves as instruments (where the measure is performance). This leads to women having high standards whilst men have higher esteem. Your self-esteem is therefore rooted in the way that you talk to yourself. It is the critical self that creates the public self and the masks that we wear, which we explored in the Lipstick chapter.

The problem with the critical voice is that it is always believed. It calls you names —some very insulting! It relives your past mistakes and it can talk in shorthand to you, like sighing or growling when you do something wrong.

What are the names that your critical voice calls you?

Often the way we talk to ourselves is far more insulting and cruel than the way we would talk to others! Therefore we must begin to eradicate the unhelpful aspects of our critical self.

Your source of your critical voice generally comes from the three main underlying feelings of:

1. **Helplessness**

2. **Hopelessness**

3. **Worthlessness**

Helplessness is about your self-confidence and the critical voice is 'my goal can be achieved, but not by me.'

Hopelessness is about your sense of optimism and the critical voice is 'there is no way my goal can be achieved!'

Worthlessness is about your sense of self-worth and the critical voice is 'my goal cannot be achieved by me because I am...' or 'because I have not...'

From the exercise above, which of the three did you recognise (if you have a critical voice in relation to your goal)?

In my coaching experience, I have noted that confidence and worthiness appear to be the most common causes. However, whichever of the three, or combination of the three, are embedded in your critical voice, they can be overturned and, in some cases, silenced for good!

Hopelessness is about lack of hope. In focusing on 'no hope' you are cutting off any future potential to achieve your goal. Therefore it is a time-related lack. Therefore, think about your goal being achieved at some future date, and then work back from that date in years or months to define just what you need to do today to move yourself towards it. A journey of a thousand miles begins with the first step. What will the first step be?

Helplessness is about lack of help! In focusing on 'helpless' it suggests that you need help to achieve your goal, therefore it is people- and mentoring- or coaching-related. Think about the goal that you want to achieve and list all of the other people who are already doing what you want to do, be or have. Not just any people, real experts and people who are already successful at being, doing or having what you want. Now write down a list of questions that you can ask them to find out exactly what they do and how they do it. Ask them to mentor or coach you or support you in your goal in any way that is appropriate. Build your network and use the network roadmap in the Pen chapter to think of questions for your helpers and mentors.

Worthlessness is about lack of worth because of something you are or are not, something you have or have not, or something that you did or did not. It is about your sense of deserving happiness or fulfilment and punishment for or denial of your happiness. What needs to happen for you to deserve happiness? Look at the statement that you made as part of your critical voice, and particularly the words that come after the 'because' word. Now change the sentence from a punishment-based one, to a recognition-focused one.

> 🍃 *When I achieve my goal of… I will feel…*

> 🍃 *I will be happy when I achieve my goal of… and will celebrate by…*

Deserving is about serving yourself with recognition and positive regard for all the small steps and achievements on the way to your goal. If your goal is to drop a dress size, and your critical voice says 'you won't achieve that because you're greedy', then imagine what you will feel like when you do achieve the goal by visualising yourself in a beautiful dress. Then use a star chart to celebrate every day that you eat healthily towards your goal and celebrate by pinning a gold star to the chart, or by putting a pound or dollar in a piggy bank every day. When you achieve your goal, buy yourself a pair of shoes or a handbag to match the dress!

The final part of the critical voice is the part that is there, in a positive way, to support us to face up to some truths. In a communication skills workshop that I run, I ask delegates to give me the name of a communicator that they admire and why. The answers are wide and varied and include people like Barack Obama, Winston Churchill, John Hurt and Judy Dench. They include ordinary people too, like teachers, grandparents, mothers and children. The objective of the exercise is not to collect the name of the person, but to reflect on 'why'. Do this exercise now, who do you admire as a great communicator, and why?

After reflecting on your answer, consider this: the things that we admire in others are often aspects of ourselves that we keep hidden inside. Equally, the things we criticise or dislike in others is also something that we dislike about ourselves. This is what psychologists call perseverating, and it works like this. Have you ever been in conversation with someone and, after they leave, you continue the conversation with them in your head? Playing scenarios of what you would really like to say to them if only you had the guts to do so? I know that I have! In my head I have had the most articulate conversations with people about how they need to get their act together and sort out their life! Or how they need to sort out their finances, or how they need to bring up their children! The act of continuing a conversation or behaviour long after the original stimulus has ended is a form of projection, and these people of whom we are critical or admiring are in fact acting like human mirrors. In future, when you hear yourself bemoaning or admiring another person inside your head, instead of listening to yourself, talk to yourself! Ask, 'what is it in me that I should face right now?' Try writing a letter; begin by writing the critical one. In this, set free your inner wicked witch! Think of someone whose behaviour drives you crazy. For example, 'Dear Annie,

You never give, you only take from me, you only ever want me when you need something! You are a user, a nasty, manipulative and self-centred user!' Let rip, really let her have all the wrath of your wicked witch – but only on paper! Then, change the name to your own and read it back. You may notice that there are times and people where you do the same, the letter now becomes the coach. Do the same for the admiration letter but this time, instead of the wicked witch, you will release your sparkling Goddess; when you're finished, reflect on the words, change the name to yours and think about all those potential and wonderful things about you that you may be holding back!

Identify whose voice it is

Sometimes critical voices can be self-limiting because they belong to someone else. 'Don't go out without an umbrella in case it rains!' 'Wrap up warm in case you catch cold!' 'Don't get too big for your boots.' These statements, said to us as a child, had good intentions behind them; however, some of them may not serve your life and its potential now. Then ask yourself, 'do I really want my mother/father/sister/teacher ruling my life today?' Again, as soon as you begin to talk to yourself, instead of listening to yourself, you can begin to make suitable choices about what is important and what is not. This will have a big impact on your worklife balance.

Identifying the internal dances that drive your image

The Dancing Queen's Exercise

What causes imbalance in your life? What are the dances that you dance to that take up your time?

In this exercise, we will assess the internal dances that you dance to and then relate those to why you become embroiled in so many dances! Make sure that you have uninterrupted time to complete this exercise and, most of all, be truthful with your answers. Really take time to reflect on them and answer as it actually is, not how you would like it to be.

	Description	Always	Often	Sometimes	Seldom	Never
1	I believe that it is necessary to gain the correct qualifications or skills before applying for a new job					
2	I should always show I am coping with the demands of life					
3	I find it difficult to say No to the demands of others					
4	People like me rarely find true happiness					
5	I find it difficult to take risks in my work or life					
6	I enjoy telling other people how to do their work so I achieve the standards I want					
7	It is important for me to put other people's needs before my own					
8	I tend to seek the permission of others before embarking on something					
9	I can be interfering, pushy or bossy					
10	I find it difficult to sit down and do nothing					
11	I avoid conflict at all costs					
12	I hate making mistakes					
13	I like to make sure that other people are happy and content					
14	I know how to take care of others well					
15	I like to have lots of change in my work and life – wherever I lay my handbag, that's my home!					

	Description	Always	Often	Sometimes	Seldom	Never
16	When friends or family visit, I enjoy making sure that I put on a lavish meal and take care of their needs					
17	I like to be in charge of the shopping, cleaning, presents and other things to do with my family					
18	I don't have time for lunch breaks in my busy day!					
19	I respond to the needs of my boss before my own					
20	There is always room for improvement in what I do					
21	I respond to the needs of my colleagues before my own					
22	It is important for me to be rushing around being busy					
23	Other people who don't work as hard as me make me frustrated					
24	My work deserves to be done perfectly					
25	I expect high standards from myself and others all the time					
26	Other people don't seem to notice or care about me or my needs					
27	I worry about people finding out that I am not as good as they think					
28	I strive to do as much as I can in a day					
29	I should keep the house spotless					

	Description	Always	Often	Sometimes	Seldom	Never
30	I like to have control over my work and don't easily share					
31	I enjoy the pressure of working up to a deadline					
32	Being productive is always more important than working relationships					
33	I enjoy it when work, hobby or life commitments really demand my time					
34	I enjoy having too much to do					
35	I hate surprises! I like to know exactly what is going on or what people are doing					
36	When studying for qualifications, it deserves the best I can do all the time					
37	I worry about failing					
38	I worry about succeeding					
39	I feel limited by my gender, sexuality, race, religion, disability or colour					
40	I find it difficult to delegate to my colleagues or employees					
41	It is so important to make sure that my family have a clean home, good food and lots of love from me above anyone else					
42	Life is always hard for me					
43	I feel that my age inhibits my ability to meet my goals					
44	I find it difficult to commit to one thing					

Description	Always	Often	Sometimes	Seldom	Never
45 *People shouldn't get so enthusiastic, it is important to live in the real world*					
46 *I feel that my personal background and upbringing limits me*					
47 *I often think about my past failings*					
48 *I feel limited by my shape or size*					
49 *I like all aspects of my life and my personal appearance to be just right*					
50 *I juggle piles of work and seem to be working on more than one thing at a time!*					
51 *I feel inadequate a lot of the time*					
52 *I feel pessimistic about the future a lot of the time*					
53 *I worry about upsetting or hurting people*					
54 *I bring myself down or am critical of myself in front of others*					

Scoring Sheet

Having completed the questionnaire, score your answers as detailed below:

ALWAYS	OFTEN	SOMETIMES	SELDOM	NEVER
10	5	3	1	0

Add up the totals for each preference and complete the attached grid. Finally, total up each column and plot your scores on the target diagram provided.

Question	Score	Question	Score	Question	Score	Question	Score	Question	Score	Question	Score
1		2		15		4		10		6	
12		3		27		5		18		9	
20		7		37		8		22		14	
24		11		39		38		23		16	
25		13		43		42		28		17	
29		19		44		45		32		26	
31		21		46		47		33		30	
36		41		48		52		34		35	
49		53		51		54		50		40	
Total (FQ)		Total (DQ)		Total (QQ)		Total (TQ)		Total (JQ)		Total (WQ)	

Plot your totals on the diagram below.

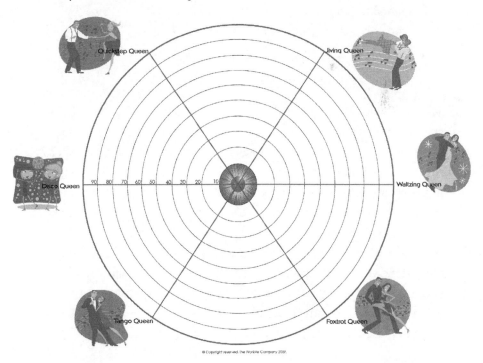

Quickstep Queen · Jiving Queen · Disco Queen · Waltzing Queen · Tango Queen · Foxtrot Queen

90 80 70 60 50 40 30 20 10

The Dancing Queen Descriptions & Action

In order to get our needs met when we were little, we often develop a range of behaviours which, although effective in our family of origin, might actually work against us as adults in the workplace or in the home. These habits literally drive our dances and can create dysfunctional outcomes if over-used. Remember, it is not a problem until it is a problem!

Depending on your scores above, your dominant score is likely to be the main driver of your dancing. In other words, a way of behaving (a habit) that helps you to get your needs met. That means that there is a part of you that internally dictates how you behave and therefore 'why' you dance to the tunes of others.

These are very loosely based on a part of psychology called transactional analysis. In this exercise it has been adapted to look at how your internal drivers maintain some of the habits that keep you dancing to tunes of others!

The most common dances are:

- **Waltzing Queens** – *who take care of others too much*
- **Disco Queens** – *who put everyone before themselves*
- **Tango Queens** – *whose lives are so dreadful*
- **Jiving Queens** – *who live life in perpetual motion*
- **Foxtrot Queens** – *who must be perfect at everything*
- **Quickstep Queens** – *who just keep moving on!*

We all exhibit parts of all of these and that is normal. However, if they become extreme, they can be a problem and cause addictive or habitual behaviour. For example, the Jive Queen can become addicted to work at the expense of her relationships outside of work. This would be reflected in the Dance floor as low scores on 'perfume' and 'photos'. Being more involved in work means that the JQ does not need to face the underlying issue of loneliness as they feel valued at work and obsess about being constantly busy. To make some changes, it is first of all important to understand what drives you, and secondly to understand what aspect of your life is impacted (the Dance floor). By identifying where your life is out of balance and relating those to the dances that you dance to, you can begin to make some analysis of where to make change.

Your internal drivers are often the real issues that prevent you from dancing your best life. However, there may also be some external factors like a sick relative, children and demanding college course. It is key that you do not look at either in isolation. For example, if you are a Quickstep mum, you may find it difficult to say No to your children. The result is that you are not only run ragged doing things to please them, but your financial situation may be poor because you cannot say No to the new toy or treat! Throughout the book we will cover each of the different aspects and look for ways that you can begin to make changes towards achieving balance – after all, if you always do what you always did, you will always get what you always got! What will you change?

Descriptions

TQ – *Tango Queen*

Folk Saying:

'Life is never a bowl of cherries!'

For the TQ, life is a bitch! If it is already bad, it is bound to get even worse. TQs feel inadequate, unworthy and undeserving of happiness. Life is meant to be a struggle from dawn to dusk and the life of a TQ woman is so hard! TQs often fear success and spontaneous mirth the most and often unconsciously create pessimism in others. They worry about everything and feel guilty about most things that they do. They will comment on the sacrifices that they make and throw water on the fires of enthusiasm. In being self-critical they will be able to catalogue their own past failings and list how things will fail in future too!

Worklife Objective: *Have fun!*

- *Allow yourself and others to have pleasure just for the sake of it.*

- *Work on your attitude: is your glass half empty, not half full?*

- *Spend the next month keeping a gratitude diary; each time you do something that you enjoy or are proud of, write it in your diary. At the end of the month read it back to yourself; it is such a treat.*

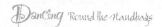
FQ – *Foxtrot Queen*

Folk Saying:

'If a job's worth doing it's
worth doing perfectly!'

The FQ is often never satisfied with what they do and how they look. Nothing is ever good enough, especially themselves! Life has to be perfect in all aspects: perfect work, perfect wife, perfect lover etc. They demand high, and sometimes unachievable, standards from others and can be very demanding managers. The FQ is prone to procrastination as they cannot hand over a piece of work until it is perfect! Therefore they tend to butt up against deadlines and can miss them for fear of failure. The self-fulfilling prophecy of not being perfect comes into play and results in them working even harder to be perfect. Their best is never good enough.

> **Worklife Objective:** *Allow things to be good enough*
>
> - *Review all the aspects of your life and do the 'shoulds' exercise from the book.*
>
> - *Allow one thing this week to go out from your desk less than perfect; no one will know how perfect it could have been!*
>
> - *Stop expecting perfection from yourself and others; we're human! Good enough is good enough! So what if the tops of pictures never get dusted or the report has no i's dotted or t's crossed?*

DQ – *Disco Queen*

Folk Saying:

'I'm just a girl who can't say No!' or
'I'll go with the flow!'

DQs take on too much. They just can't say No! Their workload is so high and they worry about upsetting people and letting people down. If you ask a DQ how they are, they invariably say 'fine', but they are like a swan, calm on the surface and paddling like crazy underneath! They never tell you when they are unhappy, stressed or overworked; they hope that you will notice! Invariably you won't and they will feel hurt and let down.

DQs hate to upset others and apologise for taking up other people's time. DQ, have you ever bumped into a chair and apologised to it?

> **Worklife Objective: *Practice direct communication***
>
> - *It is time to get your own needs met! Be direct with your communication and ask for what you need.*
>
> - *Stop apologising for taking up other people's time; if it wasn't convenient, they'd tell you.*
>
> - *Make a list of all the jobs you take on and delegate some to others. Even at home, it's OK for someone else to do the washing-up for a change!*

WQ – *Waltzing Queen*

Folk Saying:

'What would you do without me?'

WQs love to take care of others either physically (feeding, accommodation, money, driving others around etc.) or psychologically (making decisions, giving support and approving what others do etc.). They like people to be dependent on them as they want to feel indispensable. They often don't get their own needs met and complain about other people being so dependent like babies.

> **Worklife Objective: Do something for you!**
>
> - *Allow people to live their own life – let them grow up and make their own mistakes.*
>
> - *You are not a puppeteer, cut the strings and do something for you – take up a new hobby – on your own!*

JQ – *Jiving Queen*

Folk Saying:

'A woman's work is never done!'

The JQ is in a state of perpetual motion – always busy, never resting. They love the task of 'doing' above the relationships that they have with the people in their work or life and sometimes can even feel that going home spoils their rhythm and is an interruption in their day. They have an inability to relax and often say 'a woman's work is never done'. The fact is that it is usually a mask for underlying loneliness.

Worklife Objective: *Get a life! Book in me-time!*

- *Walk in the park, kick the leaves, take time out and get to know the people in your life.*
- *Try doing nothing for 15 minutes a day!*
- *In that time, get to know the real you, face your fears, think about what you're missing and then get out there and find it.*

QQ – *Quickstep Queen*

Folk Saying:

'When the going gets tough, I get going!'

QQs rarely stand still long enough to face their biggest fear – long-term emotional commitment! They wriggle out of having to communicate and when times get tough, they get going! In the workplace these might be job-hoppers, in life these people may be relationship avoiders – they don't like commitment. Wherever they lay their hat, that's their home – at least this week! A QQ doesn't stay long for fear of being 'found out' for not being good enough.

Worklife Objective: *Start to love yourself!*

- *You are OK the way you are! You are not a bad person and people do love you – warts and all!*
- *Begin to love yourself, go for a massage, a pamper day, a walk with yourself – learn to enjoy what and who you are.*
- *Learn that long-term commitment actually frees you; it does not trap you. Love and be appreciated.*

BAG - My Action Plan

BAG stands for Bin, Add and Get

B	What will I **Bin** that no longer serves my life or goals and prevents me from dancing my best life?	
A	What am I already doing, being or having that I could **Add** to or improve in order to dance my best life?	
G	What will I **Get** that will serve me well and help me to dance my best life?	

Part 2 – Your Physical Image – Your Authentic Brand

Inside my head, the real authentic me has a different physicality to the one I see if I look in the mirror. In my head I am a UK Size 12, my hair is brilliantly cut and has volume! My nails are neat and painted, my make-up looks good, my clothes are classy (usually red), my shoes are (as always) to die for, my accessories all look pulled together and I am wearing 'take me home and make me smile' underwear! She is an amazing woman – she looks and so she feels amazing too. Even when she is just doing a school run, or a trip to the supermarket, there is something that conveys who she truly is. She is in my head, and sometimes she even sneaks out. However, at other times the outside conveys something very different.

Exercise

Find some quiet space where you can close your eyes and just imagine. Allow your mind to think of the physical manifestation of the truly authentic you; from underwear to headwear to footwear, imagine every tiny detail. When you have, write it all down. Now complete the following questionnaire:

The Image Quiz

	Y	N
No matter how much weight I lose/gain, or what I do to improve myself, I still don't feel good enough		
It amazes me that people think of my size/shape/image differently to how I see myself		
On days where I am less confident, I cover up more, or wear clothes that reflect my mood		
I find it difficult to receive compliments and recognition for the way I look		
I feel larger/fatter on days when I am upset and smaller/thinner on days when I am happy and confident		
I may be feeling fine emotionally and physically, but if something negative is said to me, I suddenly feel fatter, more unattractive or ugly		
I am constantly comparing myself to others believing that they are better or thinner or more attractive or articulate		

Research reported in The Wall Street Journal stated that female executives whose clothing was described as 'extremely feminine' were typically paid less and promoted less frequently.

I saw an idea once that I would like to share with you. It was in a theatre setting, but I believe it could be adapted to suit an individual's life to build their physical and authentic brand.

First of all, find yourself a photograph album, either one of the old-fashioned plain page ones, or one with slip-in wallets; the adhesive sort won't work for this exercise. Then it is your job to fill it with images from magazines or the internet of clothes, bags, shoes, accessories that you like.

Find fabric swatches, textures and colours that you like. Find images of styles that you like and styles that you like for hair. Find make-up images that suit you, brands that you enjoy. Fill the album with your virtual wardrobe. Cut out or print words that describe your style and inspire you, like luxury, sporty, warm, cool, powerful, romantic, casual, flirty, passionate, athletic etc. Stick these words in the album where you will see them, make sure that they describe who you are! Then finally, as with all fashion shows, save the best till last. In the final pages, place images of your dream outfit, the one that you would wear to your ultimate launch party or presentation, or the one that you would wear to receive an award for the most inspirational woman of the year.

When Catherine Middleton married Prince William, weeks and weeks of speculation were focused on 'the dress' and an exquisite and beautiful dress it turned out to be –indeed fit for a Queen.

Our clothes are our feathers, and like a bird's they attract notice. As I was once told, 'dress for the job you want, not for the job you've got'. Try these tips for your image:

1. *Have your colours and style analysed! There are many image consultants out there who have a keen eye for colour as well as style to suit your body image.*

2. *If you work in an office and you're limited on money to spend, invest in good tops and cheaper skirts or trousers – you spend most of your day sitting down anyway and you can make the impact with the top half!*

3. *If you work for a company that requires you to wear a uniform or work-wear, you are limited in what you can achieve. However, this is where the accessory is Queen. Wear good-quality earrings, watch and leather shoes, belt and bag and you will look smart.*

4. *A good quality jacket – I enjoy wearing dresses, so I keep them simple – smart shift dresses – and match them with good-quality jackets that I can pull on if I need to. When I am in the office, I rarely wear a jacket and prefer a cardigan for comfort. However, if a client turns up at the door, I want to look like the MD of my company, and so I slip off the cardie and slip on my jacket. A jacket gives you power. So if you are attending an important meeting, or a meeting where you are likely to be out-numbered by men, I suggest that a jacket is a good way to pull on your personal power.*

5. *Accessory health warning! It is better to have good quality silver than tacky fake gold. Also, wear jewellery to suit your body size. I love dynamic earrings, small pretty pearls just disappear. However, make sure that your jewellery does not dangle like a bathroom flush! Dangly and plentiful earrings, or gaudy and cheap pendants, merely distract people away from your communication and lessen your power. It is better to purchase a few lovely pieces and wear them with confidence.*

6. *Someone once said to me 'If you buy a handbag, shoes and a belt in your hair colour, no matter what you are wearing, it will always look pulled together.'*

7. *Be consistent! If you change your style day by day, then people will begin to question who you really are. It is difficult to establish a style, but once you do, you can mix and match it, but always look pulled together. For example, I love textured jackets – like the traditional Chanel style. I also love floaty and chiffon and I like classic smart wear for work. I am what is referred to as a Romantic Classic; I love silk and chiffon and feminine things and can find ways of ensuring that they are part of a jacket or a dress. I have a simple linen shift dress that I wear with a Chanel-style jacket edged with silk chiffon.*

8. *Shoes – they may look fantastic, but can you walk in them? At a client meeting or presentation, it is important that all you are worried about is the content of your presentation, and not the pain in your feet! Know what you are comfortable in and what is appropriate for your place or line of work.*

9. *Handbag, briefcase, brolly, computer bag…? My suggestion would be to invest in one good bag for work that holds the lot! I have a bag that holds my computer, papers etc. and inside is a small detachable handbag that I can slip out at lunchtime, which contains my purse and personal essentials. My rule of thumb is if it doesn't fit into my left hand, then it doesn't get carried. I need my right hand free for opening doors, hanging on to underground or train handrails, hailing cabs and, of course, shaking hands. I certainly do not want to be fumbling about swapping bags to other hands if I can help it!*

10. *Always wear great underwear! I know that some of you might pooh-pooh this idea, but try it. I always wear matching items, I always wear the best I can afford and I always wear it to match my outfit or to match the mood I want to convey. For example, if I wear my sexy black silk, expensive undies to a meeting where I am competing against someone for a piece of work that I really want to do, then my undies give me the invisible anchor of added secret strength! I can stand up and present with power and if the competition were to hear the inner voice, it would be saying 'don't mess with me mister! I am wearing my black silks!' I have managed to coach more women into promotions, new jobs, better relationships and dynamic presentations all on the power of their pants!*

> *What is your authentic personal image?*
>
> *Does your outside self consistently convey who you want to be regarded as?*
>
> *Do you regularly review your style and update it as appropriate, whilst maintaining your brand?*
>
> *What will you BAG as a result of this chapter?*

Exercise

A Coaching Session with The Critical and Authentic You

I would like you to book a meeting with yourself. This meeting will last for 20 minutes the first time you do it. This meeting has to be done on a day when you can be alone, with no interruptions. The setting for this meeting is entirely up to you, but there should be no phones around to answer and you will need three chairs. If you don't have three chairs, put three cushions on the floor, or even three old magazines! The key thing is that there is an impression of three people at this meeting. The first person to sit down is you, the client, the second person is your critical self and the third will be your authentic self.

You are going to carry out a discussion with both of these people. Sit down in one of the seats. Begin to talk about an aspect of your life that you are less than happy with at the moment. Share with these other women just how you are feeling, the problem or challenge that you are experiencing and the impact of this on your life right now. When you have finished, stand up and move to the chair in which your critical self would be sitting and respond to you the client as your critical self. Allow your critical self to say all of the things that she would want to say to you. When she has finished, she will end by telling you what the positive intention of her critical voice is. In other words, what does she want for you? Move back to the client seat and feel how you feel to receive this critical input to your situation, focus on the positive intention of the critical voice, what does she want for you? For example, by being critical, is she trying to keep you safe? Thank her for her input. Then move to the chair where your authentic self is sitting. For a moment, as your authentic self, be very still and just observe the other two women. When you are ready, and having noticed both situations, what advice would you give to the client you? Step back into the client you and take on board the advice and coaching that the authentic you has given. Focus on your thoughts, feelings and insights as a result of this advice. What will you do as a result of this advice? Thank both parts of you for coming and offering insight, knowing that you can meet with them again any time.

Summary

1. *Your mirror is how you see yourself – your sense of confidence and worth.*

2. *You have three parts to self: the public self, the critical voice and the authentic self.*

3. *The critical voice can hold you back, self-limit and reduce your self-esteem.*

4. *The authentic self – the gateway to the real you! A vision of how you would like to be.*

Exercise

From this chapter, decide:

- Do you need to view yourself in a different light?

- Are you dancing to old and out of date perceptions of yourself that no longer apply?

- Do you need to de-clutter any old views of yourself from the handbag that is you?

- Do you need to stop dancing to the tunes of the critical voice in your head?

- Do you need to be clear about your brand image?

- What have you learned and will do differently as a result of completing this chapter? In the BAG exercise below, define what you will do differently.

BAG - My Action Plan

BAG stands for Bin, Add and Get

B	What will I **Bin** that no longer serves my life or goals and prevents me from dancing my best life?	
A	What am I already doing, being or having that I could **Add** to or improve in order to dance my best life?	
G	What will I **Get** that will serve me well and help me to dance my best life?	

My Phone

Introduction

The Phone chapter is about your social and professional networks. It is about who you talk to, who talks to you, who supports you, sponsors you and mentors you. It is about communication and how to influence others effectively.

In this chapter we will begin with your support network in your personal life and why it is important to retain a strong network if you are to achieve balance. We will then explore your professional network and how that supports you to grow and develop into the career that you want.

Finally we will measure your communication style and link it to worklife balance so that you can see how you work towards and away from balance in the ways that you communicate.

The phone is a metaphor for your communication networks, your social network and your professional network. In this chapter we will explore these and also communication more generally, providing you with some insight into why you gel with some people and avoid others. You will also have the opportunity to de-clutter those people from your phone who no longer add value to the dance that you wish to dance. You will further find ways to attract those who will add to your professional and social network helping you to dance your best life!

Our story ...

The traffic was horrendous. Karen was on her way home from work and had sat motionless in this queue of cars for almost 25 minutes. Karen reflected on her day. Sister had suggested that it was time for Karen to apply for her next promotion, but she'd added that Karen should improve her professional networking first. What on earth did that mean? She spoke regularly to everyone in the team, ran ward meetings and was always the first to encourage social events. Sister had explained that her 'visibility' outside of the department, and particularly 'upwards towards management', was not as good as it could be and that, as a result, others who were more visible may be considered for promotion before her. 'It's not enough nowadays to do the job well,' she had explained 'you must be seen to be visible and proactive about your professional network.' Karen wondered what on earth she should do. She was already too busy all day just doing her job, and there was no time after work due to family commitments. Maybe she would need to give up on the idea of a promotion; maybe she should be content with her current position. Her professional progress, like sitting in this traffic jam, had the brakes fully pressed on. Her mood began to sink; she felt trapped because of her inability to do more hours, to politic with the consultants and to join wretched cross-functional networks! Surely it would be easier if the system would just recognise her hard work and promote her anyway!

'How female does that sound?' came a voice from the back seat. 'I wondered when you'd show up,' laughed Karen, no longer spooked by her sudden appearance.

The two women laughed, and as they did the world around them in the car began to change, to spin, to morph into Karen's handbag once more. This time, they sat comfortably on a packet of Kleenex, staring intently at Karen's iPhone, its shiny elegant curved surface standing tall against her purse. Its mirrored face suddenly lit up like Times Square, reflecting all the must-have apps on to the faces of the two women as they peered at *the icons that promised contact with new worlds. Red-circled numbers communicated unread texts and missed calls, whilst blue notified out of date applications and tools. It was a world of hope, of contact, of 'networking'.*

Like some game-show host, older Karen broke the mesmerising spell by pressing the phone icon and opening up Karen's list of contacts – her list of favourites, and the remaining community of contacts that listed her entire communication network.

'Our first job in relation to your professional network is to create a second list of favourites – your professional favourites,' instructed fully resourceful Karen 'and these don't just include the other nurses on your ward! These include key people who can influence your career and whether you get promotion or not. You must begin to put together a list of people: their names, their contact numbers, email addresses and their actual location address.'

'Why do I need all of that?' asked Karen.

'Well, mainly to help your self-talk and to provide you with many ways of keeping in contact!' replied Karen to a rather confused younger Karen. 'Let me explain. A few minutes ago, while sitting in the car, you were clearly talking yourself out of a promotion because you didn't have time in your day and were already busy. You also said that you didn't want to politic with the consultants and join wretched cross-functional networks. Well, I believe that there are a couple of negative folk-sayings that can hold us back from progressing in our career and keep us limited in our success. Two of them relate to your communication and particularly your professional network. A person who is limited will use these sayings freely; a person who is success-focused will turn them around into positive statements of intent.

The first negative statement is, "It's not what you know, it's who you know that counts around here!" To a success-focused person, this now says, "Do I have the right networking and connecting skills?" The second

statement is, "He was just born with a silver spoon in his mouth," which to a success-focused person now says, "Do I project myself as someone who is already successful?"

'Let us look at each in turn. The first statement is about your network, and networking can be achieved not just in a face-to-face way, but also on email, SMS, twitter, blogging and good old snail mail! For example, you may be reading a medical journal and come across an article that may be useful to someone in your network. Copy it and attach a note simply saying, "Fred/Mary, saw this article and thought of you". Nothing more is needed, but it just keeps your name in their mind. When promotions come up, guess who is already in people's minds? Not only are you networking by doing this, but you are also projecting yourself as someone who is already successful (the second statement) because you are saying to them, "Even in my busy schedule, I have time to help another colleague to be successful too!" Projecting yourself as successful also means dressing for the job you want and not the one you've got, so take care of your image; look the part! Finally, learn the skills for the next job before you get the next job! Book on courses, read and make time to talk to people who are already doing the job. Instead of having lunch with your colleagues every day, book one lunch a week with someone on your career network of favourites. I will help you to develop a Network Roadmap that will help you to network successfully and build yourself as a success-focused person.'

Karen was excited by the prospect and knew that if she wanted promotion she should begin to do these things. Already she was thinking of ways to network more and project herself as a success. However, when was she going to get time to do all these other things? People demanded her time outside of work too.

'It's time to de-clutter some contacts!' announced Karen. 'Some people just take up too much of my time and that stops me from doing things for me.'

Karen began to scroll through her contact list, de-cluttering old contacts and people who 'took' from her in her career but rarely gave anything back. She built her list of professional favourites, and she reflected on her social network too. She de-cluttered old friends who were no longer in contact; she contacted others who could support her in different ways, like organising a nurse to support her parents one night a week in order to free up time to attend an evening class. By the time Karen had finished, her iPhone was in order and even seemed to shine brighter as a result of its spring clean!

Communication and You

Your professional network is a key to your success. 'It's not what you know, it's who you know that counts around here' is often true, and now means 'Do you have good networking and social networking ability?'

Using the networking tools below, begin to build your networking plan and Network Roadmap. Begin to de-clutter from your contact list all the professional contacts that no longer add value to where you want to be, and replace them with those that do.

Networking is important to secure new jobs, increase visibility in a current role, influence others, transition into a new role and for personal development. Being willing to network with others also implies the responsibility that you will be willing for people to network with you too. This is called reciprocal networking. Use the questions below to facilitate your thinking about networking.

- *What other skills, abilities and values do you want people to know you have?*
- *What new skills, abilities and behaviours do you need?*
- *When are you most willing to support others? How can you 'market' this about yourself?*
- *How could you develop yourself by supporting others?*
- *Do you have a clear idea of the ways in which you can be a good support to others?*

Networking for Your Own Development

The following table allows you to develop a plan of who you intend networking with in order to meet your personal objectives or develop specific skills. It is important to ensure that you maintain your Network Roadmap and that all outcomes are acted upon appropriately. This tool is the basis of your professional favourites list.

My professional favourites list

Name	Contact Details	What they bring me and what I can do for them

The Process for meeting with your favourites

Use the following process to support you to engage with your professional favourites in a way that will help your career or business.

Because networking is reciprocal, it is important to consider what you will give in return. We will explore this further as we proceed.

Building My Network Roadmap

Who

In this section, you will create a list of your professional favourites. You are looking for about 8 to 12 people maximum who will eventually act as ambassadors for your career. Use the following questions as prompts:

- *Who is currently on your Network List who can still support you?*

- *Who is missing? Who needs to be added?*

- *Who knows how things operate in this business/sector that you need to meet?*

- *What professional bodies or networks exist that you should join?*

How

How will you network with these people or professional bodies?

- *Face to face? Twitter? LinkedIn? Facebook? Blogging? RSS? Email? Snail-Mail? Networking events etc.?*

- *Make a list for each and try to understand how each contact may prefer to be networked with as well.*

When

Decide when you will network and how often with the same person/group. If it is face to face, book a date in their diary – one soon and one in about three months' time – so that you can follow up and share what you have done as a result of the first meeting. If it is using social network tools, be aware that communication should be regular and frequent.

Objective

What is the objective of your meeting/communication? In other words, what do you hope to achieve by meeting this person? How can they benefit you or your situation? Communicate the objective clearly when you set the meeting date. It is important that they are also prepared for the discussion.

Questions

Be specific about the questions that you want to ask. Ask open questions to ensure that you collect lots of information. For example:

'Tell me what you did to …'

'How did you do that?'

'What was the result of…?'

'Can you explain…?'

Make sure that you are clear about the questions you ask as it is often not appropriate to go back after the event to top up your information. If it is the first time that you've done this, then write down the questions to take with you. It is OK to take notes, so be prepared! Online discussion groups are also a good way to collect inputs and support for specific information. For example, on one LinkedIn discussion group, the question 'What makes a good coach?' solicited 900 pieces of feedback in the first day alone! Viral networking is a good way to collect information, but often not contacts or relationships.

Actual Outcome

- *What was the result of your meeting, what were the key learning points?*
- *Did the meeting meet your needs and objectives?*
- *Do you now have an active supporter?*
- *What more do you need?*
- *If there was any one thing that you could have done better, what would it have been?*

Key learning or actions

List the key learnings and actions that you have identified. These will form the basis for your development plan or action plan to move this forward.

- *Do you need to learn more?*
- *How will you get the information you need, who else can help?*
- *Is there any formal training or coaching available to you?*

My Network Roadmap

Who	When	Objective	Questions	Actual Outcome	Key Learnings/Action

My Network Roadmap cont'd

Who	When	Objective	Questions	Actual Outcome	Key Learnings/Action

My Social Network

In order for you to develop a good social network, it is important to understand the reasons why a social network is fundamental to your sense of community and family. Therefore, outside of work, consider those that may be on your Christmas card list or birthday list.

One of my relatives sends over 100 cards to people every Christmas. I asked how many of these people she actually ever saw. 'Oh, about 20 or so,' she said. 'Don't you think you could lose a few from the list?' I asked. 'It may never happen, but I know that if I were ever in trouble, night or day, I could call any of these 100 people and they would open their door to me,' she responded. It wasn't the act of giving a card, it was the recognition and gratitude of them being there should she ever need them.

Who would you open your door to in the middle of the night? Write down a list of people whom you regard as people you would help in a crisis. Then prioritise the list (this is difficult but force yourself to do it). Now regard the top 50, or the top 20, these are your core social network and your closest community. Could you ask any one of these to do anything for you from childcare to fixing a broken-down car?

A popular concept in a social network is the ability to job-swap in order to create balance. If you like ironing and your friend likes taking the children swimming, why not do her ironing while she takes your children to the pool?

Give and take is an implicit part of your social network. Being able to give as well as receive is essential. This is the basis of communities, and our herding instincts will encourage us to build a network or community of around 125 people.

In some cases, the size of the community is not the issue, but the willingness to ask for help, or job-swap. Why not set up a Dancing 'round the Handbags Network in your area? A group of like-minded women who get together for mutual support and to help each other to dance to their own music, creating balance in work and life. More information about Dancing'round the Handbags® Networks is contained at the back of the book.

Your Internal Chatter Box

Have you ever noticed that there are those with whom you seem to gel and those that you do not like or actively avoid? It appears that their way of communicating is so alien to our own. However, when networking it is important for us to be able to engage with others and understand the world from their perspective so that we can influence them effectively. That does not mean changing you, it just means that you can be more flexible and adapt to suit the style of the person or persons that you communicate with.

Enjoy the following exercise. It will allow you to assess your own style and then use that learning as a basis for understanding how others differ from you and how you might adapt your style to suit.

Complete the questions below, answering true or false for each, and then complete the results table:

1. *I am more extrovert and less introvert*

   a) *True*

   b) *False*

2. *I know I have done a good job because of the recognition I get from others around me, rather than how I feel about the work myself*

   a) *True*

   b) *False*

3. *I tend to focus on the big picture rather than the detail*

   a) *True*

   b) *False*

4. *I move towards goals rather than away from problems*

   a) *True*

   b) *False*

5. *I prefer options and spontaneity rather than processes and structure*

   a) *True*

   b) *False*

6. *I prefer working with people, emotions and uncertainty rather than tasks, data, facts and things*

   a) *True*

   b) *False*

7. *I relish change and get bored if things are the same for too long*

   a) *True*

   b) *False*

8. *I love being spontaneous and flexible and tend to avoid planning, organising or routine*

   a) *True*

   b) *False*

9. *I enjoy reacting to problems or situations rather than being proactive*

   a) *True*

   b) *False*

10. *I enjoy taking action, getting on with things and getting results rather than planning, considering and ensuring the best course of action before getting started*

   a) *True*

   b) *False*

On the table over, mark your scores for each of the questions above.

		Your Answer		Your Answer	
1	True	**Extrovert**	**Introvert**		False
2	True	Seeks external verification and legitimisation, you tend to seek external recognition or feedback. Often more talkative, expresses outwardly thoughts or feelings	Uses energy within, reflective, thoughtful and you tend to reflect internally about things, seeking your own sense of intuition or logic		False
3	True	**Big Picture** Generalisations, big vision, overview	**Detail** Attention to detail, focused, concentrating, specifics		False
4	True	**Towards** Focus on what you want	**Away From** Focus on what you don't want		False
5	True	**Options** Flexibility, options, choices, 'go with the flow'	**Procedures** Processes, structure, proven techniques, 'tried and tested methods', stick to the rules		False
6	True	**People** Relationships, team, friendships, feelings, values, loyalty etc.	**Task** Job, data, fact, logic, rationale, control, measures etc.		False
7	True	**Different** Change, spontenaeity, impulse, risk, challenge, opportunity	**Same** Status quo, similar, conforming, considered, settled		False
8	True				False

		Your Answer	Your Answer	
9	True	**Proactive** Action-oriented, active, movement, speed, decider	**Reactive** Reflective, look before you leap, considered, questioning, analyser	False
10	True	**Action** Just do it! Get on with it! Don't waste time!	**Planner** Consider, plan, prepare, reflect, wait	False

Meta Programmes and Communication Preference

Meta Programmes are motivational filters and are built as a result of our responses to events or stimuli (like the response you have when your boss or an old flame walks into the room). Our response to that stimulus creates decisions and actions that are rooted in our beliefs, value systems and culture. Deletions (what we don't see), distortions (what we don't want to see) and generalisations (what we always see!) about the stimuli create the filters, and the filters are built from memories, experiences beliefs and therefore expectations. For example, if you believe that your boss doesn't care, you will look for behaviours, gestures and actions that prove this from the ways in which he interacts with you. Over time, we become 'programmed' by these responses to filters and our underlying meta-programmes will eventually communicate to us unconsciously.

This is not a problem, unless it is self-limiting. For example, two millionaires may be running two different programmes inside their head in relation to their accumulation of wealth. The first Millionaire knows that she can make millions by focusing her efforts on what she wants; she has set goals since she was a young girl. Her parents always told her to strive for what she wanted. She is very much programmed to look TOWARD her future and success. The second Millionaire witnessed the despair and sadness caused by poverty and a lack of resources in her family of origin when she was a child. Her internal meta-programme is to MOVE AWAY from poverty. One is a 'towards' and one is an 'away from' internal dance.

From the exercise above, identify each of your dominant meta programmes and identify where each may be influencing your goals, choice of jobs, living your life and building relationships with others. Is there anything that you need to change? For example, if you run a meta programme that demands a need for procedures, processes and systems, explore your ability to be chaotic, as well as your need for structure. Do this, imagine that there is a dancefloor in front of you. On one end of the floor, there are couples dancing perfectly to ballroom dances. At the other, is a writhing spasm of people dancing in their own way. Look at each end of the spectrum on this dancefloor and ask yourself 'What does dancing like this get for me?" For example, on the chaotic end of the dancefloor, you may suggest that it gets you freedom, creativity, spontaneity etc. at the other end, it gets you structure, flow, coordination etc. Now apply this to the workplace, you will need to have different people for different situations – all dancing the same way does not add value to the organisation!

Your Communication Preferences

By looking at the list of words below, tick or highlight all of those that best describe you. Be aware, this is not how you would like to influence others, but rather how you do. You should seek to tick or highlight at least 40 words, not less than 30, and no more than 60. Then, add up the total numbers of the corresponding letter and write it in the scorecard at the bottom. Remember, be honest with yourself, you'll get better results that way, which will help your personal development.

My Preferred way of influencing others is to be:

No.	Code	Word	No.	Code	Word	No.	Code	Word
1.	IS	Intense	33.	JE	Relaxed	65.	AL	Sociable
2.	AL	Stimulating	34.	CH	Determined	66.	JA	Contemplative
3.	IS	Analytical	35.	JE	Team focused	67.	KA	Impatient
4.	SY	Dynamic	36.	CH	Task/Target driven	68.	JE	Caring
5.	CH	Driven	37.	KA	Assertive	69.	SY	Impulsive
6.	SY	Persuasive	38.	SY	Fascinating	70.	AL	Intuitive
7.	KA	Demanding	39.	SA	Loyal	71.	CH	Insistent
8.	JA	Detail conscious	40.	JA	Organised	72.	JE	People focused
9.	AL	Chatty	41.	SA	Passive	73.	JA	Secretive
10.	AL	Enthusiastic	42.	SA	Tranquil	74.	SY	Charming
11.	CH	Tough	43.	AL	Chaotic	75.	AL	Attention Grabbing
12.	IS	Systematic	44.	KA	Direct	76.	IS	Factual
13.	SY	Restless	45.	JE	Patient	77.	JA	Enigmatic
14.	KA	Powerful	46.	JA	Reasoned	78.	KA	Vigorous
15.	SA	Calm	47.	SY	Spontaneous	79.	SY	Motivating
16.	AL	Energetic	48.	KA	Commanding	80.	IS	Meticulous
17.	IS	Tenacious	49.	IS	Questioning	81.	AL	Emotional
18.	JA	Formal	50.	CH	Competitive	82.	CH	Unflinching
19.	AL	Excitable	51.	AL	Passionate	83.	SA	Distant
20.	SA	Reserved	52.	JA	Cautious	84.	KA	Heroic
21.	KA	Adventurous	53.	SA	Quiet	85.	SA	Accepting
22.	JE	Flexible	54.	KA	Goal oriented	86.	SA	Peacemaker
23.	IS	Critical	55.	AL	Fun	87.	SY	Influential
24.	CH	Formidable	56.	CH	Authoritative	88.	SA	Respectful
25.	JE	Good tempered	57.	SA	Charitable	89.	SA	Courteous
26.	SY	Provocative	58.	JA	Methodical	90.	JE	Inclusive
27.	JA	Private	59.	JE	Tolerant	91.	JA	Rational
28.	SY	Collaborative	60.	CH	Unwavering	92.	IS	Logical
29.	JE	Devoted	61.	JE	Trusty	93.	CH	Single-minded
30.	CH	Intimidating	62.	IS	Investigative	94.	JE	Encouraging
31.	IS	Judicious	63.	KA	Challenging	95.	JA	Inquiring
32.	KA	Achieving	64.	IS	Vigilant	96.	SY	Inspiring

Below, write your total scores from the table on previous page.

IS	JA	SA	JE	AL	SY	KA	CH

Now, plot the scores on the answer grid shown below. This grid is available to download from the website, by registering your membership (free of charge).

Proactive, Towards, External, Tell, Impulsive

Kate

Sylvia

Chris

Options
Relationships
People
Big Picture
Different

Procedures
Detail
Same
Task
Data/fact

Ali

Isabel

Jennie

Jane

Sarah

Reactive, Away from, Internal, Questioning, Considering

Interpreting your Scores

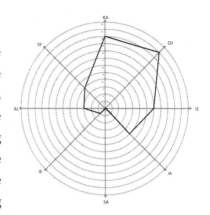

If you are like most people, you will have scores in all areas, and when you join up the dots, will observe a dominant preference, like the example shown here. However, some people have equal scores in each box, showing no dominant preference, and others score zero in certain areas, showing an extreme lack of preference. There is no right or wrong answer; it is just your preference.

It is sometimes beneficial to ask others to complete the questionnaire in order to provide you with feedback, as their perception of your communication style can be enlightening as well as developmental. For example, if your boss perceives you differently to your employees, or you communicate differently to male colleagues than female, then this insight may help you to reflect on the appropriateness of adapting your style in different situations.

The power of this tool is its ability to provide you with invaluable input about how you influence yourself and others. Should your preferred style not work with a certain individual or team, imagine how useful it would be to have a tool at your fingertips that would support you to adapt to suit their style instead?

Being able to recognise another person's style just by the way they speak, the language they use or their body language towards you could be invaluable in an interview situation, or an important presentation. By adapting your style to suit the receiver of your communication, you will ensure influence – you're talking my language! In NLP circles, there is a presupposition that states 'the meaning of your communication is the response that you get' – by adapting to suit the language of the receiver, you will engage their attention, and encourage their buy in to you and your needs. Balance comes from the ability to recognise and influence from the receiver's frame of reference. By communicating more effectively, and asking for your needs to be met in the language of the receiver, you

reduce your own stress, improve relationships and ensure the outcome that you desire!

Based on the true - false questionnaire that you completed earlier in the chapter, as well as the above questionnaire, you can now see not only which communication style you use naturally, but also the underlying unconscious communication drivers that are programmed within. These programmes, like any other, can be amended or adapted for yourself, or in the process of communicating more effectively with others.

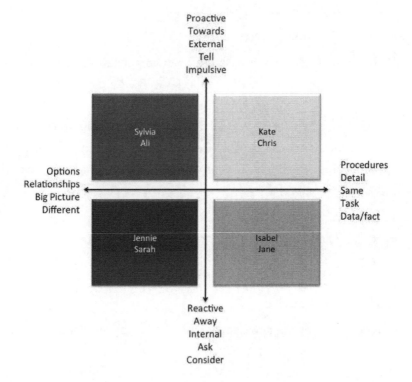

Below are the style profiles and they are grouped into twos, as shown by the diagram above. You should read your closely matched profile and make additional notes if you have any secondary preferences. For example, you may show strong preferences for both Chris and Isabel. They are in different quadrants, but they are both on the side of procedures, detail and task. This suggests that you have more of a task than people preference.

The Style Profiles

Summary of Chris and Kate

Your non-verbal communication indicators include direct eye contact, pointing, cutting and pushing hand gestures, and tend to walk at a fast and determined pace. You can have a focused gaze, and will tend to control your facial expressions and command a rigid posture when communicating with others. Kate is less driven that Chris, but if you are either, you know what you want and are determined to get it!

Chris

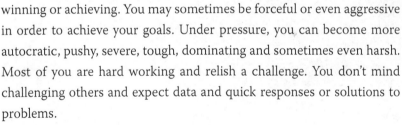

Summary: If you scored highest in Chris, you prefer strong processes and procedures, you have attention to detail, look for what is the same during change, are task focused and results oriented. You proactively move towards goals, are externally focused, usually extrovert and quick to make decisions.

If you are a Chris you are likely to be business-like, forceful and determined. You enjoy taking risks, making quick decisions, taking initiative and focusing on winning or achieving. You may sometimes be forceful or even aggressive in order to achieve your goals. Under pressure, you can become more autocratic, pushy, severe, tough, dominating and sometimes even harsh. Most of you are hard working and relish a challenge. You don't mind challenging others and expect data and quick responses or solutions to problems.

You don't value personal relationships at work as much as getting the job done. You keep your emotions locked in and under control preferring to focus on what has to be achieved. In some cases, you can even be dismissive of the need to engage or motivate. Chris tends to be a poor empathiser and therefore not so good at listening. Your reduced non-verbal acuity and general distraction caused by your impatience to achieve performance can mean that she misses out on the importance of ensuring buy-in from the team. 'My way or the Highway' becomes the outcome and this will not be motivating for Ali, Jennie and Sarah.

Kate

Summary: You prefer strong processes and procedures, delegate effectively, are fast moving, look for what is the same in change, are task focused, goal oriented and externally focused. Yu are usually extrovert, spontaneous, adventurous, like to control self and others and are commanding with an audience.

If you chose Kate, then you would have selected words like: Demanding, powerful, adventurous, achieving, assertive, direct, commanding, goal oriented, challenging, impatient, vigorous, and heroic. Others regard you as straight-talking; someone who calls a spade a spade and expects high performance at all times. You usually like to control the action plans,

activities and work of others and can debate until you get your own way. You will recognise performance and achievement, but may lack a people focus. Under pressure, you can become more autocratic, pushy and demanding. She value people that get the task done, recognising who your high performers are and will often utilise them to the exclusion of others. You prefer to avoid emotional decision-making, but can be commanding and persuasive. You, Like Chris, can be a poor listener, often distracted by your own fast moving brain, which is focused on achieving the next thing! Take time to engage with people like Sarah, Jennie and Ali, who can offer the people aspects that will help you to be even more successful.

Adapting your style to suit CHRIS or KATE

DO'S	DON'TS
Be clear, specific, brief, and to the point.	Don't ramble on, or waste their time.
Stick to business.	Don't try to build a personal relationship.
Come prepared with all requirements, objectives, support material in well organised "package".	Don't forget or lose things; do not be disorganised or messy; do not confuse or distract their mind from business.
Present the facts logically; plan your presentation efficiently.	Don't leave loopholes or vague issues – if you do not want to be put down.
Ask specific (preferably "what?" and "how") questions.	Don't ask rhetorical or irrelevant questions.
Provide alternatives and choices for making their own decisions.	Don't come with a rigid decision.
Provide facts and figures about probability of success or effectiveness of options.	Don't speculate wildly or offer unachievable deadlines.
If you disagree, take issue with facts, not the person.	If you disagree, do not let it reflect on them personally.
If you agree, support results, not the person.	If you agree, do not reinforce with "I will support you".
Motivate and persuade by referring to objectives and results.	Don't try to convince by "personal" means.
Support their conclusions.	Don't direct or order.
After talking business, leave.	Don't stay for a personal chat after finishing business

Summary of Isabel and Jane

Both of you prefer strong processes and procedures, have attention to detail, look for what is the same in change, are task focused and enjoy problem solving (goals are usually moving away from something you don't want, rather than something you do). You tend to be reactive to the needs and tasks of others, ask lots of questions and need time to consider responses, therefore decisions are well thought through, even though they are not instant.

In terms of verbal and non-verbal behaviour, you are slower, more deliberate, focused on data and fact, often monotone, but softer than the louder tones of Chris and Kate. You often focus on historic detail, proven methods for problem solving and refer to past examples. You often don't make regular eye contact, dropping your head or looking away when thinking or talking to another. Your facial expressions and most gestures are controlled, and show little emotion.

Isabel

If you scored high in Isabel, you would have ticked words like: Intense, analytical, tenacious, systematic, critical, judicious, standards focused,

factual, meticulous, vigilant, questioning, logical and investigative. You are perceived as a thinker, a technical expert, an introvert, detailed focused, deliberate, constrained and logical. You focus on data, fact, standards; a processed focused problem solver who is disciplined in their approach to work. Isabel listens well, weighs up all the options and bases decisions on proven methods of problem resolution. Your quiet and restrained nature means that you show very little emotion when dealing with others. Isabel remains guarded and only builds relationships once trust is ensured. You avoid close emotional or physical contact with colleagues.

Nervous of public displays of emotion or public recognition, you will tend to remain silent about your achievements. You can be critical of the standards and outputs of others. For example, you can be critical of timekeeping, untidiness and chaotic methods. This can lead to a moralistic view, arrogance and aloofness. However, you expect things to be done properly and to exacting standards, therefore the output of your work can always be depended on. Be aware that keeping your distance can be regarded as coldness, especially by Ali, Jennie and Sarah.

Jane

If you are a Jane handbag, then you would have highlighted words like: Detail conscious, formal, private, methodical, organised, reasoned, cautious, contemplative, secretive, enigmatic, rational and enquiring.

Jane likes structure, proven methods, certainty, detail, and seeks evidence before committing to a course of action. You are self-disciplined, often aloof and prefer to let others take initiative in social settings. You enjoy working alone, often seeking tasks or work that requires serious attention to detail. You demonstrate little emotion, preferring to influence others with data and fact, which helps to decrease the risks in decision-making. You prefer time to reflect on decisions before making them, and would say 'good decisions and judgement cannot be rushed'. You are conscientious about doing the

right thing right first time, organised, a planner, enjoy problem solving and adhering to proven standards. Personally, you are generally quite private, preferring to keep home life and social life separate from work. You avoid physical contact at work, but are less emotionally distant than Isabel. You can be critical of the standards and outputs of others. For example, you can be critical of timekeeping, untidiness and chaotic methods. This can lead to a moralistic view, arrogance and aloofness, which will not go down well with Sylvia, Ali and Jennie.

Adapting your style to suit Isabel or Jane

DO'S	DON'TS
Prepare your "case" in advance.	Don't be disorganised or messy.
Approach them in a straightforward, direct way; stick to business.	Don't be giddy, casual, informal or loud.
Support their principles; use a thoughtful approach; build your credibility by listing pros and cons.	Don't rush the decision -making process.
Make an organised contribution to their efforts; present specifics, and do what you say you can do.	Don't be vague about what is expected of either of you; do not fail to follow through.
Take your time, but be persistent.	Don't dilly-dally.
	Don't leave things to chance or luck.
Draw up a scheduled approach to implementing action with a step-by-step timetable; assure them there will not be surprises.	Don't provide special personal incentives.
	Don't threaten, cajole, wheedle, coax.
If you agree, follow through, because they will check progress to plan.	Don't use testimonies of others or unreliable sources; do not be haphazard.
If you disagree, make an organised presentation of your position.	Don't use someone's opinion as evidence.
Give them time to verify reliability of your actions; be accurate, realistic.	Don't use gimmicks or clever, quick manipulations.
Provide solid, tangible, practical evidence.	Don't push too hard, or be unrealistic with deadlines.

Summary of Sylvia and Ali

You are a goal oriented, forward focused individual who is fun to be around, engaging, people focused, empathetic and relationship based. Externally focused usually extrovert, quick to make decisions, can be impulsive, likes to see the 'big picture', limited attention to detail, easily bored, embraces change, likes to create change and difference.

Your verbal and non-verbal behaviours include a varied and sometimes melodic tone of voice that conveys feelings and moving towards something. You can talk fast or loud when excited, and non-verbal gestures can be dramatic in line with emotions. You often use open hand gestures, pointing, pushing and curled hands to convey a point. You make direct eye contact, lean forward and relish face-to-face communication. Your posture is often casual, open and warm and you will touch colleagues and show emotion in words and gestures.

Sylvia

If you are a Sylvia you would have highlighted words from the following list: Dynamic, Persuasive, restless, provocative, fascinating, spontaneous, impulsive, charming, motivating, influential and inspiring.

You are the life and soul of the team. You collaborate, build networks, identify sources and resources and are generally forward focused and visionary. You enjoy fun, laughter and camaraderie, believing that a team that is engaged and happy can achieve amazing things. As a people orientated extrovert, you like an audience and the public recognition that it brings. You are passionate, competitive and high-spirited, valuing open and honest communication and preferring spontaneity. Sylvia is future-oriented, with a risk-taking entrepreneurial spirit like the Kate. You are creative and value quick decision-making and innovation in others. You are less chaotic or disorganised than Ali, making sure that events or presentations are right, but more importantly, goal focused and inspiring. You love a celebration of achievement and your extrovert nature means that you are happy to take centre stage and play to your adoring audience. You are the party bag!

Ali

If Ali is the name on your bag, then you would have highlighted words like stimulating, chatty, enthusiastic, energetic, excitable, chaotic, passionate, fun, sociable, intuitive, attention grabbing and emotional.

You love to tell stories, talk about your ideas, dreams and goals and ensure the buy-in of the team towards a compelling vision. You believe that leadership is about creating great teamwork in a culture of trust, empowerment and playing to people strengths. You enjoy building relationships and making sure that small talk and chatter are experienced before getting down to the job at hand. You make decisions based on feelings and Intuition and can be very passionate, excitable and motivating. Your warmth, involvement, encouragement, responsiveness and friendliness creates a sense of belonging in a team, ensuring a safe and comfortable environment for others to take risks and achieve results. You may be regarded as a bit chaotic and disorganised by those who like control and structure, so be careful to ensure that your enthusiasm is tempered with Isabel, Jane and Chris.

Adapting your style to suit Sylvia and Ali

DO'S	DON'TS
Support their dreams and intuitions	Don't suppress their ideas and contributions
Leave time for socialising	Don't be impersonal, cold, or aloof
Talk about people and their objectives; opinions they find stimulating.	Don't concentrate on facts and figures or go into details
Do commit them to courses of action	Don't leave decisions up in the air
Ask for their opinions and ideas – particularly about people	Don't stick too rigidly to the agenda

DO'S	DON'TS
Provide ideas	*Don't talk down to them, do not patronise*
Use enough time to be stimulating, fun-loving, fast-moving	*Don't be dogmatic or inflexible*
Offer incentives for quick action, risks and competitiveness	*Don't forget to recognise and reward their contribution*
Give them space to perform, be creative and mark their space with their brand!	
Recognise them publicly with reward, applause, and gifts!	

Summary of Jennie and Sarah

If you are a Jennie or a Sarah you are someone who achieves your goals by building relationships and establishing strong supportive alliances and networks. You are perceived as warm, involving, a good listener and easy to engage with. You are someone who enjoys being with others and building a culture of shared responsibility, support and encouragement. Your challenge is to focus on task, data and structure, as you prefer relationships, teamwork and tranquillity.

Your verbal and non-verbal behaviours include soft vocal inflected tones, warm, slow pace, casual body language, some indirect eye contact, touch and a tendency to seek cooperation through gestures that ensure personal security and compliance.

Under stress, you will tend to back down and become compliant with others. Strong assertive gestures do not come naturally to you, as you prefer quieter and gentler approaches.

Sarah

As a Sarah you will have highlighted some of the following words: calm, reserved, loyal, passive, quiet, charitable, reserved, accepting, peacemaker, respectful and courteous. You avoid unnecessary risk taking or impulsiveness, preferring to ensure everyone's buy in and support before moving ahead. You are cooperative, loyal and private, adapting to the needs of others to minimise interpersonal conflict whenever possible. You naturally display empathy to others and trust people to do a good job,

resulting in the confidence and engagement of others. Your people approach results in a strong dedication to others and team success and wellbeing. You tend to go with the flow and will conform to what others want. Sometimes you lack confidence in your own ability, or are too shy to assert your own agenda or needs and therefore are likely to become a little too dependent on others. Be careful that you do not become too gullible or soft with others who are likely to manipulate your good nature, that have a more demanding or impulsive style like Chris, Kate and Sylvia.

Jennie

Jennie is less private than Sarah, and would have highlighted some of the following: Flexible, devoted, relaxed, team-focused, patient, tolerant, trusting, caring, people focused, inclusive and encouraging. Jennie prefers to develop strong and close relationships with her team. Jennie

shares a lot about herself personally, and prefers others to do the same. Jennie uses relationships and the strength of them to avoid and move away from conflict. Jennie likes to play hard as well as work hard, and is good at celebrating success in her team. She is supportive, collaborative and very dependable. She can become a bit of a mother figure in the team and must be careful not to use this strength with people who would not value it, like Kate, Chris and Isabel.

Adapting your style to suit Jennie and Sarah

DO'S	DON'TS
Spend the first few minutes talking at a personal level to break the ice	*Don't rush headlong into business or the agenda.*
Show sincere and authentic interest in them as people	*Don't force them into quick decisions*
Patiently work with them to help achieve objectives	*Don't debate about facts and figures.*
Present your case informally, and listen well	*Don't be too pushy and fast.*
Ask "how?" questions to draw out their opinions	*Don't make decisions for them and care-take them into becoming ineffective*
If you disagree, look for an emotional response (sadness or hurt)	*Do not isolate them with no support, or make them work alone*
Recognition and reward should be delivered one-to-one and should be for personal contributions	

Each person adds value to the organisation or to any personal interaction. If we always view people from our own map of the world, then we may not experience the diversity of styles and possibilities that others can bring from their perspective. By observing others and improving your own acuity, you too can become more influential. For example, if you know that you are an Sylvia, and that you have a boss who is an Isabel, then you will now know that boss needs data, fact, analysis and a bit of time to consider her decision. Pushing, motivating, inspiring and cajoling them will not go down well; as will not having ideas backed up with hard facts! Frustrating as it might be, if you want your own needs met, influence them in a way that they expect to be influenced! It is not 'treat others as you would expect to be treated yourself, it is 'treat others as THEY would expect to be treated.'

Learning comes from being aware of other people's communication style and being flexible enough to adapt yourself to their map of the world. In a communication situation, recognising others' styles and communicating to suit them, builds rapport and supports a positive outcome.

Exercise

Download two copies of the above diagram from the website. On the first, plot your dominant scores in one colour and the person you most get on with (in life or work) in another colour. Why do you get on well? What is it that you have, or do that is complementary? What is it about both of your styles that make you gel?

Now do the same on the second sheet, but this time plot the scores of the person that you get on with least? What is it about their style that is incongruent? How would you have to adapt your style to suit theirs and achieve a better outcome?

Exercise

Make a list of the key people in your work and life and then next to their name, decide how you might change the way you communicate in order to achieve a better relationship or outcome with them in future. Before meeting them, think of some ways in which you may speak to them differently. You can use this tool for both personal as well as business use.

Work Colleagues

Name	Style	Action

Life relationships

Name	Style	Action

*Remember, if you always do what you always did,
then you'll always get what you always got!*

BAG - My Action Plan

BAG stands for **B**in, **A**dd and **G**et

B	What will I **Bin** that no longer serves my life or goals and prevents me from dancing my best life?	_____ _____
A	What am I already doing, being or having that I could **Add** to or improve in order to dance my best life?	_____ _____
G	What will I **Get** that will serve me well and help me to dance my best life?	_____ _____

7 My Purse

Introduction

Of all the Handbag chapters, the Purse has been the most challenging to write. For a long time, I explored and questioned the metaphor and its meaning. Is it about change? Credit? Money? Resources? Flow? Wealth? All of these things, or something altogether different? It wasn't until I was wandering around a museum, being followed by a rather unscrupulous-looking character, that I really discovered its true meaning. It was my behaviour in response to my stalker that truly inspired my thoughts. As he followed me closely from room to room, shadowing my moves from exhibit to exhibit, I became a little more concerned. He was very close, observing, but being far enough away to not be too weird. Instead of confronting him, escaping to a ladies' toilet or alerting staff, I simply zipped up my handbag and drew it closer to my body! I had in my imagination a feeling that he intended to steal from me. I sat down on a nearby viewing bench to think and consider why I had done what I had done. The man who was following me continued on his journey around the museum, and I saw him some time later catching up with his family and chatting about favourite exhibits. He had turned out to be completely innocent, but his behaviour and my suspicion had in fact helped me to

become a little less reflective about the museum treasures and more about the treasures within my own handbag. Why did I zip up my bag? It was of course to protect my purse! If it were stolen, the loss would run deeper than the loss of any other item like, for example, a lipstick! The purse is more important than any other item; it contains credit cards, cash and change. It may also contain receipts and, if you are like most women, photographs of the people that the purse cares for. I suddenly realised that this chapter was not about how much money a woman had; it was much more important than that. The purse represents 'choice' and 'change'. As part of those two most important aspects, we can also explore currency, credit, sacrifice and your receipts of gratitude. Had my purse been stolen that day, it would have removed a lot of choices for me in the short term – money to get home being one. It would also have created change in me at a deeper level; maybe I would have become less trusting, or maybe I would have changed my behaviour towards people. In speculating and contemplating these things, the content of the Purse chapter evolved.

Our story ...

Karen had just experienced the week from hell; the hospital was busy, Josh had a viscous cold and, to cap it all, James's parents were 'visiting' from York. Karen liked his parents but 'visiting' meant that they were 'on holiday', and whilst on holiday, they expected to be looked after and nurtured. For a whole week, they had lounged around, read newspapers and the air of expected service floated around them. Did they offer to wash up? No. Did they offer to take everyone out for tea? No. Did they look after Josh while Karen went to work? No. In fact, they were astounded that Karen had even considered going to work at all when her son was poorly! By Thursday evening, Karen was seething inside and as she cleared away the dishes from yet another meal, she observed the scene in this 'hotel' she had created. She listened as her in-laws bickered about what to watch on TV, Josh coughed into his

Playstation (oblivious to the world, caught up in some cyber-space war that demanded every second of his attention), Tilly was engrossed in Facebook 'walls' that allowed virtual street-corner gatherings with her chums, and James in a flurry of 'see you later!' marched out of the front door to play another testosterone-filled game of squash. Karen gently laid down the tea towel, put on her jacket and quietly let herself out of the back door.

It was a lovely summer's evening and the pale lemon sky was just beginning to turn to a peachy glow against the deep blue above. Karen loved this time of day. She meandered along the path that stitched the rear gardens of the houses on to the open common in a neat row of suburbia. She would often walk this route, either going to or returning from a shift at work. Tonight was her night off and so the pace was less demanding, but her mood was different too; she felt sad and there was a nagging sense of injustice about the lack of support at home and her inability to get any of them to even notice the imbalance of workload.

'Can I join you?' The voice made Karen jump and she swung round, wiping the moist tears that had begun to rise in her eyes. It was Tomorrow Karen, but where had she come from this time? Karen wondered. 'Yes, of course, and don't make me jump like that!' she scolded laughingly. The two women continued across the common in silence towards the boating lake. There was no need to talk; Karen wanted to enjoy the freedom and the thoughts that were swirling around in her mind. Eventually they reached the edge of the water where they sat down on a park bench and stared across the glassy surface dappled like glitter on a seasonal card by the last rays of the setting sun. Geese, ducks and swans glided across the mirrored surface towards the two women, anticipating a bonus snack before sundown. But nothing was forthcoming and soon they grew bored and faded off into distant rushes, pencil-like striped ripples of water drawn across the surface in their wake. As they did, the older Karen pointed out the grace of the swan, its long white neck elegantly poised above

heart-shaped wings of soft arctic-white down. It cut through the water gracefully, leaving merely a faint trace of it ever having passed. 'The swan looks so elegant!' offered the older woman. 'Yes,' said Karen 'but you can't see the thrashing that's going on underneath the water!' This gave the older woman her opportunity. 'A bit like you and your life?' she commented rhetorically. 'Exactly like me and my life!' retorted Karen in an instant.

'Tell me more...' said Tomorrow Karen empathetically, anticipating the explanation that was to come.

'I do everything for them, and you know what? Right now, they probably don't even know that I have left, gone out for a walk!'

The stress and tiredness in Karen's face was etched against her skin, and in the fading light looked more intense as the scars of tiredness etched craggy paths under her bright blue eyes.

'I am so fed up with the whole thing! I sometimes think that I will paint HOTEL on the front door, just to make my point!'

The older Karen took her hands in hers. 'Tonight we are going to look at your purse. Your purse represents the costs and sacrifices you make. It is about credit; who takes credit? It is about receipts of gratitude and recognition, and it is about change. We will explore your earnings – not real money, but how you earn respect, dignity, support. As we look at what you earn, we will also reflect on the cost of being you.'

The two women walked for a while, arm in arm and in silence. The dusk around them deepened and they continued forward on to a small side path overgrown with shrubs and low trees. The path grew darker and darker and their pace became more and more hypnotic and unconscious. As they reached the clearing, the path had all but disappeared and they were once again enveloped in the satin surrealism of Karen's handbag. There, poised like a locomotive of leather, stood Karen's long green purse – a bit battered and worn but unconditionally respected and, in an odd way, a true part of her.

'Shall we open it up?' beckoned Tomorrow Karen, striding towards its shiny gold stud with outstretched hands. Karen felt a sudden pang of protection for her most private of items, and strode ahead of the older woman as if to block her way and shield her purse from those intrusive hands.

'I'll do it!' she announced. 'It's...' She caught herself before stating an obvious lie that the purse belonged to her alone. The older woman respected her need for control and stepped aside to allow Karen clear access to it.

'Do you see the power that this item commands?' The two women contemplated the purse for a moment, recognising its potency and contemplating its power. The purse was indeed important; it demanded special protection as it provided the continuous resources for life's day-to-day needs. Losing a purse would jeopardise our ability to pay bills, feed our families and buy the occasional treat. However, more than all of that, in the hands of someone who doesn't own it, they have the power to ransack its content, taking what is not theirs to have; raping the very essence of who we are. Karen shivered with the recognition of its unique potency.

Karen respectfully opened the purse and pulled open the inner tabernacle of secrecy. The plastic window, intended for a name and address 'in case of loss or theft' had been replaced with a photo of Karen, James and the children. Karen observed this now giant poster of her family and understood that her purse indeed funded their needs.

'Let us begin with change and choice, the credit cards, receipts and of course money itself. Is there anything else in your purse that we should explore?' asked Tomorrow Karen.

'There is my secret pocket with the emergency £10 note and of course the purse itself!'

'Indeed! Let's get started then, we have a lot to get through!'

Many women dream of leaving a relationship or job that is withering them, but cannot because they do not have the resources – either financial or internal – to make the move. That is true until the heat gets turned up to a point where they can no longer stand it and they must leave for their own survival. For many years I have read or heard about women living in abusive marriages, partnerships or jobs and have asked myself 'why don't they just leave?' I couldn't understand why they would stay in a toxic relationship in which they were being regularly physically or mentally abused. I now realise that the choice is not always about the relationship, but rather the lack of resources (financial or confidence) to actually make the move. These women become a slave to the very thing that would also liberate them – money. Having financial independence brings choice, the ability to liberate yourself from debts or relationships, bad management, jobs that don't inspire you or living environments that are less than happy. The money resource is important as it provides the decision-making capability to do what you want. In the Dance chapter we explored the meaning of work and life. Work was defined as a source of income, the 'wherewithal' to live life. Life, we agreed, was about family, friends, leisure, learning and self. Interestingly, the source of income tends to be spent in that order as well, with money for self often at the bottom of the list. This is also true for time, and will be explored in the Diary chapter. Money for our own needs, especially our long-term needs, is generally left at the bottom of the list. Many women, if their confidence is already jarred by poor relationships or work, feel less than deserving of the scraps of money that are left. It is a continuous cycle and one that is difficult to break out of unless, like my friend Anna, one day you wake up and decide to make a change for your own emotional or physical survival.

For years my husband had verbally and emotionally attacked me. I felt destroyed. I had no self-esteem and was becoming more and more reclusive. My only saving grace was my job. I had worked for a large public sector department for many years and was an expert on specific crime information. I decided that I would put all of my energy into work and away from Steve's abuse at home. I opened a separate bank account in an online bank and managed it from work. He had no idea. Each month, I squirrelled away a percentage of my salary, and each time I received a bonus or pay-rise, I put all of it into the account. Steve and I had always had a joint account to pay the bills, so it was easy for me to hide extra income in another account. It wasn't much, but it soon became enough. I had saved enough for 12 months' rent on another house. I knew that would be enough to get me started and of course I would manage the rest out of my existing income. I also started moving bits and pieces that were important to me out of the house – little things, but things that had sentimental value. I moved them into a friend's garage. One night, Steve came home in a foul mood and spent an hour lashing me with his tongue. It was interesting, because every word seemed to make me stronger, every insult broke the links in the chain of my imprisonment in this relationship. The next morning, he rose and left before 8:00 a.m. I knew that he would be gone for about 12 hours. I packed all of my remaining belongings and those of my son, I loaded my car with that which was important to me and I left. That was two years ago, and I am now happy. Squirrelling was so important, and I encourage every woman and man in a relationship like that to save enough money to just get them out of the door. Looking back now, the material things were not important; my well-being and that of my little boy was.

Money, Money, Money

Many women I speak to are less than focused on the long-term availability or growth of their money. Even here, in our advanced western culture, we earn on average about 17% less than men and we contribute less to pensions as well. For every £1 a man earns from his pension, a woman earns 32p. How much do you focus on your long-term wealth and what would happen if you were suddenly in need of a regular income from a pension or savings? Many women abdicate responsibility for this, still believing that their husband will provide or that they will worry about it later. Some women who do not have husbands but are in relationships with opposite or same-sex partners have told me, 'I really should sort something out, even if it is just life cover for us in case anything happens, but I have just never got round to it.' I suspect that we are all just so busy with the 'now' that we never get round to focusing on the 'then'. I was guilty of this too, but have recently begun to invest a small amount a month into savings – something I should have done in my 20s! Back then I was more interested in holidays, clothes and buying my first home than worrying about long-term sustainability. We are in an ageing population where, by the time we retire or need care, a lot more of the UK population will be in the same position. This means that we will need improved caring and residential facilities for eldercare. Fewer young people than older will put strain on the caring professions and, unless something different is done, many women could be facing a bleak future in their old age. It is important that we plan for that time by investing now. Let me put it in context. If you are 35 years old today, you will work (based on current legislation) until you are 65. That equates to 30 years or 360 months. If you saved £100 a month in a shoebox under your bed, and ignoring any tax liability on these savings, or interest gained if you were to save it elsewhere, you would have £36,000 to last you until you died. Based on current death predictions for women, you are likely to live to see your 100th birthday and beyond, which means that you would need that £36,000 to last for about 40 years... which in my sum book is about £90 per month. As women, we must begin to realise that we either have to work longer or we have to save more – and in smart ways. That also means not putting all your eggs in one basket but spreading your wealth in ways that provide a good return on your investment. My advice would be to find a really good IFA and work with them now to invest and save effectively. If you are already wealthy, or have investments, review your wealth regularly and make sure that you have appropriate funds available to you should you need them. Do not abdicate responsibility for your long-term well-being, do something today.

In the museum, I was protecting my purse – my ability to resource. If it had been taken, it would have removed all choices from my life. The violation of a person's choices can be devastating. I think of women around the world who live in societies where they have little choice, little voice and no liberation. Having choice creates positive flow, we feel good and we feel liberated. We then feel free to flow all of our resources, whether it be money, love, support, nurturing or any other resource that is paramount to who we are.

By having choice, we can make change. Change is the second part of the purse's metaphoric meaning. Making change happen is either about moving towards what you do want, or moving away from what you don't. Each of us will prefer one of these methods and you can measure your preferred approach in the Phone chapter. However, for now just be aware of your intuitive preference for either moving towards something better or moving away from something that you no longer want. Each change horizon, marked by towards or away from, is the first part of change. Complete the diagram below to think about your preference. Which end of the continuum is easier to complete; what you do want, or what don't you?

What do I no longer want?   *What do I want?*

In your journal, draw the above line and list all of the answers to each question about any change that you are keen to make in your life. Which is easier to complete? Then ask yourself 'what needs to happen for me to achieve each of these?' You will then have some clear strategies for moving towards what you want.

Transitioning Towards What You Want

The second part is the journey or transition from where you are to where you want to be. This can be challenging as we transition away from what 'was' to what 'could be'. An amazing lady called Elizabeth Kubler Ross studied the effects of loss due to death; her book On Death and Dying documents her findings. She discovered that people tend to transition through the grieving process in a similar way, from shock, through denial, emotional chaos, depression, acceptance, testing and finally integration. This is shown on the diagram below.

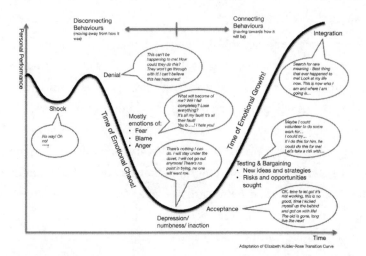

Adaptation of Elizabeth Kübler-Ross Transition Curve

Organisational specialists and psychologists have also studied Elizabeth's transition curve in situations of change in any context (not just death of a loved one) and have discovered that we transition in the same way for any change or loss. Consider a simple example like losing your car keys from your handbag:

1. **Shock:** *'I'm sure I left my keys in my bag!'*

2. **Denial:** *'I've looked through this bag three times and still can't find them! They must be here somewhere!'*

3. **Blame:** *(Internal and external) 'That's typical of me! I'm always losing my keys!' or 'Who's moved my keys?'*

4. **Anger:** *(Internal or external) 'Why can't I ever get organised?' or 'Why can't people leave my stuff alone?!'*

5. **Depression:** *'OK, they're not there, now what am I going to do, it's hopeless!'*

6. **Acceptance:** *'OK, they're gone, so what are my options?'*

7. **Testing and Bargaining:** *'I'll borrow my partner's and find my own later.'*

8. **Integration:** *'That's taught me a lesson for the future!'*

Think about any change situation in your life and you will recognise the transition curve process. We transition in this way whether it is a perceived positive or negative change. That is because we view change as loss of some sort and must move away from loss and towards a new horizon. Even positive changes like getting a promotion, moving to a new house, getting married or having a first child all incur loss of some sort as we let go of what was in order to gain what is new. For example, when we marry, we lose the single lifestyle. When we get a new job, we miss the old.

The curve is divided into two halves, the first showing the 'disconnecting' aspects (i.e. letting go of the old) and the second depicting the 'connecting' aspects (i.e. moving towards the new horizon and new life). When going through change in your life, recognise that all of your emotions are legitimate and only become a problem if they are too extreme. Be kind to yourself, knowing that what you are feeling is OK, and when it gets tough, keep yourself focused on the new horizon, the benefits of what you will get once you have transitioned.

In the section below, think about changes that you are currently going through. Journal where you are on the curve, how you feel and what you can do to move to the next transitional phase.

The Transition Action Plan

Changes I am going through	How I feel, what I am experiencing	Which part of the curve is this?	What needs to happen for me to move forward?

A final point: change is inevitable in your life, how you deal with that change is key. Throughout this book you will be making decisions about what and how to change specific aspects of you and your life. Understanding the change process is a good tool to have in your handbag!

Credit Cards

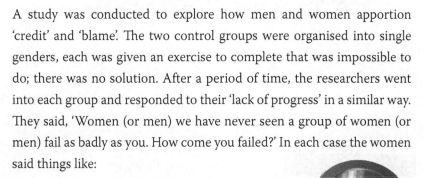

> 🦪 *Do you take credit for work done?*

> 🦪 *Do you accept compliments graciously?*

> 🦪 *Do you blame others or circumstances for mistakes, or do you blame yourself?*

A study was conducted to explore how men and women apportion 'credit' and 'blame'. The two control groups were organised into single genders, each was given an exercise to complete that was impossible to do; there was no solution. After a period of time, the researchers went into each group and responded to their 'lack of progress' in a similar way. They said, 'Women (or men) we have never seen a group of women (or men) fail as badly as you. How come you failed?' In each case the women said things like:

1. *Sorry!*

2. *I didn't listen well enough*

3. *I have never been good at this sort of thing*

And in each case, then men said things like:

1. *There is something wrong with the exercise!*

2. *There is something wrong with your instructions*

3. *If you think you are so clever, you do it!*

Then they gave each control group an exercise that was simple and clear; the solution was evident. Again, they spoke to each control group in a standard way and said, 'We have never seen a group of women (or men) succeed as well as you! This is impressive; why have you succeeded to this level?'

The women said:

1. *I was lucky*

2. *It was easy*

3. *You gave us such clear instructions, thank you!*

The men said:

1. *Yes, I am good at this sort of thing*

2. *Ever since I was a child I have been good at this sort of thing*

3. *Just as well we knew what to do straight away*

The results of the study were consistent, and showed that women and men tend to apportion credit and blame in different ways, as shown on the diagram below.

Credit - External

Blame - External

Blame - Internal

Credit - Internal

If something goes wrong, women tend to blame themselves (internal). If things go right, women often credit that to something outside of themselves (external). Consider the phrase 'I was lucky' compared to 'I am good'. When we take credit for strengths authentically, we sound and appear more confident; however, when we give credit away, we sound as though we lack confidence or self-assurance. For example, have you ever complimented a woman friend on something that she is wearing? How did she respond? Is she likely to give your compliment away – for example, 'I got it in the sale!' or 'Oh, I've had it for ages!'? Compare this with accepting the compliment graciously – 'Thank you, yes I like it too.'

Credit Exercise for the next month, six months, year or life

1. When someone pays you a compliment just say 'thank you'.

2. When you do a piece of work, put your name on it, and your contact details; new bosses need to know how to get hold of you for promotion interviews!

3. When you produce or do something that you are proud of, drop a pound, a dollar, a euro, a few dirham – whatever your national currency – into a tin or piggy bank. I call mine my 'handbag fund'. On my birthday each year, I empty the handbag fund and I buy myself a gift with the contents of the tin. The most special part is not the gift but emptying the tin and looking at all those coins that represent times when I have felt proud throughout the previous year.

Dealing with Self-Blame

Have you ever seen a woman bump into a desk and apologise to it? Or walk into the path of a stranger in a shopping mall and apologise as if it is her fault for getting in the way? Or blame herself for domestic abuse, marriage breakdown, business failure and world poverty? Self-blame has big repercussions for women in business and in getting her needs met. For example, if a woman's life were out of balance, whose fault would it be – hers for not coping or the organisation's for loading too much work on? Migrating towards self-blame can lead to feelings of guilt and shame when things go wrong or life is out of balance and, instead of asking for support or letting go of too many tasks, we merely try harder. Trying harder does not solve the issue; it merely improves our ability to juggle! We must stop juggling and start balancing work and life, and that includes managing self-blame.

Reflect on how the men responded in the previous exercise. Their blame was external; it was the circumstances, the 'puzzle' and not them. Therefore, if you regard the imbalance in your life to be external to yourself, not your fault, it creates a more pragmatic and practical approach to dealing with your challenges. For example, if you have too much workload that is driving long hours and imbalance, 'too much workload' is the issue, not your personal ability to cope with all the work! Take a leaf out of Emma's book ...

> I was one of those women who apologised to the chair
> if I bumped into it! I was always bringing myself down.
> Colleagues would say, 'Emma, you did a fantastic job on
> that sales project, you should shout about it!' and I would
> say, 'No, it was a team effort and everyone helped.' Over the
> years, I would see people being promoted ahead of me and all
> because of the work that I was helping them to achieve. But
> still I wasn't assertive enough or confident enough to project
> myself. In meetings I would watch as people stole my ideas,
> took ownership for them and afterwards I helped them to
> implement them! Then one day I decided to work with Lynne
> and she taught me all about attribution, assertiveness and
> coached my confidence. I began saying 'thank you' when
> people complimented my hair, or my clothes. It was hard
> at first, but I soon began to feel good. Then one day there
> was an important meeting announced. Our VP of Sales was
> coming into the UK to run a focus group to collect ideas for
> market growth. The meeting had no sooner been announced
> but my peers were on the phone saying, 'Emma, have we got
> any good ideas to suggest to Bob?' The alarm bells began to
> ring – have 'we' got any good ideas? What they really meant
> was, 'Emma, can you come up with some ideas that I can call
> my own at the meeting with Bob?' I decided that I had four
> options open to me:
>
>   a) I could give them all my ideas and let them take credit
>   b) I could say No
>   c) I could tell them I would think about it and get back to them
>   d) I could ask a question back

I decided that a) was not an option any more. I decided that my values would not allow me to do b) to a colleague even though it was tempting! I decided that c) would only result in more interruptions another day and so I went for option d. Therefore, when they said, 'Emma, have we got any good ideas to suggest to Bob?' I replied, 'Well, I don't have any right now, but how about we each write down a few ideas and email them to Bob ahead of time?' This immediately bounced the ball back in their court to come up with some ideas too. Those that didn't have any ideas or options said, 'Let's have a meeting to brainstorm some ideas this week.' Of course I declined due to workload priorities. I then set aside time to really think through my ideas. I had worked in sales a long time and knew the market well. I pulled together a list of options with some pros and cons, some market trends and some historical data. I suggested specific strategies for market growth and I signed it in MY name, not the team's name. I then emailed these to Bob with a message saying, 'In light of our forthcoming meeting in the UK, I have put together my list of ideas for market growth. I am happy to discuss these with you before you get here or, if you prefer to review them on the plane, we can have a discussion on your arrival. You will see that I have given you some additional research and my knowledge of the market to augment any further ideas that my UK colleagues also may come up with prior to the meeting.' Needless to say, Bob did not harvest too many ideas from the rest of the team and, as a result, Bob invited me to work directly for him to grow the market in line with my ideas. That was two years ago, the market has continued to grow and I am now VP of sales in the UK. The rest of the team? Oh, they all work for me and we have a collaborative culture that rewards team as well as individual effort!

Blame Exercise for the next month, six months, year and life

1. Sometimes it is appropriate to talk about 'we', but not always, especially when others are more likely to take credit for your work, so take credit or be proud of what you do.

2. Blame the circumstances that you are in and list what those are in order to fix them. 'Too much workload' or 'unhealthy relationship' or 'commute time'. It is not about you!

3. Collect compliments! Put them in a box, read them now and again and celebrate your talents.

Cost and Sacrifice

What is the cost of giving up family in favour of career? The cost of giving up career in favour of family? What is the cost of giving up? What do we sacrifice?

In this section of the Purse chapter, we will explore our sacrifices. Look again at your Dance floor. Begin with health (the Tissues) and, working clockwise around the floor, define what you sacrifice in each of these areas and what the cost is to you on the table below. For example, in the Tissues area, do you sacrifice time for regular exercise? If so, what is the cost of that to you? Try to think of those costs in terms of short term (now and the next year), medium term (in the next three to five years) and long term (greater than 10 or 20 years). You decide the timescales for short, medium and long term. For each aspect, write down the sacrifices and costs, then decide what you are going to do to stop sacrificing these things. Some may be more important than others, so you may have to prioritise your final list; there is a column at the end of the table to decide the priority order. These can then be transferred on to your goals (the Pen chapter). In order to stop sacrificing, we often have to de-clutter another aspect of our life. For example, finding time for exercise may involve letting go of.

Cost and Sacrifice Table

Category	Action	What do I sacrifice?	What is the short/medium & long-term Cost?	What needs to Change?	Priority?
My Tissues –	Health & Wellbeing				
My Lipstick –	Stress & Authenticity				
My Mirror –	Emotional & Physical Image				
My Keys –	To Success & Heart				
My Purse –	Choice & Change				
My Photos –	My relationships				
My Phone –	Social & Professional Networks				
My Diary –	Work & Life Time				
My Snack –	Personal & Professional Development				
My Perfume –	Spiritual & Feminine				
My Pen –	Work & Life Goals				

What do I need to bin in order to achieve the priorities that I have set above?

_____

_____

_____

Many women that I have spoken to say that they feel trapped in the work they do due to the family's need for money. Others say that they cannot leave toxic relationships because they do not have the money to leave (especially if they have dependants). Others say that they cannot change career because they don't have the skills or experience to do what they really want to do. All of these things relate to the belief that they 'cannot', because they do not have the 'wherewithal' to dance their best life. Whether it is money, skills, confidence, love, experience or knowledge, all of these represent the 'currency' to dance your best life. 'Lack of' is the focus and traps you in the belief that you are a victim of circumstance. You are not; you can make change happen. 'I can make change happen!' Say it loudly, every day!

Review your Dance floor; what currency do you need for health, career, dependants etc.? Do you have these? If so, you already have the currency that you need. For those areas where you don't have the currency, you need to make change! Change is the small stuff – the coins that, if plenty, add up to lots of money, i.e. lots of currency! Making small change, penny, dime, cent or dirham a time soon adds up to lots of change and soon your purse is full! When you look back on a time when your purse was empty, you realise that it was up to you to create the change; no one else could do it for you. It was in your grasp, a coin at a time!

On the table below, write down all the currency and small change that you already have. This will provide you with an idea of the start point. Don't worry if you do not know where you want your life to be in the future; for now, you are just looking at what you have and what you need to change.

Be Thankful

Towards the end of the table below you will see a column dedicated to gratitude. It is important to be grateful for those things that you do have. Even if these areas are a challenge at the moment, take time to note what you are thankful for. Notes of gratitude provide us with the cash to keep going, even when it gets tough.

> *My husband died suddenly leaving my two young children and me. The pain and loss was intense. I began to keep a gratitude diary to help me to get through. Small things, like being thankful for nice weather, to big things like the hugs and comfort of good friends. We struggled financially, had to sell the house and the children had to change school. It felt desperate some days and I missed Paul so much. I cried myself to sleep most nights from exhaustion, grief and loneliness, but I would pick myself up by thinking about what I was grateful for, like the laughter I had with the children watching them play with our pet dog! It sounds crazy, but these small acts of gratitude gave me hope, kept me going. It still feels lonely without Paul, but I am living each day, one step at a time, and I am thankful for what I do have, right now, today.*

Gratitude creates hope and will also help you to remember what you do have, rather than the 'lack' of something in your life. What you focus on you get more of, or what you think about, you bring about. I believe that focusing on gratitude is better than focusing on lack and loss.

> *I was desperate to find a man to love, to be with, to share things with. I never met anyone, never went on a date – not even a blind date! I focused on my lack all of the time and this resulted in me focusing on the lack of a man in my life. I focused on my empty apartment, my empty social life and turned down parties because I couldn't face my friends who*

were with someone significant in their life. I felt lonely and wallowed in my lack every day. Then one day, I woke up and decided to change my thinking. Instead of focusing on the lack of a man, I focused on attracting the right man. I made a note to myself of all the things I wanted in the right man, even down to his feet! I put the note away and got on with my life. Now and again I would look at the list; sometimes I added something but more often than not it remained the same. It felt more positive because I was focusing on what I did want instead of what I didn't have. Six months ago, a colleague fell sick and I had to step in at the last moment to replace them at a business conference in Dubai. The first morning of the conference, I sat beside Jack, we got talking, found out that we had lots in common… we have been together ever since. I found the note last month when I was packing up to move out to Dubai to be with him; I laughed out loud – every single thing on the list was a clear description of Jack, right down to his shoe size!

Make a note, and bank it! What do you want?

Category	Action	What currency do I already have?	What change do I need to make?	I am grateful for Priority?
My Tissues –	Health & Wellbeing			
My Lipstick –	Stress & Authenticity			
My Mirror –	Emotional & Physical Image			
My Keys –	To Success & Heart			
My Purse –	Choice & Change			
My Photos –	My relationships			
My Phone –	Social & Professional Networks			
My Diary –	Work & Life Time			
My Snack –	Personal & Professional Development			
My Perfume –	Spiritual & Feminine			
My Pen –	Work & Life Goals			

Summary

The purse is the heart and essence of you because it represents the internal resources that you have to be able to dance your best life.

Now is the time to step back, look at your purse, see it in detail and decide on your action plan. What does your purse now look like? Has it changed? Is there a new style, colour, content?

What have you learned and will do differently as a result of completing this chapter? In the BAG exercise below, define your actions.

BAG - My Action Plan

BAG stands for **B**in, **A**dd and **G**et

B	What will I **Bin** that no longer serves my life or goals and prevents me from dancing my best life?	_____ _____
A	What am I already doing, being or having that I could **Add** to or improve in order to dance my best life?	_____ _____
G	What will I **Get** that will serve me well and help me to dance my best life?	_____ _____

Dance your Best Life!

8 My Snack

Personal and professional development is the flavour of the Snack chapter. The snack is about nutrition for the mind, and subsequently your development and growth!

Developing yourself in whichever direction you dream of going is often not a priority for women as they juggle the demands of work and life. However, as women begin to manage their diary more effectively, and strip out the time demands of others in order to spend more with themselves, the subject of personal or professional development nags like a pang of hunger inside. Feeding your own personal and professional development is key to growth – but this is one snack that won't add inches to your hips!

As an advocate and supporter of strengths-based leadership, I will begin with a story, a story dear to my heart and one that sums up my approach to personal and professional development. When I first became a manager, I was managing a team of about seven professional development consultants. I was Head of Learning & Development for Hewlett Packard. I was proud of my promotion but scared stiff, not only of taking on responsibility for the development of hundreds of people, but more so, the development of my small team; I had to practise what

I preached! One morning, early in my new role, I came into the office to discover the Head of Marketing sitting in my office cubicle. 'I have come to share with you my wisdom of leadership!' he announced, before I had even taken off my coat! This was a manager that everyone respected, loved and enjoyed being with, so I knew even before he began that this would be a lesson worth learning! 'I am listening!' I responded curiously.

'It is very simple, you must remember "The Art of Ping Pong Management!"' he announced with pride, continuing and ignoring my apparent confusion. 'The British team always win the European Championships at ping-pong, but the Chinese always win the World Championships. The British team decided that they would benchmark the Chinese team's coaching practice to adopt it for their own and thereby give themselves more competitive advantage. First of all, they looked at their own coaching practice and, as they watched their players, they found themselves saying things like, "Nick, your forehand is fantastic, your backhand is not so great, what we need to do is to improve your backhand and we will do whatever it takes to help you to do just that".

'After a while, they noticed that Nick's backhand had improved a bit, but not to the same standard as his forehand. No matter how much money and time they invested, Nick just didn't improve. Exasperated, they visited the Chinese coach who watched Nick play. "Nick, your forehand is amazing," acknowledged the Chinese coach, "your backhand is less good. My advice is to forget your backhand and become world-class at your forehand".

Instead of trying to improve a weakness and make Nick average at both, the Chinese recognised that it was more important to literally play to strengths. In business, so many performance management systems focus on the improvement of weakness in favour of developing strengths! As a result, many organisations are continually focused on people's 'lack' rather than their unique talent, and yet it was that unique ability that probably got them the job in the first place. I have experienced this too: managers who have continually focused on my lack of planning and organising skills, whilst ignoring my talent for communication. As a result, I have been on more Time Management training courses than I care to remember, and today I am still not very good at managing my time and priorities, although I can train others! This investment in my weakness was not only an expensive waste of money for my organisation, but a disengaging and demotivating experience for me! As I looked around me, other people could manage to organise and plan; why couldn't I? Then I noticed that there were lots of demotivated people, people who couldn't present, people who couldn't write reports, people who couldn't strategise! All of these people losing energy and money worrying about what they couldn't do, whilst hibernating inside of them was an amazing untapped talent. This was brought home to me very soon after my conversation with this manager. My L&D team were a very diverse bunch of individuals, all of whom, whilst they had similar jobs, delivered them in different ways. All of them – apart from our department administrator whose role was unique to her and therefore not comparable to others. Jill was rarely happy and had gained herself the reputation of being a bit of a Rottweiler with other members of the team and in the wider business. She continually looked sour and only delivered that which was expected of her, never a penny more! She did her job, complained all day, and went home at 5 o'clock to her dog and her life outside of work. She rarely socialised with any of us, never took on extra projects and was generally miserable. Now, as part of my role as Head of L&D, I had to produce reports for the business, showing development linked to performance, training delivered, return on investment stats etc. This was not a strength for me. I knew that it was important, but doing this task was always a chore for me. I left it until last, I moaned and complained and dreamed of doing other things like staging world-class conferences, or engaging top speakers, or designing a new leadership programme. Reporting on training stats, based on my ability to be disorganised, was not an exercise that I relished! One day, I walked into our office, everyone was out apart from Jill, I must have looked more miserable than she did, and noticing, she said, 'Lynne, can I help you with that report?' I was shocked, but gracefully accepted Jill's offer of support. In the next two hours, Jill cut through my piles of paper, course evaluations, booking references and financial tracking sheets like a chef fan-slicing cucumber! She was a miracle worker! She set up files, systems, cabinets, spreadsheets and a reporting system that would all but automate my reporting process. At the end of the day, we had a report that deserved a purple cushion; it was a work of genius! As I believe in the importance of giving credit where credit is due, I put Jill's name on the bottom of the report front cover and sent it off to the Leadership Team. They were astounded. 'Jill did this? Stroppy, mouthy, miserable Jill?' 'Yes, I replied 'and hopefully it won't be a one-off act of charity!' I laughed. The following month, and with Jill's systems firmly in place, I still felt very miserable about the prospect of doing the report, but as soon as I mentioned this to Jill, I saw it; I saw what you must look for in all of your people, I saw the TWINKLE FACTOR! As soon as I complained that it was that time of the month again to produce the Leadership Team Training Report & Analysis, her eyes twinkled! She could not wait to get stuck into those numbers! I handed it over to her as an owned activity and I set her free to make it her own. In the four years that I was in that role, Jill was promoted five times. When I left, she was company analyst for our site. On LinkedIn recently, I saw that she was now Global VP of Business Reporting. I am very proud; had she not asked to help that day, and had I not seen the twinkle factor in her eye, she might still be an administrator and I might have played to her weaknesses and sent her on an interpersonal skills workshop to improve her attitude at work.

Play to your strengths, find your TWINKLE FACTOR!

The danger of playing to weakness in favour of strengths impacts both the organisation as well as the employee:

- *Employee disengagement – sense of failure as managers constantly focus on what they are not good at.*
- *Increased cost for the organisation of wasted development activity focusing on weakness.*
- *An organisation that is far from world-class as they focus on making everyone average at everything.*
- *Employee fear – performance management seen as a punishment, rather than development.*

It is time to set you free from 'weakness focus' and begin to develop your world-class skills and abilities.

Our story . . .

Karen stomped through the park on her way home, the rain steadily crying down, weeping like she was. It had been an awful day; not only was the ward infested with yet another virus, but she had been plagued by another annual performance review with her manager. She hated performance reviews! Not only were they a complete waste of time but they were the most demotivating and anger-inducing meetings in her whole year! Karen deliberately smashed her foot down into each puddle, actively releasing her frustration and pent-up tears. She didn't care that her trousers were becoming soaked; each splash of flying water droplets exploded into the air and reminded her of the force it would take to break through the glass ceiling of discrimination she was trapped under at work. Every single year since Karen could remember she had been picked up on her inability to do admin! Did they comment on her care? No! Did they comment on her medical skills, bedside manner, communication skills? No! They weren't as important as filling out rotten forms, balanced scorecards and Gantt charts of drug dispensation! 'I HATE THIS JOB!' she screamed as she kicked the next puddle of water, spraying shards of water scurrying into the grass. 'Then leave!' screamed her future self, bringing Karen back from the world of self-righteous indignation with a jolt! Karen stared out of bloodshot eyes, and wiping the tears and snot from her nose, composed herself as best she could. Then she crumpled into tears again as she thought that she could no longer face a job that didn't value what she did.

'Let's find somewhere dry to talk,' said Tomorrow Karen, motioning her younger self towards the refuge of the bandstand. The autumn rain was doing its best to push the fallen leaves back into the earth to feed and re-nourish the soil for future seasons. The two women sat huddled from the rain inside the old bandstand; no music today, but the ghostly sounds of the autumn wind and rain dancing on its rooftop. 'The autumn is a wonderful time of sharing the harvest, re-nourishing the earth and

slowly winding down towards the winter of sleep and replenishment,' commented Tomorrow Karen. 'How can you take this time to realise that you have reached the autumn of your career in this place, you have given everything you can, and now you must nourish yourself, use this as a period of rest, so that when the time comes, you can once again burst into new bloom, and a new career?'

Karen loved the analogy of the seasons, and immediately saw that her career had indeed come to that point where she had harvested and it was time to let go. Just like a tree lets go of its leaves, Karen knew that it was time to let go of her nursing job and begin to move into a new phase. 'I don't have the skills yet to do what I really want,' she announced. 'And what needs to happen for you to get those skills?' asked Tomorrow Karen, not being drawn by the critical voice of the younger woman who was beginning to find excuses to do nothing and stay with the safer option.

'I would need to go to college, probably day or evenings, get some practice, learn the business side…' Karen continued to list all the activities that would need to occur for her to do the work that she wanted to do and, as a result, was oblivious to the fact that the bandstand had disappeared and the two women were now sitting inside Karen's handbag once more.

'Oh!' she said, suddenly realising that the rain and wind were now replaced by the cosiness of her warm velvet bag. 'This feels nicer, I must say!' The two women laughed.

'Your personal development is key, and down here in this lovely autumn bag we need to find your snack. Your snack represents personal development because it is the way you nourish your personal and professional growth,' said Tomorrow Karen. The two women stood up from their makeshift seat on the purse and began to root around for Karen's snack. 'I may have already eaten it!' she exclaimed 'after the day that I have had!'

She suddenly found it lurking behind some dead batteries from Josh's games console. Its shiny green wrapper and tempting graphic of juicy nuts, seeds and fruit promised healthy contents. Tomorrow Karen pushed the muesli bar on to its side, exposing a giant linear barcode and a list of ingredients, additives and energy information. Tomorrow Karen explained, 'The content of your muesli bar is more than just a satisfier of hunger, it also provides energy and nutrition which help you to grow or be strong. Personal and Professional Development help us too; they are also about growth and strength, but in a different way. In order for you to grow into the person that you want to be, you must feed not your body, but your mind and your self-awareness. The food of the mind and personal growth is learning through formal methods like courses, qualifications and workshops, and other ways that support self-awareness and come from methods like coaching, mentoring, observing etc. Now, Karen, you want to be a garden designer and run your own garden design business?' Tomorrow Karen asked rhetorically. 'In order to do that, you must develop different skills from the ones that you have as a nurse! Let us see what they might be!'

The two women looked down at the muesli bar and, as only happens in the handbag, the ingredients began to change and there on the label under ingredients was a whole list of skills and qualifications that Karen needed. Under 'Additives' was a list of additional experiences and workshops she could attend, including coaching and mentoring from garden design networks. Under 'Preservatives' Karen read all about the job vacancies in nurseries and garden centres that were paying about the same money that she was already earning and would preserve her sanity more than nursing! When she was younger, she felt that nursing was the career for her, but now, after all these years, she had just run out of passion for the job. The caring aspects were what motivated her, but the bureaucracy, admin and autocracy had just worn her down and drained her desire to keep on doing it.

James had suggested that she just packed it in, but she knew that the family needed her income to make ends meet. However, James's encouragement had inspired her to look, and so finally, as Karen's eyes

fixed on the package's 'Energy' information, she saw that energy came from her motivation to do something she cared about; energy came from James's support and energy came from her desire to make a difference.

It was all there in black and white for her to see. She knew what she had to do, and she would certainly take the bait and bite into this huge development opportunity. First thing tomorrow, instead of moaning and complaining about her current job, she would redirect that energy into what she did want, and that was to become a garden designer and horticulturist. She would book on to the next course, she would resign from her current job and, for once in a very long time, she would dance to her own tune!

Dancing To Your Own Tune

Let us begin by reviewing your strengths, and particularly those related to when you dance at your best.

Have you noticed whether you are the type that either enjoys coming up with the ideas or enjoys planning those ideas, or maybe you are the type that likes implementing the plans or reviewing how things went? If so, then the following exercise may just give you an indication of 'where in time' your strengths lie. This insight will be good at home as well as in work and will allow you to play to the strengths of the people around you, to make sure that you use others effectively too. In addition, I have designed this Dance floor exercise to highlight your natural tunes, the tunes you might dance to now and again, and the tunes that you will sit out for your own good! Enjoy this exercise; I am sure you will find it useful!

Dancing in Time Questionnaire

Below is a list of statements followed underneath by three options. Read the statement and the options, then decide the order of preference for the three options. Rank the choices in your order of preference putting 5 for 1st, 2 for 2nd and 0 for 3rd. Do not leave any blank. For example:

Scoring

For every answer, score as follows:

1st preference = 5
2nd Preference = 2
3rd preference = 0

For example:

The best way to ensure that you have a good party is to:

A Encourage everyone to contribute to the party as it is happening	B Provide a good invitation with a clear agenda of activities	C Encourage everyone to clear up afterwards
2 = 2nd preference	5 = 1st preference	0 = 3rd preference

1. The best way to start a project or plan an event is to:

A	B	C
Imagine what it would be like if it was successful and communicate your vision and ideas to others	Sit down and write a plan of action and a plan of required resources, dates, a time line and a budget	Pull together the right team of people and solicit inputs and feelings about how to make it successful

2. When decisions have to be made, I like to:

A	B	C
Provide the team with data and ideas to inform the decision-making process	Make a quick decision and tell the team what it is	Encourage others to contribute to the decision

3. When motivating or getting the buy-in of others, I prefer to:

A	B	C
Share my passion, motivation and feelings about the job, so that it encourages them to feel enthusiastic too	Show them that it is OK to be innovative, take risks and look for new ways to do things	Be a role model, a coach and mentor for others so that they can learn my expertise on how best to do the job

4. My preparation as a leader can be recognised by:

A	B	C
My planning and organising skills	My vision, creativity, ideas and innovation	My ability to pull together the right team

5. When the party is over, or the project complete, I like to:

A	B	C
Ponder about or review what went well and what could have gone better	Ensure that loose ends are tied up and that we are good to close it down	Celebrate success with a personal 'thank you' or celebrate project achievements with the team

6. My performance as a leader can be best exemplified by my:

A	B	C
Expertise at my job and skills and abilities to make it happen	My ability to motivate and engage a team	My ability to take risks and make quick decisions

7. When I sense that things are not moving forwards quickly enough my preference is to:

A	B	C
Pursue a new course of action or take a new risk	Find out what needs to be done next and produce an action plan	Incentivise the team to motivate and engage them in action

8. When I have never done something before, I tend to:

A	B	C
Take a risk, try it, pursue a new adventure, just do it!	Find someone who has already done it and ask them to coach me	Research best practice and look for the best way to do it, prepare accordingly

9. If someone is upset, after an event, meeting or party I tend to:

A	B	C
Listen openly to their distress, make no judgement, and coach them to find the positive things from the outcome	Suggest that there is no point in crying over spilt milk, and should focus on what they are doing now and let go	Solicit information about their state/ problem, understand their needs and help them to draw conclusions and learning from what happened

10. If I wanted a cake for a special event, I would be the type who would:

A	B	C
Design the cake, have an absolutely clear idea of what I wanted and then get someone else to do it	Buy the ingredients for an existing design and get on with it myself	Hire a team of cooks or cake company to create something appropriate

11. If I were organising a party, I would be the type who would:

A	B	C
Intend to have a good time, participate in the dances and hand round all the great food that I had prepared	Be life and soul, get to know as many people as I could and introduce them to others	Decide the detail - where it would be, a theme, the guest list, organise the catering and the entertainment etc.

12. If I were organising my own funeral, I would be the type who would:

A	B	C
Write or record a synopsis of my life and a conclusion about the legacy I left behind to be played at the ceremony or given as a gift	Organise every detail of the flowers, words, venue, after-party, order of service and really dot the i's on every detail	Encourage everybody to celebrate, have fun and give me a good send-off

13. When balancing work and life, I prefer to:		
A	**B**	**C**
Organise how I will spend my time, make decisions about what will not get done and look for opportunities to delegate	Just get on and juggle it all! My practical, pragmatic and can-do approach means that I can usually juggle it all	Engage with family and colleagues to ensure they share the load and that it is not all on my shoulders!

14. At the end of the day, just before I leave the workplace to go home, I tend to:		
A	**B**	**C**
Spend time chatting with colleagues, engaging with them to celebrate everything we have achieved, then go home	Think about all the things that I achieved that day and review what went well, and what didn't and plan tomorrow's schedule of activities	Complete, switch off and go – other things to do outside of work

15. When I retire from work, I want to be remembered as someone who:		
A	**B**	**C**
Got the job done, achieved loads, wasn't afraid to roll up my sleeves and do the job well	Was a great person to work for/with; someone who created a good culture to work in that motivated the team and recognised their contribution	Had great ideas, could pull together a great strategy, made decisions and knew what worked

Now on the table below you will see all of the question numbers mixed into new categories. Transfer your scores on to the table below, add up the totals and transfer those on to the final score sheet!

Your Preferred Dance floor Beat

Question	My Score	Question	My Score	Question	My Score
1c		1a		1b	
4c		4b		4a	
8b		8c		8a	
10c		10a		10b	
11b		11c		11a	
Total (Pop)		Total (Jazz)		Total (Classic)	
2c		2a		2b	
3a		3b		3c	
6b		6c		6a	
7c		7a		7b	
13c		13a		13b	
Total (Rock)		Total (Punk)		Total (Soul)	
5c		5a		5b	
9a		9c		9b	
12c		12a		12b	
14a		14b		14c	
15b		15c		15a	
Total (Disco)		Total (Blues)		Total (Reggae)	

	People Leader	Resources Leader	Task Leader	Time Preference Total
Initiator	POP =	JAZZ =	CLASSIC =	Pop + Jazz + Classic =
Producer	ROCK =	PUNK =	SOUL =	Rock + Punk + Soul =
ulminator	DISCO =	BLUES =	REGGAE =	Disco + Blues + Reggae =
Preference Total	Pop + Rock + Disco =	Jazz + Punk + Blues =	Classic + Soul + Reggae =	

Score Interpretations

High Pop Music - The Includer

Pop music is called this because it is popular! It is wide and varied, diverse and flexible, but easily recognisable and fun to hum along to. Pop music has a clear identity and includes lots of different types. You are The Includer!

Strengths – The Includer knows exactly where she is heading, and pulls the right team together, develops the team brand or identity, builds a sense of belonging, collaboration and trust. She creates a culture of common purpose towards a goal and works with everyone to develop their skills to achieve the goal. She is caring, inspiring and inclusive. She creates a family atmosphere, manages conflict and builds a support system for everyone in the team.

Challenges – Your challenge is to actually 'do the task'. You prefer to empower others to deliver on task. You may also forget to review what does and does not work. Find people in your team who can deliver this. You may get bored easily and look for the next opportunity for searching out people and resources to deliver a task. Look at your Producing and Culminating scores to identify weaknesses.

Development Opportunity – Find a role that requires the buy-in and collaboration of a global team or a disparate team to challenge your abilities in this area. Maybe a cross-cultural team would be an opportunity for you while you develop your people skills further. Avoid roles that expect you to work alone or with too much isolation from people.

At Home – Don't always be the one who organises family or friends get-togethers, let someone else do it for a change! Hobbies that may suit you could include being part of a sports team, a team cause or an activity that requires the coordination of the right people to develop or deliver something – maybe a local amateur dramatics group, a fun-run for charity or a women's network.

Worklife Balance Tip – Don't beat yourself up for not getting everyone bought-in to your goals, you'll only spend too much time trying to convince those that just don't get it. Instead work with those that do and, sooner or later, the others will come on board too; after all, you cannot push a rope!

> *How else do your strengths and challenges impact your work, life and achieving goals?*
>
> *Use the BAG Action Plan to make change relevant to you.*

High Rock Music – The Engager

Rock music gets people on their feet! Just consider 'We will Rock You!' by Queen. At concerts it became a sing-along anthem – everyone on their feet, clapping hands in unison and chanting the beat together. Rock music creates group engagement. You are The Engager!

Strengths – When times get tough, or workload seems high, or the team doesn't think it can do any more, in comes The Engager! The Engager motivates, cheers people on, inspires everyone to keep going and to achieve great things! The motivator appears during the time of doing the work, not creating the work, and so differs from The Includer because they don't need to find the resources, just keep them involved. Your strengths lie in your focus on people performance. You can incentivise, recognise and reward the behaviour that leads people to implement, do

and act. You can create a competitive spirit too, and if need be, a culture of winning through team focus. Your measures of success are action, doing and achieving results through people.

Challenges – Your challenge will be if you scored low in Culminating, as you may forget to collect and analyse the big picture impact of what you do. For example, your team may be doing well, but what about the overall company? Lifting your head above the action and looking back at what you have learned and what you could do differently may be an issue. In addition, you may find that you get frustrated with those that seem to lack energy, drift into conceptual thinking and idea-creation, without ever getting off their rear and actually doing anything!

Development Opportunity – Play to your strengths in a role where targets and teamwork is core to success. Managing a Contact Centre team, a sales team or a sports team would suit you. The key is to find a role that combines the need for performance and teamwork. Avoid roles that are conceptual, creative and include lots of time working alone.

At Home – Well, I bet you have more parties, more visitors and more things to do than any other profile in this test! How about having a weekend with nothing to do? Or weekends where you are the visitor and can just enjoy being and not doing?

Worklife Balance Tip – Don't beat yourself up for not constantly being the happy one in the team! You need time out too, to recharge your batteries so that you can motivate others. Take time to pamper and indulge yourself, reward yourself for your people skills.

> *How else do your strengths and challenges impact your work, life and achieving goals?*
>
> *Use the BAG Action Plan to make change relevant to you.*

High Disco – The Celebrator

Disco music allows everyone to do their own thing to a beat that encourages fun, celebration and uniqueness. Recognition and achievement comes from the beat of dancing your way. Having a good time is key; you are The Celebrator!

Strengths – Allow me to hereby officially announce you as the party animal! You enjoy the ability to celebrate what people have achieved! You enjoy the ability to recognise, reward and celebrate success. You recognise those people in your team who deserve recognition and you are keen to make sure it happens. Being people-focused, you also recognise that there are people who prefer private and quiet recognition, and those that prefer public. You also know how to celebrate in appropriate ways; small milestone celebrations are blended with big achievement celebrations. You will work well in roles where you have the accountability and autonomy to create a culture of improvement, change and celebration. Being able to motivate and incentivise people towards achievement that is linked to completion of a goal is essential. Your celebrations are triggered by completion, not by beginnings. You prefer to say 'thank you' or 'well done' as opposed to 'you can do it' and 'go for it', which is the language of the Engager.

Challenges – Whilst quick to celebrate, you are not quick to find the right team in the first place or work with them to develop a clear vision, unless you scored high in those areas too. Look at what you scored lowest in, and find someone in your team who is good at what you are not.

Development Opportunities – Find a role that plays to your strengths of celebrating achievement. This could be a charity role, fundraising, etc. and has an element of people aiming towards the achievement of something worth celebrating. Avoid roles that require you to focus just on task and not on people.

At Home – Find time to recognise and celebrate your achievements, and not others' all the time! Get involved in hobbies where recognition of achievement is important, like charity fund-raising, school activities, fairs, fetes and appeals.

Worklife Balance Tip – Definitely get yourself a handbag fund! A money bank where you can drop a coin in each time you do something that you are proud of. When it is your birthday, buy yourself a celebration gift.

- *How else do your strengths and challenges impact your work, life and achieving goals?*
- *Use the BAG Action Plan to make change relevant to you.*

High Jazz – The Visionary

Jazz is an eclectic mix of creativity, innovation and desire to be different. It is creative and compelling just like a goal or vision. You are The Visionary!

Strengths – Creative, ideas person, flexible, innovative, looks for new ways to do things, have things or be.

Challenges – Easily bored, short attention span, dislikes the mundane, prefers big picture, forgets to carry out reviews. Low attention to detail on tactical plans and implementation. Can often get bored and moves on before a project is complete.

Development Opportunity – Find roles with lots of variety, opportunity for change, autonomy and ability to innovate. Make sure that the role does not require focused attention to detail; if it does, make sure that you have the ability to delegate and influence others to take on this task for you. Surround yourself with a team that has different strengths from yours so that they can fill in the gaps of what you are not good at.

At Home – Look for me-time activities that play to your strengths of creativity and need for variety. Make sure that if you're the only one in the family that enjoys lots of new things to do, you retain some semblance of routine for others not like you.

Worklife Balance Tip – Stop beating yourself up for what you are not good at, and deliver what you are.

- *How else do your strengths and challenges impact your work, life and achieving goals?*
- *Use the BAG Action Plan to make change.*

High Punk – The Risk Taker

Punk is risky, challenging, loud and opinionated. The Punk likes to tell, to take risks and to challenge the status quo. It is different, out of the ordinary and energetic. You are The Punk!

Strengths – Risk-taker and fast decision-maker, sees opportunities, entrepreneurial, fast-moving. Great delegator, good at prioritising.

Challenges – Could be impulsive if risk-taking is extreme, could forget to take into account the needs of others. Planning and attention to detail may be a challenge, and you may become frustrated with people who take time to make decisions.

Development Opportunity – Find roles that will allow you to seek new ways of doing this, or a sales or marketing role that plays to your entrepreneurial spirit. Make sure that there is opportunity for you to work alone, have autonomy and then, through your opportunity-focused approach, set goals for yourself and others. If you are considering running your own business, or already do so, make sure that you engage with people who can implement your ideas and have enough attention to detail to follow things through on your behalf, otherwise there will be a lot of unfinished work and projects!

At Home – Take time to just enjoy the 'now', take me-time that is focused on being and not doing. Listen to music, meditate, read a book – but just read the book for reading's sake, not to read ten in a week!

Worklife Balance Tip – Stop beating yourself up for what you don't get done in a day, just enjoy the day itself. Some days are just plain old boring, with no adventure or risk. Look on this as time to rejuvenate.

> *How else do your strengths and challenges impact your work, life and achieving goals?*

> *Use the BAG Action Plan to make change relevant to you.*

High Blues – The Reviewer

Strengths – Measures what went well and what didn't, reviews what happened and draws conclusions from outcomes. The Reviewer says what it does on the tin, you are good at reflecting on situations, tasks and events and analysing what went well and what you would do differently in future. A Reviewer is invaluable in the workplace because in our fast-moving environments we can often forget to draw breath and just look back at the landscape we have created. You have good attention to detail and like to tidy things up and draw conclusions. You can be the anchor of reality in a team asking well-considered questions and commenting on observations.

Challenges – Your ability to let go, make quick decisions, say that something is now good enough. Sometimes you will be challenged by your inability to set goals, look forward and visualise or strategise.

Development Opportunity – Look for roles where your analytical and monitoring skills are valued. Look for opportunities where you can work as part of a project team where you will be expected to collect, analyse and report information as part of an ongoing process that forces you to let go of milestones regularly. Work on projects and in roles where there are clear endings.

At Home – Take on those roles that encourage you to look for improvements in the way the family works, or community projects that would benefit from your strong reviewer and analytical ability.

Worklife Balance Tip – Don't beat yourself up for not always being spontaneous or visionary. You are a Reviewer, what was the best thing that happened to you last month? Learn to celebrate or journal achievements.

> 🐚 *How else do your strengths and challenges impact your work, life and achieving goals?*

> 🐚 *Use the BAG Action Plan to make change relevant to you.*

High Classic – The Planner

Strengths – Creates strategies and plans, clarifies timelines, resources and tools. A real skill for converting goals and vision into plans. This skill supports you to deliver to a deadline, as well as understand all the resources that will be required to execute the plan. A Planner is a thinker and often considers resources as well as tools and tactics. The Planner is a good lateral thinker and can coordinate people, materials, jobs, tasks and deadlines into a big schedule that ensures things happen on time. The planner loves events and projects to plan, with great attention to detail, they ensure that nothing falls through the net.

Challenges – Planners often believe that the plan is also a communication tool, being a more than adequate way to inform people about courses of action and deadlines. A plan is generally not a good communication tool and may not motivate or fire people up when things are getting a bit stuck. Find someone in your team who scores high on Rock (Engager) or high on Pop (Includer), who can support you to find the right people to do the task, and then engage and motivate them towards success.

Development Opportunity – Look for roles that require coordinating activities, tap into your planning skills and ability to find resources. This can be in traditional planning roles, or can be in event management, event coordination or other management roles that require detailed organisation.

At Home – Take time to be more spontaneous, or leave the social planning to someone else! Delegate specific plans to others in your family or friends network so that you are not always expected to organise everything. Plan to do one thing for you this year that is alone and gives you time to think about you and not everyone else for a change.

Worklife Balance Tip – Don't beat yourself up for not always pleasing everyone, please yourself for a change. Go for a walk, enjoy a nice view, have a spa weekend, indulge in a good book!

> *How else do your strengths and challenges impact your work, life and achieving goals?*
>
> *Use the BAG Action Plan to make change relevant to you.*

High Soul – The Implementer

Strengths – The Implementer rolls up her sleeves and gets stuck in! Why delegate when you can do it yourself, and do it well! The Implementer is pragmatic, practical, action-oriented and has a can-do attitude.

Challenges – Delegation! How will anyone ever learn when you do it all for them? Your workload may be high and your in-tray even higher! You are a girl who may be challenged to say No, you love action and enjoy the thrill of being busy. Even at home you may do things for others, sometimes when they can do it for themselves, or when you could outsource it to others! Sitting still is not enough sometimes, and that is a challenge.

Development Opportunity – It is good to be practical and you should find a role that allows you to share the load as part of a team. In order to not get worn out, make sure that you learn to say No to too much workload.

At Home – Share the load; it's OK for things to be less than perfect. Take time for you to be silent, still and not doing anything!

Worklife Balance Tip – Don't beat yourself up for having nothing to do! Enjoy the peace and the moment.

> *How else do your strengths and challenges impact your work, life and achieving goals?*

> *Use the BAG Action Plan to make change relevant to you.*

High Reggae – The Finisher

Strengths – The Finisher does just that, finishes things off! You hate loose ends and unfinished business. You like to dot the i's, cross the t's and wind things up. Your desire is for a sense of achievement in work and in life! In fact you are probably the type of woman who prefers to stand back and appreciate the joy of a clean house rather than actually doing the housework! Appreciation of the sparkling taps in the bathroom is one thing, but if you still have to empty the waste bin, then there is no sense of achievement – yet! You will tick off your checklist to ensure that everything is completed neatly, on time and in budget. Once complete, then the sense of achievement is evident.

Challenges – You don't deal with procrastinators and dilly-dally behaviour that stops things from being completed and disbanded. You are sometimes forgetful of influencing the emotional side of ensuring buy-in, believing that people should stick to the plan and get things done. You prefer working on the completion of tasks, so can be challenged by those around you who are more conceptual, creative and airy-fairy.

Development Opportunity – To play to your strengths, find a role that has attention to detail, implementation and completion as key factors in its success. Avoid free-thinking and experimentation roles that never provide you with the sense of achievement that you most desire. Short-term, quick-fire projects with tangible completion of deadlines will suit you better than open-ended drifting projects with no real goal in sight.

At Home – Decide which things can drift and be less controlled. Involve yourself in activities that play to your strengths; maybe community projects that require detailed completion would be good, or involvement in local events.

Worklife Balance Tip – Don't beat yourself up for not getting everything done today! Enjoy the peace and the moment.

> *How else do your strengths and challenges impact your work, life and achieving goals?*

> *Use the BAG Action Plan to make change relevant to you.*

From the exercise above, you now have an idea of some of your strengths and when they will be put to best use. It is important to also reflect on those overall areas where you scored lowest, and therefore what you should avoid, delegate or develop. Use the table below to add up your total scores for each column and row to identify (on the vertical axis) if you are a people leader, a resources leader or a task leader, and (on the horizontal axis) whether you are of more use at the beginning of a project (Initiator), during a project (Producer) or at the end of a project (Culminator).

You can also use the development plan beneath this to create actions for your ongoing development. Use the table to also plot those in your team, to identify those around you that have strengths where you might not. These are perfect opportunities for delegation and development of others.

	People Leader	Resources Leader	Task Leader	Time Preference Total
Initiator	POP = Includer	JAZZ = Visionary	CLASSIC = Planner	Pop + Jazz + Classic =
Producer	ROCK = Engager	PUNK = Risk-Taker	SOUL = Implementer	Rock + Punk + Soul =
Culminator	DISCO = Celebrator	BLUES = Reviewer	REGGAE = Finisher	Disco + Blues + Reggae =
Role Preference	Pop + Rock + Disco =	Jazz + Punk + Blues =	Classic + Soul + Reggae =	

	Category	Suggested Action	My action plan
1	Strengths	Develop this strength	
2		Develop this strength	
3		Develop this strength	
4	Could do at a push!	Develop this quality	
5		Delegate or develop	
6		Delegate	
7	Avoid at all costs!	Delegate	
8		Delegate	
9		Delegate	

My Development Plan

Writing a development plan is actually quite an easy task. It requires you to look both long and short term, truly engage in what you should be doing (your strengths), include personal as well as professional development and it should focus on both work and life.

It was once said 'A vision is where you are going, a plan is how you get there!' If the vision is the destination, and the plan is the map, then all we need do is follow the map! However, as we know, a map is not the territory, and even though your map may show a destination of where you want to get to, it rarely shows the up and down, round and about, backwards and forwards, rough and smooth terrain to get there. On your journey of personal and professional development, you may meet people along the way who will guide you towards your vision, and those that guide you into the thorns where you get lost and are not sure where to go next. You may trip over financial or time obstacles, climb high mountains of learning, and rest on the beach of self-awareness. Whatever the terrain, your development plan can never allow for the terrain, only the map. However, we can accept that the terrain will be wild and varied, and if we are able to keep on developing, learning, growing and achieving, we will reach our destination of personal potential and, as we look back, we will see that the terrain that we have passed through is part of our development and learning too. Thomas Edison, who invented the light bulb, was once asked by a snooty journalist, 'How does it feel to have failed to invent the light bulb 2,000 times?' In a flash, Eddison responded, 'No sir, I did not fail to make the light bulb 2,000 times, I discovered 1,999 ways how to not make a light bulb!' We can learn two things from Edison's example. First, we must be tenacious; through his own experience we see that, if we want something badly enough, we will or could fail on a number of occasions before we reach our goal. Each time we must pick ourselves up, dust ourselves off and keep on trying. After all, the learning is in the wobbling. By that I ask you to consider a baby who is learning to walk; she stands up, she balances, she totters forwards, she loses her balance and drops on to her bottom. She doesn't think to herself, 'Do you know what? I'm not very good at this walking thing, I think I'll give up and leave others to walk instead, walking is clearly not for me.' In reality she pulls herself to her feet once more and, with all the determination and focus that her little self can muster, she wobbles, walks, drops, stands a bit more and soon becomes proficient! Learning a new skill means that you will wobble when you start, you may fall down and lose confidence, but it is important to keep on trying until you find out if it is a strength; how would athletes discover they had a strength for running unless they tried walking first?

Paul Hersey and Ken Blanchard's situation leadership theory describes this in wonderful detail and suggests that we don't become unconsciously competent about doing something unless we have moved through the other stages. Take for example learning to drive. When you first get in a car, you are unconsciously incompetent – you don't know what you don't know! Then, after a couple of lessons, you realise just how much there is to learn, you are now consciously incompetent – you know what you don't know! Then, as you approach your driving examination, you move to the third stage, which is consciously competent – you know what you know! Finally, and sometimes a few months later, you become unconsciously competent – you don't know just how much you know! This theory can be applied to most new skills in work and in life. The important thing is to know which development intervention you need for each stage. At the early stages it should be more focused and supervised, but it would be highly inappropriate to closely supervise an expert!

Development Plan in Action

A Professional Development Plan has four distinct parts as shown on the diagram below. Each of these is then underpinned by ways in which you can achieve this development. It is not always through training and qualifications; it could be through coaching, reading, mentoring, benchmarking and a myriad of other ways. We can learn at a bus stop if we just take time to open our eyes and ears!

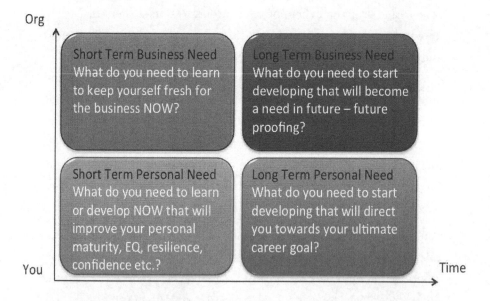

For many women, knowing what that ultimate destination looks like is a real challenge. Therefore, we will begin with the bottom right-hand quadrant and, as a result of that, will be able to clarify the content of the other three.

Exercise

Picture This! Do You Know Where You're Going To?

Note: you can download a copy of this exercise as an audio file from the website.

1. *Write down today's date.*

2. *Write down the date when you want to be living and working at your full potential. If you don't know, then guess! Write down the first date that comes to mind.*

Now work back from that date by one year (if the date is longer than a year from now) or six months (if medium-term) or one month (if short-term). For example, if your goal is to be working and living at your best in three years' time, take a year off that date. If your goal is to be there in one year, take off six months and if your goal is three months, take off one month.

Now, as you consider that new date, in your imagination we are going to go shopping. I want you to close your eyes and become aware of your breathing. With each outward breath, relax. In your imagination, look at the calendar on your wall or on your desk. See the date on that calendar (it is the new date that you set above). See the date clearly in your mind. I want you to imagine that you have the day all to yourself and that you are going to go shopping. I want you to see that you are in your house, you are ready to go, and you are just about to leave. There is a knock at the front door and, when you open it, there on the doorstep is your future self. She will be your companion for today; she smiles, excited by the prospect of going shopping! Look at how she is dressed, her demeanour, her mood, physical presence. She is your full potential! Listen to the excitement in her voice, her eagerness to shop with you and her passion for spending the day with you.

Listen to the sound of your front door closing and watch as you move out and into your shopping trip.

Imagine now that you have arrived at the place that you will shop. Where have you chosen? What is around you? Take time to notice every detail. As you turn around in your imagination, there, behind you, is a wonderful handbag

235

shop. The shop is full of every type and style of handbag that you can imagine. Your future self grabs you by the arm and marches you into the shop. The smell of leather and fabrics, the explosion of colour and texture splash across your senses, evoking emotions of pleasure, desire and satisfaction.

You separate, each taking time to browse the selection of temptations and possibilities. This is no ordinary handbag shop though, this shop is called the 'Handbag of Your Potential'. The handbag is a representation of who you want to become, the woman you are truly capable of being. Take time now to walk quietly around this shop, looking, feeling, smelling and touching every handbag that you are drawn towards.

Suddenly, and without warning, your future self runs towards you, she grabs your hand and pulls you towards a stand near the back of the shop. Before you get there, she playfully covers your eyes with her hand, telling you not to look until she removes her hand. Silently, and before the handbag, she gently lets go and slowly drops her hand from your eyes. As you look forward, there in front of you is the handbag of your potential. What does it look like? Fabric? Colour? Smell? Texture? Size? Handles? Locks? Fasteners? You can see this handbag now. As you look at this handbag, how does that handbag inform you about your future self? What do all the elements say about who you can become? Take in every detail and how this informs you about your potential. Look at the outside, inside, top, bottom, everything!

Now, in your imagination, take this handbag down from the stand, hold it, and in your own time take it to the desk where the shopkeeper will assign it to you. No money changes hands in this shop; every bag of potential is priceless. After all, if you were to place a price tag on your potential, how much would it be worth?

The shopkeeper opens a huge book on the counter, she swiftly flicks through the silken white paper pages until she turns the one that displays a picture of your chosen bag. Listed beneath the picture are all the attributes and qualities of potential that it bestows on its owner. She registers your name in the book as the proud owner of this potential and asks you to sign the page as a commitment to receiving and releasing this potential in you. You take the pen from the shopkeeper and sign your name as a commitment to your *potential. The shopkeeper proudly hands the bag to you, it is now yours to have and yours to become.*

As you walk outside of the shop, you become aware that you are once again outside the front door of your own house; your future self is no longer there but she will come again when you need her most. Once again, become aware of your breathing, and as you count from seven to one, come back into the here and now and open your eyes.

What sort of bag did you choose? Write down everything that you remember. Then, take time to think about what each detail represented, and what the potential was for you. Some aspects may already be a part of you but some may need to be developed. For example:

Bag Detail	What does this represent for me?	Current quality or expertise?	Development need?
Fur	Soft and warm	No, I can be a bit harsh with people	Yes, I need to develop my ability to be warmer and more accommodating to my team/family
Gol	Gold is money and buckle is keeping it locked up!	No, I spend like water! I have too much month left at the end of my salary!	How to save my money, how to keep it and not spend it

Remember, really explore what each thing represents for you! A button on your bag may mean keeping things buttoned up and safe; on another person's, it could represent keeping quiet (button it!). So, be careful not to go along with the expected representation – fur could be wild not warm!

The next step is to take your completed table and add the next two columns:

What will I be doing, being or having as a result of this development?	How will I get this development?
I will be more empathetic, better at listening, better at picking up their needs and showing more emotion myself	I will find a coach who can help me to develop empathy. I will also attend a course to improve my listening and interpersonal skills
I will be wealthier, and I will not be worrying about saving for future needs	I will make an appointment with my Bank Manager to set up a savings account that I don't touch. I will ask for advice about how best to save. I will find myself an IFA to help me with long-term financial planning

After you have done that, the next step is to decide what the measure or goal will be and when you are going to do it by:

Measure	Deadline Date
Positive feedback about my leadership style from the team	October 15th
Saved £1,000 by the end of the year	December 30th
Started to save towards a pension	January 8th

Once you have completed the long-term personal plan, you can then begin to understand what you need to do as a priority in the short term (bottom left-hand quadrant, short-term personal need) that will project you towards your long-term goals. The next step is to think about the two upper quadrants (short-term business need and long-term business need) on your development plan and take into account what the business needs from you now, and in future. Your completed development plan will take into account all four of the quadrants and will look a bit like this:

Blank copies of this form can be downloaded from the member area on the website.

As you move into the Pen chapter, you will also learn about goal setting; your goals can be added to this plan, or you may wish to add aspects of this plan to your vision board or goal sheet.

Development Tactic	Best Development Option	Measure/Progress	J	F	M	A	M	J	J	A	S	O
Identify Coach for personal assertiveness	Coaching	☺ Identified ALLY Coach, had first meeting	14									
Register on 'Finance for Non-Financial Managers' course	Course	☹ No more courses until next quarter, will look outside at local college courses instead					X					
Understand and document route to become Marketing Communications Manager	Mentor - Alicia Foyle	☺	12	24	22	21	21	17	22	21	26	23
Identify cross-functional committee/project I can join to develop my project management skills	Boss - David Hind	☹ David and I struggling to find suitable project with space		23								

Learning to learn began when we drew our first breath. It is the continuous and never-ending aspect of our life and will continue until we draw our last breath. Make every breath count from now until the end, dance your best life!

BAG - My Action Plan

BAG stands for **B**in, **A**dd and **G**et

B	What will I **Bin** that no longer serves my life or goals and prevents me from dancing my best life?	_____ _____
A	What am I already doing, being or having that I could **Add** to or improve in order to dance my best life?	_____ _____
G	What will I **Get** that will serve me well and help me to dance my best life?	_____ _____

239

My Keys

The Keys chapter is about two things:

1. ***The Keys to your heart*** – *your home and lifestyle are projections of you*

2. ***The Keys to your success*** – *creating the success linked to your core values*

Keys to Your Heart

The word 'heart' has a literal as well as a metaphorical meaning, and so we use it in many different contexts. It is the beating, life-sustaining organ in our body but also the heartfelt seat of emotion (I love you), the core of something (the heart of the matter), the house of compassion (have a heart), and the spirit itself (her heart lives on). The keys to your heart are all of these aspects of the heart and how they relate in your life. In many ways it is the culture of how you live. The heart of your home and your lifestyle are all projections of who you are, and therefore a manifested symbol of whom you are. It has been said that home is where the heart is, and also that it is men who build houses and women who create homes. Therefore, in this context, could it be said that our home is a representation of our heart?

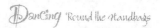

Our story ...

It had been a good day; Karen had enjoyed the interaction with patients, had a good time with her colleagues and Sister had awarded her a pay increase! It was good; she was feeling motivated and strong; her heart sang! Even when doing the most undesirable tasks, she did them with commitment and loyalty to her work, her team and with the support of her manager. Karen began to think about other things that made happy, how they made her feel; she drifted off into her own thoughts as she meandered from the hospital and slipped out into the balmy summer air. It was still light, but the indigo blanket of night was slowly and deliberately being pulled across the sky. She decided to walk the long way home through the town. Her stroll took her past her favourite shops where, of course, she paused to escape into their content of shoes, dresses, accessories and handbags. Her route meandered through many of the little side alleyways. The street lamps flickered on in the dimming light, casting ghostly shadows deep into their wake. Karen began to think about her lifestyle – too much work, not enough me-time! She thought about her home – too cluttered, old-fashioned, things wearing out. As she looked at the temptations in the shop windows, she began to dream about how her life would be if money were no object! She dreamed of the house that she would live in, the furnishings, designer kitchen, luxury en-suite for her and James, en-suite shower rooms to the children's bedrooms, a proper utility room and boot room, a lovely dining room that opened on to a beautiful decked area for entertaining friends. A study for James and a room in the garden for her where she could get me-time to design the garden, sew, paint, read and meditate. She could see this house in every detail, from door-knobs to bed-knobs! She saw her, James and the children enjoying social time, and most of all being a happy family. She saw herself running her own garden design business with a full order book and expanding to hire new staff to help her out. Her life was looking great!

'Wow! Sounds like you have been busy in that head of yours!' said a familiar voice beside her. Karen looked and there was Tomorrow Karen, looking very lovely in her summer eveningwear. The sunglasses propped on her head were the latest Chanel and her handbag was the latest and most amazing Lulu Guinness…

'You look fantastic!' admitted Karen.

'I look like you would look if you were to manifest these dreams that you have been having! I must admit I do feel good and it would have been inappropriate to turn up in High Street after that little fantasy of yours!'

The two women laughed and indulged in the details of Tomorrow Karen's new-found image and lifestyle.

'You have begun to look at the keys to your success and the keys to your heart. I think it may be time to unlock your potential in order that you can make this a reality for you. The keys to your success are about living to your values and doing what is important to you in your life – it includes work and relationships. The keys to your heart are about creating the home and lifestyle that reflect who you are, your identity. As a woman, your home is a reflection of your identity. Think about how no two homes of your friends are the same, their style is unique; even if the bricks and mortar are the same design, each is unique to every woman. I agree that James and the children have all made their own mark on the home, but it is you who is the centre of the home, you that decides what goes where, when things need to be cleaned, tidied or overhauled! It is you who creates the home and you that creates the feeling of home. As you and I walk tonight I want you to think about your home, and ask yourself if you are proud of it. What would you change about it? What needs to happen for it to become the home that you desire? And most importantly, what needs to happen for it to be a true reflection of the woman you are today?' Karen pondered for a minute, wandering through each room in her mind – the lounge, the dining room, the kitchen, each bedroom, bathroom and corridor.

'It is a bit shabby in places, it could do with upgrading, de-cluttering and a lick of paint!' She continued, 'I love the garden, I love my little potting shed and I like the haven that I have created for myself there, but much of the rest of it is not who I am any more!'

As the two women turned the corner into the square, their meandering, quiet world was filled with the bustle of people enjoying the summer evening at local wine bars, restaurants and cafés. Karen loved this time of year and revelled in the cacophony of laughter, chatting, chinking glasses and clattering of plates around her. She scanned the scene and saw families – parents cajoling children to accomplish the achievement of an empty plate, good table manners and minimal noise! She saw couples staring longingly into each other's eyes over the flicker of tiny dancing tea lights, and couples that were less happy, bickering in muted tones. She saw business people, engaged in serious politicking and point-scoring, and then, as she scanned the comings and goings of all the relationships in the town square, her eyes fixed on a couple whom she recognised. Her eyes were fixed, but her mind took a moment to catch up. Alarm bells were ringing, her rational logical self was trying to justify the sight she saw, and yet her emotional self was screaming. It was James… with her friend Lucy. They were tucked into the corner of a wine bar, both enjoying a bottle of something red, and holding hands. Karen stood transfixed, trying to find explanation, and yet part of her wanted to stride in, calling to both and envisioning her great day ending with the clink of three wine glasses and laughter with two people she loved. However, her feet stood transfixed as her mind raced from panic, to fear, to tears, to hurt, to rational friendliness, to hurt, and the same over and over again. She searched every nuance of their behaviour, their looks, their eye contact and body language for clues to the relationship between them. If she had seen James looking concerned and comforting a tearful friend, she would know that Lucy had a problem and James was just being there as a friend – especially as she, Karen, had been working a lot recently and had little time for any time with friends. In which case, she would join them for that nightcap and add her support. As she stared, searching for these clues, the relationship she actually saw presented in emotional technicolour screamed sex, attraction and desire. Karen felt sick. She watched as James slowly reached out and entwined Lucy's long dark hair between his fingers, enticing her towards him and the reward of a long, slow, passionate and yet gentle kiss.

Karen felt herself crumble; her knees were like jelly and her heart and stomach sank in a deep dread. She wanted to scream, to release the pain of splintering shards of grief within her. She stared, tormented and tortured by the truth of their liaison; tears spilling down her cheeks, she ran from the restaurant, her stomach cramping from the pain of betrayal, humiliation, dismay, hurt and white-hot rage. She was blind to everything around her as the scene of James and Lucy engulfed her mind, replaying its hideous, stark reality. She was oblivious to everyone, no longer caring about any relationship but her own; faster she ran, instinctively heading for home in a fog of searing pain and tears. She didn't even notice Tomorrow Karen running with her until she reached her front door. The two women stared at each other, both feeling, both knowing, both wanting none of this to be true. Tomorrow Karen reached out and Karen sobbed uncontrollably. There was no need for a visit to the handbag tonight, Karen knew the lesson of her keys and, in the arms of her future self, knew that the fragile dance of the heart and loved ones, and security and life friendships, were often tested to the hilt of pain, pleasure, rage, despair, laughter, fun and ache. Love hurt so much and no relationships felt it so acutely than those that held a key to your heart and your success. As both women stood silently in the dark, Karen knew that the dance that was to come would either bring her family closer or it would rip it apart, splintering and tearing the heart of all that she held dear. She loved James, loved her children and loved Lucy, so this must be worth fighting for? Her head throbbing, her eyes swollen, her stomach churning, Karen began to sink deeper and deeper into that familiar place that she always travelled to with Tomorrow Karen; today it was into the

Lulu Guinness handbag. When she opened her eyes, she was lying on a soft rose-covered tissue and, slowly focusing on her new surroundings, knew that there was a new lesson to be learned and new work to do. She removed wiped her eyes with the tissue, and began to observe the contents of this luxury bag. It was beautiful, like the inside of a silken Bedouin tent. It was cool and dark, purple silk draping her like the night sky over a mystical desert landscape. For Karen, an oasis in a desert of pain, humiliation and panic.

Tomorrow Karen beckoned her to where lay a bunch of keys. Their shiny brass surface glinted in the subdued light within the bag, each key held together by a brown leather key ring announcing the word 'MUM' branded into its skin. The key ring had been a gift from the children after a recent trip to the seaside and provided a label for her most important role. Karen's stomach turned and tears began to flow as she thought about what might happen to them in the weeks to come.

'Two keys, one for success and one for heart. Which would you like to begin with?' interrupted Tomorrow Karen in a determined tone.

'Let's start with my heart shall we, it seems fitting as that is what I was thinking about when you turned up looking as glamorous as Joan Collins!' The two women laughed together like firm friends, the best of friends.

Tomorrow Karen picked up the Key to her Heart, stretching it in front of her. 'Then let's begin…'

Before returning to the reality of her life, Karen knew that she could no longer dance to the old music of her and James's relationship; from tonight, that track no longer existed. Together they would have to learn a new dance – together or apart. A new score would play, one that would change tempo time and again as they mastered the rhythm that was about to beat through their marriage. She had to be strong, whatever happened next; she would learn this dance for the sake of her marriage, her children and her friendship. This was the key to her heart and her success.

'Home is where the heart is' – this was brought home (excuse the pun) to me recently when we sold our family home. Financial decisions and a downturn in my business meant that we could no longer afford to keep the home that we had lived in for 14 years. It was the home that my children had been brought up in, a home that my husband and I had worked hard to buy, a home filled with memories, not just stuff. We sold and we were forced to rent. The rental property, a nice house in our local town, promised to give my husband and me the lifestyle that we now desired. We wanted to have more time together, walk out to restaurants, enjoy the freedom of the town and all of its facilities. The children would have easy access to friends and I could pack away the sign for the top of my car marked 'MUM'S TAXI'. I treated the house with the respect that it deserved, but it did not feel like home. It was the property of someone else, not me. When you live in someone else's house, you must abide by their rules of décor, choices and restrictions. It is their heart, not yours. My family did not settle and, in fact, we moved very soon. I discovered that not only was I living in a house and not a home, I was also living in a community in which we did not belong. The house we live in now is more like 'who we are' and hopefully we will be able to buy it and truly make it somewhere I can call my own. Until then, I will do what I can to make it a home and thereby give it a heart.

Your home – large or small, mobile or static, rented or owned – is an outward projection of who you are, who you have been and who you wish to become. When I was packing to leave the house that we had lived in for many years, I recall the process of reviewing every item of furniture, ornament and clothing and deciding whether it should be packed to go with me, donated to the local charity shop, sold, given away or binned, by asking myself, 'Is this who I am today and who I want to be regarded as?' There were literally hundreds of items that were de-cluttered from my life because I announced, 'This is not who I am any more!' It is the most liberating experience because the question and announcement allowed me to overcome the sentimentality of keeping 'stuff' because it was given to me, because it might come in handy, or that it was expensive. Just as we can collect cholesterol around our physical heart, we can collect clutter around our virtual heart. Therefore, by de-cluttering you can free yourself up to be the person that you are meant to be. De-cluttering my home was so cathartic and so energising! We donated so much to a charity that they have been able to raise literally thousands for their cause. I sold most of our furniture, gave away a lot, and shed years and years of collected stuff; I suddenly felt lighter and open to newness! The virtual cholesterol was gone and my life was flowing once more.

There is all sorts of clutter in most of our lives. Sometimes it is physical, sometimes psychological and sometimes emotional. The easiest to spot is the physical and getting rid of this can have a significant impact on all our other areas of clutter. Emotional clutter is dealt with throughout the book, therefore physical clutter is the focus for this chapter.

First of all we need to recognise it as clutter. Start by looking around your home. Take a notepad and visit each room as if you are inspecting it. For those rooms that you have little influence over (like a teenager's bedroom) just close the door and leave that one out – for now. While standing in the centre of each room, look around you and ask, 'Is this who I am any more?' Material objects are only useful if they are serving you in some practical, emotional, or aesthetic way. When you start serving them, that is when they become clutter. What do I mean by 'serving them'? I mean keeping them, cleaning them, having them because you feel you have to. Imagine if you were buying a new home that had no storage cupboards. You would have to de-clutter or have all of your stuff on show! If you buy a property or an item of furniture for its storage ability, then maybe it is time to save your money and de-clutter instead. I hear of many women who get to the age of about 50 and suddenly have the overwhelming desire to throw away lots of clutter.

All this sounds pretty obvious but it is amazing how trapped we can feel by the things around us. It feels so difficult to make a start that we end up doing nothing at all. You don't have to throw everything out. Keep the things that are really important to you. Getting rid of clutter is not about throwing away things that are meaningful to you; it is about throwing out stuff that is no longer relevant to your life, thus leaving space and time for things that are more meaningful.

The Clutter Quiz

	Yes	No

1. *Do you receive catalogues, manuals or magazines and subscribe to things that you know you will never buy from or look at?*

2. *Are you a reading pile person? Do you create a reading pile that you never quite get the time to look at?*

3. *Do you have piles of paper on your desk that is not 'current' work?*

4. *Do you misplace important papers, bills, information and worry that one day it will bite you in the bottom?*

5. *If you were looking for a new house, would you turn it down due to lack of storage space?*

6. *Do you fill the storage spaces in your car too?*

7. *Do you buy things that you don't need with money that you don't have to impress people that you often don't particularly like?*

8. *Do you often feel embarrassed by how your home or office looks when visitors turn up unexpectedly?*

9. *Do you worry about opening the door to cupboards in case something falls out?*

10. *Have you ever missed an appointment or phone call because you either forgot to put it in your diary or double-booked it?*

11. *Do you have trouble saying 'No'?*

12. *Do you have more than one 'to-do' list?*

13. *Do you forget to get back to someone because you lost the message?*

14. *Do you pack extra things 'just in case' when going on holiday?*

15. *Do you hold on to clothes 'just in case' you fit in to them again some day or they come back into fashion?*

16. *Do you hold on to presents that were bought for you even though you don't like them or don't need them any more?*

Sort all of your clutter into four piles: rubbish, charity shop, sell or give away. Use the following questions to decide whether an item is clutter or not:

- *Do you have lots of nice but useless things gathering dust? Consider how much they really mean to you. Could you get rid of some of them? You probably won't miss them and will enjoy the time you have saved from dusting them regularly.*

- *Are old papers and documents cluttering your desk and stopping you from having a clear space to think and work? File what is important, do something with the stuff that needs attending to and throw the rest away. If you are a paper- or pile-pusher, use the three-dot method – when you pick up a piece of paper for the first time, put a red dot in the corner, then when you pick it up for the second time a few days later, but still don't know what to do with it, put a second dot in the corner. When you pick it up for the third time, it now has top priority and should never be given a third dot! Act on it now and then get rid of it or file the paper as actioned.*

- *What about the linen cupboard? Is it full of sheets, pillowcases and towels that you never use? If so, pass them on to someone who can use them.*

- *What about those kitchen drawers? Are they full of gadgets that looked so good at the time you bought them and you have never used since? How about all those appliances – pasta makers, bread makers, egg boilers – how often do you use those? Who would get better use from them?*

- *How about your sock drawer? Are you still waiting for that missing sock to turn up? Other drawers? Wardrobe? Do you have a wardrobe or area with clothes that were expensive but you've never worn, or clothes that some day you may get back into? Sell or charity shop for all of it!*

Here is a handy tip. When you get something new, get rid of something old. It is easy to put into practice and will help you to keep your clutter manageable.

Once you get into the swing of it and start to feel the rewards of less clutter in your life, it will get easier and easier.

Psychology of Clutter

We are bombarded with advertising that suggests having more of their product will build our self-esteem

Write down ways in which you receive this message

_____

_____

We struggle to say 'No'

In what way does not saying 'No' create clutter for you?

_____

_____

Empty spaces and empty cupboards often make us say 'what could I keep in here?'

What do you fill up that creates clutter for you?

_____

_____

We don't like to hurt people's feelings

In what way do other people's feelings or needs create clutter for you?

_____

_____

We might need it some day, or it might be valuable some day, or it might come in handy some day, or it may come back into fashion some day?

Or it may fit me again some day…?

What 'might…some day' talk creates clutter for you?

_____

_____

Be brutal with that clutter, give it away, throw it away or sell it! Your home should be a reflection of who you are, who you want to be. As you look around, even if it is just with your wardrobe to begin with, be certain of your style now and get rid of those items that may come back into fashion, may fit again and one day you might just suit!

C – *Clear your home, your diary and your mind of clutter*

L – *Let go of everything that no longer reflects who you are*

U – *Unleash the Goddess of Clutter Liberation from within you!*

T – *Take things to charity shops*

T – *Take things to car-boot or nearly-new sales*

E – *Earn money from your clutter to buy time away with your loved ones or friends*

R – *Ruthless with sentimental and out-of-date, out-of-size stuff!*

Home is where the heart is – Part 2

Once you are rid of your clutter, it is time to make your home into a reflection of you now. If you are like most other people, disposable wealth is limited and sometimes we just cannot afford to replace everything all at once. Therefore, make a decision about things one room at a time, starting with the room that is most important to you. When I moved into the house that we currently rent, I decided that my bedroom had to be the first room to reflect who I was. Prior to moving, I began to collect things that I would put in my new room. I painted it as soon as I moved, and with the inexpensive addition of new curtains and bedding, created a room that reflected who I am. It feels nice! Beyond that, I make sure that I keep it that way. On a recent radio discussion, I heard the singer Beverley Knight tell the DJ, 'I make my bed every morning when I get up, it makes me feel like a lady.' I could understand what she meant. I do the same, and that got me thinking about what other things I do, and do not do, that are a reflection of who I am. For example, I do not like getting up to dirty dishes in the morning; cleaning up before bed makes me feel as though I can end the day and start a new day fresh!

What do you do or not do, and how does it make you feel? Really explore what is important to you, what is at the heart of the matter; when exploring this, remember not to get caught up in 'shoulds'! Shoulds trap us in negative behaviour patterns linked to guilt and are more focused on what you don't want. Instead, focus on things that get you what you do want at a heart level. To support you with this, ask yourself, 'What does that get for me?' In the Beverley Knight story, making her bed was not about 'I should do it because that is what is expected of me' but rather 'it makes me feel like a lady'. If I were coaching Beverley, I may ask her, 'And what does feeling like a lady get for you?' By asking that question, you can begin to see that it can get to the heart of her behaviour.

What is important?	What is at the heart of the matter here for me?

Keys to Success

I heard a line in a song on the radio once and it was, 'Be yourself because everyone else is taken'! It is a simple line, but profound in its meaning. We have spoken about authenticity throughout the book, but the key to success is being authentic and true to your needs right now. I spoke to a girlfriend on the phone yesterday. She has had some time out of work due to stress and pressure, and yet her son is continually nagging her to pull herself together and get back to work 'in case she loses her job'. I asked her if his words were a projection of his own fears and insecurities, but also asked if she had been specific about how he could support her to meet her needs. 'If he doesn't know what you need, then he will continue to judge, whereas if you ask for his support, he has a vested interest in a positive outcome for you both,' I suggested. Key to success is being true to your needs, and asking for what you want. Often we can be indirect communicators, we expect people to know what we want by osmosis! But what if you do not know what you want? What if you have been dancing to the same tunes for so long that you just don't know what your purpose is any more? Your purpose is underpinned by your identity, which is defined by your beliefs and values. The key to success begins with the commitment to your core values, your beliefs and then you will know who you truly are and have clarity about your purpose. Throughout the remainder of this chapter, we will explore values and in the Perfume chapter you will explore identity and purpose.

What is a Value?

A value is a deeply held belief about what is important. It drives your behaviours, educates your capability and, step-by-step, moves you towards your identity and purpose. In other words, your values and beliefs underpin or drive your behaviour and lead you to your purpose in life. The reason so many people keep on repeating the same patterns in their life is lack of understanding of their core values and therefore what behaviours they need to change in order to make life better.

For example, think about being asked to change in some way; unless you truly believe in the reason for the change, you won't. This has big implications for workplace change, as often the reason why change projects fail is not because people don't know 'how' to change, but rather more to do with 'why' it is important that they do change and what it will get for them if they do. Values seek to answer what is important, and good leaders know this and explain importance in terms of consequence. For example, I am often asked to justify the need for worklife balance in the workplace. Leaders of businesses say to me, 'We are already successful; offering worklife balance and flexible working might negatively affect our bottom line. Everyone will want flexible working and they will become less motivated by work and more motivated to stay at home under the duvet!' As I listen to their language, I hear the values that they unconsciously extol, like financial success, work ethic, commitment to work, and I reflect in my answer the importance of these and how the benefits of a worklife balance culture can also be aligned with those values. 'I can see that financial success is evident as well as important to you, and I can show you how worklife balance can positively impact your bottom line by ensuring an even stronger work ethic of people committed to work through increased motivation, reduced cost due to improper absence and increased productivity due to a healthier work and life balance'. By using their values in my statement, they rarely reject, or have space to reject, my words as in their mind I am speaking truth. This then allows me an opportunity to provide the business case for moving towards worklife balance, as well as their ultimate purpose, in a way that is congruent with their values. Communication works well when it turns the key to unlock the person's values and why they are important.

If your beliefs drive your behaviour, they can also keep you stuck. Just look at the word 'belief'; in the middle is the word 'lie'. Beliefs can be lies we tell ourselves that prevent us from looking at life with a different perspective. We see this all the time in society where people have beliefs about others that are untrue or in some way exclusive. Religions, borders, skin colours etc. can all create 'beliefs' that may indeed be 'lies'. At an individual level, beliefs are so deeply held that sometimes we don't even know that we have them, never mind how they impact us. Beliefs can cause rigidity, and that means that the person with most flexibility is usually most successful. Who do you know that is stuck in their ways and unwilling to change? When we believe something so rigidly, it prevents us from seeing alternatives. What do you believe? Is it true beyond doubt?

I love the quote 'A belief is not merely an idea the mind possesses, it is an idea that possesses the mind'. Thoughts are things, and if embedded long and often enough, form strong neural pathways that are regarded as fact, truth and ultimately believed. Beliefs lead to self-fulfilling prophecies – you get what you think! Like 'all men are unfaithful' or 'all families quarrel'

Write down a list of specific beliefs that you have in relation to the headings given on the next page, then in the right-hand box, decide how you might view them differently:

	My Belief	How I could think
Old people		
Christmas		
Marriage		
Men		
Women		
Children		
Terrorists		
Wet weather		
Alcohol		
Foreigners		
Flying		
Gay people		
Cancer		
Chocolate		
Fast drivers		
Large Corporates		
Death		
Spiders		
Rich people		
Poor people		
Sales people		
Fast food		
Young adults		
Fat adults		
Fat children		

Our beliefs drive our actions, and actions are either away from something that we don't want, or towards something that we do.

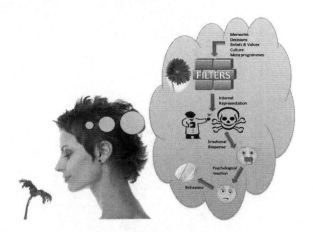

Generalisations create filters which are built from memories, decisions, beliefs, values, culture and therefore the action we take as a result. For instance, in the example shown above, the woman sees a flower, this triggers her memory about flowers and her belief that it will give her an allergic reaction. The filter then creates an internal representation in her head that warns her of the danger and suggests chemical imbalance in her system. This creates an emotional response which, in this case, may be worry or anxiety, and that leads to a psychological reaction of 'feeling ill' or 'feeling depressed'. The resultant behaviour is to take a tablet.

In coaching this woman, I would work with her at a belief level in order to re-align her filters and subsequent responses.

My Values Exercise

Think of a time when things were going really well for you; life was going great, work was going great, or both.

For each of the stated values below, decide whether you ALWAYS value it, OFTEN value it, SOMETIMES value it, SELDOM value it or NEVER value it. Try to be strict with yourself, aim to have NO MORE than four in the always category, seven to nine in the often and the rest spread over the remaining options. A full version of this exercise is available on the website and as part of the Dancing 'round the Handbags® workshops and retreats.

My Values

	Always	Often	Sometimes	Seldom	Never
Achievement					
Friendships					
Effectiveness					
Market position					
Helping other people					
Upward promotion & Advancement					
Efficiency					
Meaningful work					
Having a family					
Ethical practice					
Merit					
Adventure					
Privacy					
Excellence					
Affection (love and caring)					
Accumulation of Money					
Arts					
Wealth					
Reputation					
Quality environment					

	Always	Often	Sometimes	Seldom	Never
Honesty					
Supervising others					
Job title linked to high status					
Job title linked to expertise					
Job title linked to wealth					
Challenging problems					
Independence					
Excitement					
Personal development					
Variety					
Influencing others					
Loyalty					
Truth					
Spiritual growth					
Intimacy					
Inner harmony					
Customer excellence					
Trust					
Community involvement					
Social development					
Flexibility					
Stress free					

	Always	Often	Sometimes	Seldom	Never
Growth					
Purity					
Innovative					
Pioneering					
Pleasure					
Quality					
Power					
Expertise					
Risk taking					
Integrity					
Fame					
Teamwork					
Working outdoors					
Physical strength					
Physical agility					
Physical stamina					
Emotional resilience					
Intellectual status					
Fast living					
Wisdom					
Competition					
Co-operation					

	Always	Often	Sometimes	Seldom	Never
Involvement					
Conformity					
Fast-paced work					
Tranquillity in life					
Job tranquillity					
Work under pressure					
Knowledge					
Teamwork					
Structure					
Proximity between work and home					
Creativity					
Financial security					
Respect					
Decisiveness					
Controlling the work of others					
Controlling the way people live					
Authenticity					
Democracy					
Ecological awareness					
Stability					

	Always	Often	Sometimes	Seldom	Never
Personal freedom					
Freedom to act					
Freedom					
Balance					
Change					
Security					
Happiness					
Family					
Qualifications					
Job satisfaction					
Love					
Laughter					
Negativity					
Attention to detail					
Big picture					
Recognition					
Rules and procedures					
Diversity					
Joy					

Now focus on the four ALWAYS valued and prioritise them from 1 to 4, where 1 is the most important.

1. _____

2. _____

3. _____

4. _____

When we are in an environment where our core values are being met, we feel a sense of true identity; we can be ourselves. Identity comes from values and is explored in the My Perfume chapter. When our core values are not being met, this is often indicated by a sense of things not going well, feeling out of place or a real sense of resistance. This resistance usually means that instead of 1 leading to 2, to 3 and to 4 above, it actually indicates that not having 4 drives an outcome that prevents 3, 2 and 1. Try it for yourself in the diagrams provided below.

Then, as a result, ask, 'Am I living to my values in work and in life?' If the answer is No, then what are the keys to your success that will allow you to begin to live to your positive cycle?

Example:

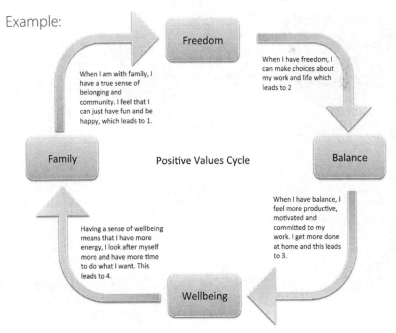

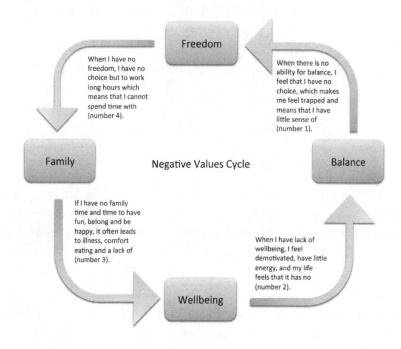

Negative Values Cycle

Freedom

When I have no freedom, I have no choice but to work long hours which means that I cannot spend time with (number 4).

When there is no ability for balance, I feel that I have no choice, which makes me feel trapped and means that I have little sense of (number 1).

Family

Balance

If I have no family time and time to have fun, belong and be happy, it often leads to illness, comfort eating and a lack of (number 3).

When I have lack of wellbeing, I feel demotivated, have little energy, and my life feels that it has no (number 2).

Wellbeing

BAG - My Action Plan
BAG stands for Bin, Add and Get

B	What will I **Bin** that no longer serves my life or goals and prevents me from dancing my best life?	
A	What am I already doing, being or having that I could **Add** to or improve in order to dance my best life?	
G	What will I **Get** that will serve me well and help me to dance my best life?	

Dance your Best Life!

10 My Photos

The Photos chapter is dedicated to relationships and four key relationships in our lives: our marriage/partnership, our dependants (children, animals, other dependants), family and friends. To decide who falls into these categories, especially if you're not sure, these people could be on a photograph and held somewhere in your handbag. Work colleagues, neighbours and acquaintances rarely make it to the handbag and so are dealt with in the social and professional networks of the My Phone chapter.

Our Photographs are about the significant life relationships you have: your dependants, family, friends and of course your partner or spouse. On your Dance floor, these aspects take up four of the segments and represent a very significant part of your sense of well-being, belonging and community. The processes and outcomes of relationships can be different for each of us, but the bottom line is the same; we are relationship-based for a very good reason. This will be explored in this chapter.

> *To dance is to be out of yourself; larger,*
> *more beautiful, more powerful."*
>
> -Agnes De Mille

Our story ...

The Egyptian sun shone down on Karen's face as she lay comfortably in a lounger by the pool. This was the first time that she and James had been away alone – no kids, parents, friends or pets – since their honeymoon. It was bliss! Even though she missed the children and felt the odd pang of guilt about leaving them with her sister, she knew that this holiday was a well-earned rest and 'couple time' for them both. The lessons of recent months were all too stark and painful and they both needed a break. They needed time out just to re-connect with one another and rebuild their marriage. Karen watched as James meandered up and down the pool, keeping cool and enjoying the respite from the midday sun. Karen observed his features, his sopping mop of wet curls snuggled against his tanned neck and face. He pushed them back, running his slender fingers through the spirals of dark brown hair. Karen felt desire to make love with him there and then and imagined sliding into the pool and enjoying his body, out of view from other poolside sunbathers of course! She hadn't felt those desires for a long time. Sex had become something she did, not something she wanted. Sex had descended to that once a week, in the dark, when the kids were asleep routine, and, if she was true to herself, something that she was keen to get over and done with so she could sleep. Here, with all the pressures of life evaporated in the heat of the desert, Karen's desires were returning, and with them the lesson that time together on their own was important and something that they should have done a long time ago. She loved him very much, and although times had been tough, the love was still strong. Changes had to happen, not just in their relationship though, but in other relationship and also in the way they lived their life. All of it had become shabby and taken for granted, and that had led to the problems of James having an affair and Karen focusing entirely on work and the children.

Karen began to think of her relationships, how was she to keep on improving her marriage when they returned to real life? The children, her parents, her friends; all of them needed a part of her. If she was to balance the relationships in her life, she would need to let go of certain things and ask for help with others.

"Asking for help is rarely a sign of weakness." Announced a voice next to her. Karen looked round, and there, resplendent on the lounger to her left was Tomorrow Karen, wearing the most exquisite beachwear and sun hat. Her Chanel sunglasses reflected the golden desert sun and looked fantastic against her bronzed and toned body.

"Wow! Look at you!" chuckled Karen, "you look lovely!"

Tomorrow Karen reached down into her new Mulberry beach bag and extracted a small magenta pink wallet. She gave it to Karen. "A present for you!" she smiled. Karen opened the pink leather wallet, to reveal four photos; one of herself with James, one with the children, a third with her parents and a fourth with her friends.

"This is lovely, thank you!" Karen said.

I am glad that you like it, for it is also the basis of our work today; we are going to review your photos, which represent the key relationships in your life – your marriage, dependants, family and friends.

Karen dropped the leather photograph wallet into her handbag, and as she did, she too descended into the depths of her bag, for the next lesson with her future self.

Marriage/Partnership

Often referred to as the 'significant other', 'other half' or 'life mate', the partnership with this person is very significant. Some people choose not to include such a relationship in their life. My friend Jo, for example, has chosen to dedicate her life to her religious beliefs, and whilst she has sworn a vow of dedication and celibacy, she is happy with her choice. Another friend has no relationship in her life and would dearly love one; she would regard herself as unhappy right now. Therefore, any relationship could be regarded as:

1. *In one and happy*

2. *In one and unhappy*

3. *Out of one and happy*

4. *Out of one and unhappy*

Each state suggests that different action may be required. Look at the score that you gave marriage/partnership on your Dance floor in Chapter 1. If you scored it high, then you may be in a state of 1 or 3 above. Like my friend Jo – she is out of one and happy, she has chosen not to have this kind of relationship in her life. My friends Louise and Elaine have been together 18 years and are as happy now as when they met. Or you may be in one and unhappy, or out of one and unhappy. Loneliness can be an issue in both scenarios. My friend Janie has been internet dating for a while and cannot seem to find the right one, whilst my friend Anne is in a loveless marriage.

How would you describe your situation?

Marriage/Partnership Diagnostic

In the following diagnostic, you are going to assess what is important to you in your relationship with your partner, and how satisfied you are with each. If you are not in a relationship and would like to be, then this may provide you with some indication of what you would most like from your ideal partner.

The bigger the gap between importance and satisfaction, the more likely it is that there will be a conflict or incongruence that you may want to address. Once complete, you will highlight the major issues and then create an action plan to communicate and resolve them. It may be beneficial for you both to complete the questionnaire and then work together on an action plan for the gaps. You may also want to add your own questions.

By assessing the importance versus satisfaction, you will gain insight into any imbalance. For example, if you have marital challenges happening in your life, then this does impact your work? For both men and women, troubles in relationships drain our motivation and engagement. Therefore, doing this exercise together may provide you with a starter for discussion and resolution.

One more thing: if your results show a positive large gap, i.e. you score it low on importance and high on satisfaction, then you may view this as a bonus, or something not to explore. You may choose to just recognise the satisfaction and be grateful, or you may want to explore why it is not important. The keys to success may be able to help with this exploration and provide answers for you.

Score where 1 is low importance/satisfaction and 5 is high importance/satisfaction.

	Importance (1 to 5)	Satisfaction (1 to 5)
1. My partner and I find time every day to communicate with one another		
2. My partner and I are good friends		
3. My partner and I enjoy physical intimacy that does not involve sex		
4. Sex is good and enjoyed equally		
5. My partner supports me emotionally as well as physically		
6. My partner and I enjoy social time together – either alone or with friends		
7. My partner and I believe in the same approach to bringing up children		

	Importance (1 to 5)	Satisfaction (1 to 5)
8. My partner and I both agree(d) about having children or not		
9. My partner and I share the same values on most things		
10. My partner and I manage disagreements and conflict between each other appropriately		
11. My partner and I make important decisions together		
12. My partner and I share responsibilities in the home		
13. My partner and I manage our finances together		
14. My partner and I take responsibility for the health and well-being of ourselves and family seriously		
15. My partner and I discuss serious issues like one of us dying or leaving and plans for such events		
16. My partner and I encourage each other to be the best we can be		
17. My partner and I encourage each other to be involved in hobbies and interests without the other		
18. My partner and I trust each other		
19. My partner and I love each other		
20. My partner and I are in love with each other		

Write down below those areas that have the largest gaps and then work with your partner on an action plan to resolve them.

1. *Which areas are most critical for you?*

   _____

   _____

   _____

2. *Which areas are most critical for your partner?*

   _____

   _____

   _____

3. *If your partner were to make one change to satisfy your needs, what would you ask?*

   _____

   _____

   _____

4. *If you were to make one change to satisfy your partner's needs what would they ask you to change?*

   _____

   _____

   _____

5. *What is your action plan for moving forward?*

   _____

   _____

   _____

I always said that my marriage would not be like my parents'. I wanted something different from theirs. I observed theirs and didn't like a lot of it; I observed boyfriends' parents and saw some things I liked and some things I didn't. As with many lessons in life, we learn by observing, watching and mimicking those that we perceive to be more powerful or senior to ourselves. Have you ever heard yourself say, 'I sound just like my mother?' At an unconscious level we observed how our parents related to each other and thought that was the way it should be done. Sometimes, we consciously say 'my marriage/partnership will never be like my parents', especially if it was very dysfunctional; however, at some level we often manifest those similarities. If you lived in a single parent family situation or with people not your parents, you would still observe those around you to look for ways to run your relationships. There is no manual, no best way, but be sure of one thing: your children may never listen to a word you say, but they are always watching what you do. What lessons are they learning about marriage/partnership by silently watching you and your partner?

I would also like to explore the 'out of one and unhappy' state. So many of my friends feel as if they are not whole unless they are in a relationship. I have seen many friends jump from one relationship straight into another, living each one with the mask of expectation firmly in place; an expectation that they will behave in a way that they believe their partner wants them to. Living to the expectations of others, or playing a role, soon becomes exhausting and cannot be sustained. However, so many of the people that I have seen do this truly lose who they are, and therefore define themselves by the person they have on their arm. They are terrified of not having someone in their life and many accept partners that are incompatible rather than have no one attached. Instead of panicking and rushing around trying to find another appendage, I believe that it may be healthier to build a lasting relationship with your true self first. A counsellor friend of mine once said that it is good to have a gap of at least five years between significant relationships in order to not just heal but to get to know who you now are. Once you have done that, then going into a new relationship means that you are taking you into it, not some inauthentic expectation of who you should be. At 73 and after a big gap between relationships, Jane Fonda learned this lesson well; she said, 'I am not losing myself in this relationship, I am bringing myself to it.' Let's take a leaf from her book now, and not wait until we are 73 to do so. Work on being in love with you, be curious to get to know who you truly are, what you enjoy, what you want to do. You are never alone when you have your fully resourceful self.

Coaching from Within

Identify which of the four states you are in right now. Then, find some space in a room where you can lay out these four imaginary states a bit like on the diagram below. You can use cushions or magazines or bits of paper to signify positions 1, 2, 3 and 4.

Begin by standing on position 1 which signifies you now, today, the present and current you in or out of a relationship (see diagram below to decide which one you are in now). As you stand on that position, there should be three other positions around you that are not you (as shown on the diagram).

From your position, imagine that you could get advice or support from the other three versions of you standing on the other three positions. That is what we are going to do.

From position 1, communicate to all of the other three (as if they were there) what life is like for you right now in the relationship that you are in or not in. Once you have done that, look at the other three positions and decide which one of these you would like to have coaching from first. Step on to that position, and facing the quadrant that you have just come from, truly feel what it feels like to be that you in that place. In your own time, give mentoring/support or advice to the woman in position 1 from your new position (2, 3, or 4). What would you tell her to do from this perspective? What advice would you give her? Give it now. Step back into position 1, and really take on board the advice given to you from the other version of you. Thank her for her advice. Move to each of the others in turn, repeating the process above until you have had advice or mentoring from all of the three positions.

As you stand there in your original position, reflect on the three pieces of advice or support you have had, be grateful for their insight.

Now, step off position 1 and stand back so that you can see all four positions. From that position, outside of all four, is there anything else that you would tell the person in position 1, or indeed any of the other three? It is now time to consider what steps or actions you are going to take and when you will take them.

The quadrants are shown in the diagram below, and an example of getting started.

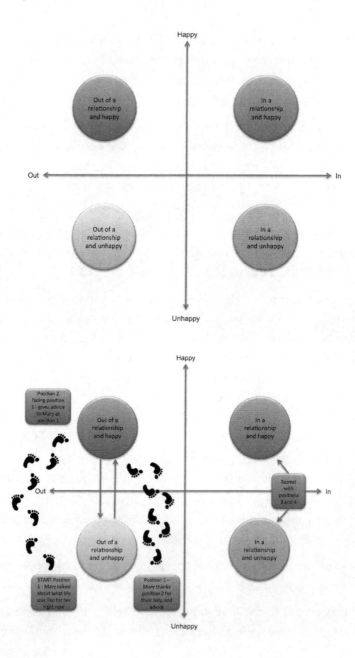

Dependants — who'd have them?

A dependant is someone or something that is dependent on you for their day-to-day well-being, survival and support. Dependants are usually thought of as children, but can also be other family members or pets. My friend Deborah has cared for her disabled sister since her parents died. My friend Judith cares for a whole yard of six horses, two ponies, three dogs, two cats and an ostrich called Kelly, not to mention the various chickens, sheep and other farm animals that appear to be dependent on Judith for their survival. A dependant is just that – someone or something that would perish if it were not for your care. Because of that bond, the dependent person or pet takes priority and becomes the central focus for care and consideration. In this regard, there are reasons and seasons of care; whilst a pet's might be constant throughout its life, care for a child changes as it grows. In my presentations on worklife balance, there are a number of things that I communicate in relation to worklife balance for people with caring responsibilities. First of all, and the most important is – life comes first! The responsibility to the child or children comes before the job, the salary or the organisation. A very good friend of mine was VP of Sales for a very large electronic manufacturing company. He earned a fantastic salary and had the lifestyle to go with it. For years they had enjoyed the fruits of his hard work. Then one day their world fell apart. Their young son was diagnosed with cancer. The family took him to the best hospitals and consulted with the best doctors. An aggressive course of chemotherapy seemed to be the only option open to their son. My friend was devastated, terrified and wanted to take this away from his boy. Frustration that none of his money, power or success could buy this from his boy, he wanted to take it away from him, to go through it instead of him; he and his wife were distraught. My friend Patrick decided that he would stay with Adam throughout his treatment; he would be there every step of the way. On the Monday morning, he went into work, met with his boss and said, 'I need six weeks out of the business, my son has cancer and I want to be with him to support him through his treatment.' His boss replied, 'Patrick, this is not a good time to ask. We are coming up to year-end and we need our VP of Sales here to help us make the numbers! Don't you have a wife at home who could look after your son? After all, we are probably paying for him to be in the best place, and there's probably nothing you can do anyway! You would be better off focusing on work, it'll keep your mind off things, Patrick, and your son will get better without you worrying about your quota performance and P&L!'

Patrick walked from his boss's office in silence. He walked purposefully back to his own, wrote his resignation, left it on the desk and walked out; he never went back. Patrick did stay with his son, and did help him through his treatment. When Adam was well, Patrick looked for a new role and since then has created a very different work ethic for himself and his family – one focused on life and work balance. Adam is now grown up and in fact has just graduated from university, ready to build his own career. The lesson from this tale is clear: LIFE COMES FIRST! There is no amount of thousands of pounds of salary, bonus, big office and status that would keep anyone away from their dependants if they needed to be there.

Review the score that you gave to the dependants section of the Photographs part of the Dance floor. Like marriage/partnership, you may have scored it based on any of the following options:

1. ***Don't have dependants and happy about that*** – *maybe you have made choices to retain your levels of independence, do not want children or pets, or maybe your children have grown up and are no longer dependent.*

2. ***Do have dependants and all is well and happy*** – *maybe you do have children and pets, but all is well and there is no imbalance.*

3. ***Don't have dependants and unhappy*** – *maybe you have been trying to have a child, or long to have a child or something dependent on you but, for whatever reason, you have not managed to create that in your life yet and it is making you unhappy.*

4. ***Do have dependants and unhappy*** – *maybe you are currently experiencing a short-term issue with one of your dependants, or a long-term issue that is causing imbalance. Maybe the issue is not the dependant, but your ability to manage their needs because of work or life circumstances, like an inflexible employer, lack of support or lack of resources.*

If you answered 3 or 4, define the current situation below, your level of satisfaction with it, the cause of the imbalance and more than one option for addressing the imbalance.

Current Situation	Satisfaction Level (1 to 10)	Cause	Options

Flexible working is one of the ways that supports the reasons and seasons of people's lives. Reasons are situations like my friend Patrick's above. Or it could be a less serious illness, sporting commitments, delivering a charity challenge or a specific need/emergency. The reasons that people need time out are usually irrelevant; it is how the organisation copes with those needs that is important to create a sense of give and take and balance for both the company and the individual. Reasons for flexible working are generally short-term and don't affect Terms & Conditions of Employment. For example, your child may have a cold and you need to take a few days out to look after her; working from home would allow a balance between the work and caring. Not all jobs allow the option to work from home, but there are probably things that you could do if you and your employer focused on looking for ways it could happen, rather than ways it should not. Saying No to flexible working is an easy response; saying 'OK, how can we make this work?' is healthier for employees and bottom lines. When give and take happens, employees are generally about 27% more productive and around 39% more loyal. Increased productivity and engagement positively impact the bottom line.

Then there are seasons of people's lives in which they need to work flexibly in order to deal with a more long-term need. For example, a mother may wish to work part-time when her baby is young, but when the child goes to school her contract may change to part-time in a term-time approach.

I can honestly say that I have worked a number of ways during the growth of my children, every option from compressed working week, home-based working, full-time and, during one occasion when my daughter was sick, not at all for three months. However, consider this: if a mother or father has an 18-year-old son with a drug problem, or an 18-month-old-baby who is keeping them awake at night, this will have an impact on the person's work.

Work is something you do, and less and less becoming a place that you go. Managers of people should begin to look at work as a contribution, not as hours of input at a desk in an office or factory. More and more we are seeing the growth of crowdsourcing; the unleashing of a strategy in micro parts, a bit like throwing all of the pieces of a jigsaw puzzle into a crowd and watching as they all come together to make it into a picture. Wikipedia is a great example of crowdsourcing, and many organisations use this approach internally to encourage innovation and change; they don't give a damn what your job title is, how old you are, how senior or how big your parking space is, they care about your contribution. If you became measured on that, the 'nine to five' dinosaur mentality would become extinct. I believe that this would free people to work when it suited them, to deadlines set by the organisation and customer/market. This would attract and retain amazing talent able to deliver whatever their personal talent was. Imagine how work would change! Instead of hierarchies of status, corridors of power and job roles that keep people pigeon-holed into boundaries of mediocrity, work was freedom to work towards a vision that played to people's strengths, allowed personal growth and team development in a collaborative way. One is a masculine culture, the other a feminine culture; balance between both is key for our future success.

Balance of culture would naturally allow people to manage the needs of dependants in a long, and short-term focused way. The diagram below provides ideas on which flexible working options would work for those with either a short-term or long-term need, and those with the need to reduce hours at work, or just re-arrange them.

The adaptable thing about flexible working is that it can change as life circumstances change. The key with carers of dependants is having a working pattern that allows them to plan ahead; chaotic, last-minute meetings and re-schedules can be difficult for the carer to adjust to.

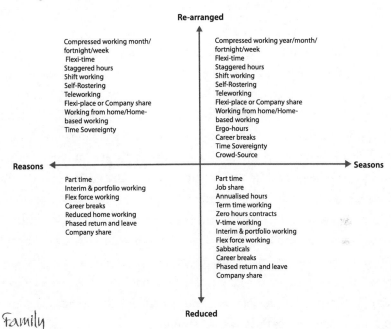

Family

Family is what you define as family. Family for you could be a traditional environment with mum, dad, siblings, aunts, uncles etc., or it could be your next-door neighbour, an old teacher, a departed relative or a partner's family. Families are wide and varied, and family relationships are unique to your environment.

Look at how you scored family on your Dance floor, was it a perfect 10? How do we assess 10? 5? 1?

In general it is about relationships, or lack of them, that makes us score higher or lower. Sometimes it is worry about the health or well-being of a family member. My friend Helen's mother had Alzheimer's. As her mother's illness progressed, Helen became more and more concerned. Her work performance began to drop and Helen became particularly agitated at certain times – like appointments, or financial transactions that her mum needed to manage. Helen's boss, David, noticed that she was becoming more distressed and, without interfering, asked Helen how he could help her. 'I worry most when she has to collect her pension, or go to the bank. She often leaves her money and bank book on the counter as she has no idea why she is there,' explained Helen. David could see and sense Helen's anxiety and asked what would make life easier for her. 'If I could go with her to get her pension, and find ways that I could become a signatory for her account, and if I could be there with her for appointments and not let it affect my work too much, that would be great,' said Helen. Helen and David worked out a pattern of flexible working where Helen worked a compressed working week and took every Thursday morning to deal with her mum's finances and attend any appointments. Sometimes appointments came outside of that time, and Helen just managed it with David. He also put her in touch with a solicitor who helped Helen to become legally in charge of her mother's affairs. David recognised that Helen was a good employee, he wanted to support her and so, by relieving some of her pressure through flexible working and practical advice, he knew that work for Helen would sort itself out again. He was right; Helen's performance, loyalty and support of David more than increased! Helen's mum has since passed away and Helen feels sad about the loss, but knows that she did all that she could to support her mum in those last few months.

Family impacts work! How does your family life impact yours? How does work impact your family life? The long-hours culture in the UK puts particular pressure on people, and that impacts family life. I was talking to one man just recently who said, 'I am frightened to call my son these days. He is so busy with work, he has no time for me. I have started asking my neighbour to help me with little chores that I can no longer do myself. I don't want to interrupt my son from his work. I know he is busy, but sometimes I just want to talk to him. If I call he becomes impatient with me and always thinks I want something from him. I don't, I just want to know he's OK. I know that he has a very big important job, it's just sad that I have dropped to the bottom of the heap of things that are important in his life.'

There is a quote that I use in presentations and it is this: 'One of the symptoms of an approaching nervous breakdown is the belief that one's work is terribly important.'

On the diagram below, place the names of key family members in the spaces provided and as shown in the example. Now score each relationship where 1 is awful, up to 10 – fantastic. Then for each, define what would need to happen for it to reach a 10.

Relation	Score 1-10 or N/A	Relationship	Action
My relationship with my mother	3	Mum has always been a challenge for me, she is quite controlling and it is her way or the highway	Recognise that her intention is positive, and it is her way of showing her love to her family. Allow her to control some small things, but be assertive for what is important to me
My relationship with my father	9	Love my dad!	
My relationship with my brother	6	Love my brother, but he is opinionated like my mother	Choose my battles
My relationship with my aunt	8	Love my aunt, but need to spend more time with her	Free up one Saturday a month to take her shopping and make lunch for her

Relation	Score 1-10 or N/A	Relationship	Action

Remember, the difference between relation and relationship is the word 'ship'.

Ships should have direction, be steered and should never be forced to sink!

Friends

Friends are for reasons, for seasons and for lifetimes. I once read the following and want to share it with you as you move forward from today into tomorrow and onwards, to dance your best life.

'People come into your life for a *reason*, a *season* or a *lifetime*. When you know which one it is, you will know what to do for that person – and for you.

When someone is in your life for a *REASON*, it is usually to meet a need you have expressed, either outwardly or in your heart. They have come to assist you through a difficulty, to provide you with guidance and support, to aid you physically, emotionally or spiritually. They may seem like a godsend, and they are. They are there for the reason you need them to be. Then, without any wrongdoing on your part and at a convenient time, something will be said or done to bring the relationship to an end. What we must realise is that our need has been met, our heart's desire fulfilled, their work is done. The reason has been answered and now it is time to move on.

Some people come into your life for a *SEASON*, because your turn has come to share, grow or learn. They bring you an experience of peace, companionship, support or make you laugh. They may teach you something you have never done. They usually give you an unbelievable amount of joy. Believe it, it is real but only for a season. When their work is done, one day, and not always suddenly, you notice that they are no longer there or no longer wanted. The season has passed and now it is time to move on.

LIFETIME relationships teach you lifetime lessons, things you must build upon in order to have a solid emotional foundation, to live your purpose, to be the person you are able to be. Your job is to accept the lesson, love the person and put what you have learned to use in all other relationships and areas of your life. It is said that love is blind but friendship is clairvoyant.

Thank you for being a part of my life and for allowing me to be a part of yours; whether I was a reason, a season or will be a lifetime, please …

Are my friends reasons, seasons or lifetimes?

The following diagram allows you to decide where you will place your friends in terms of whether they are reasons, seasons or lifetime friends. To begin, I believe that it is important to define who your friends are, and what level of friendship you have with them. I have a small handful of true, core friends that I would lay down my life for, be there in the middle of the night for and allow them to live in my home at any time. Then there are social friends that I can enjoy good times with, but wouldn't think to talk to them about my inner secrets and desires. Then there are those who are on the outside of the boundary of friendship and are more like chums. I may see them now and again, I may like them a lot, I may work with them, but they only get so close because they and I have our own friends.

True friends want the best for you, they can show empathy and sympathy – like two bodies with one soul. They have compassion for you and you for them. Only they can point out your faults and problems when other people might find it difficult to do so. There is honesty and trust and no fear of being judged – as Mother Theresa once said, 'If you judge, you have little time to love.' Friends love each other unconditionally and develop reciprocity of love, give and take love and humour that is core to them. Helen Keller once said, 'With every friend I love who has been taken into the brown bosom of the earth a part of me has been buried there; but their contribution to my being of happiness, strength and understanding remains to sustain me in an altered world'.

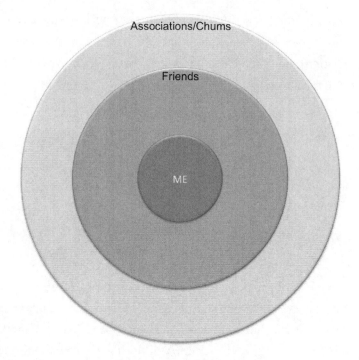

Now transfer their names on to the relevant part of the diagram below:

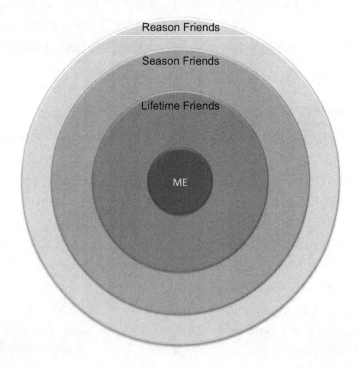

Summary

🍃 *What have you discovered by doing this exercise?*

🍃 *Which friends do you wish to invest more time into?*

🍃 *Which friends take up too much of your time and need to be managed differently?*

🍃 *Which friends do you need to let go of that no longer need to be a part of your life?*

BAG - My Action Plan

BAG stands for Bin, Add and Get

B	What will I **Bin** that no longer serves my life or goals and prevents me from dancing my best life?	_____ _____
A	What am I already doing, being or having that I could **Add** to or improve in order to dance my best life?	_____ _____
G	What will I **Get** that will serve me well and help me to dance my best life?	_____ _____

285

11 My Perfume

Ask yourself: 'When things are going well and I am working/living at my best, who do I become?' I ask this question to senior women as part of my Lipstick Leadership Research, and they say, 'I am me!' or 'I become the best of me'.

Identity – knowing who you are and what your purpose is – is the focus for this chapter. It blends the feminine and the spiritual aspects of you, so that you may know your identity and purpose in life.

Identity is a clear understanding of what we stand for (our values and beliefs), the behaviours that we portray, the skills and capabilities that we use, all in an environment of work and life that is blended together to create a solid and sure image of who we truly are. In relation to this book, your identity is your music and your purpose is the tune that you want to dance to in order to dance your best life.

> *"The journey between who you once were,*
> *and who you are now becoming, is where*
> *the dance of life really takes place."*
>
> - Barbara De Angelis

Our story ...

The wind howled outside and Karen lay there in bed listening as it competed with James's snoring. She wondered which howled louder but knew that, either way, she couldn't sleep and decided that instead of fighting it, she would go downstairs and read.

As she emerged on to the landing, she caught a whiff of the new paint on the walls and the earthy smell of the new wooden floors drifting up from downstairs. She and James had worked tirelessly since their return from holiday, and now in late October with the autumn winds doing their best to blast any remaining leaves from the trees and hurtle the naked branches into a season of winter chill, the renovations were complete and the family could enjoy their lovely new home. Karen was proud of what they had achieved; it had breathed new life into their home as well as their relationship. Karen reflected on the recent times and the renewed vows that she and James had taken never to take each other for granted again. She was happy in her relationship and loved the house, but she still had a nagging gap within her that suggested that there was more for her to do and be. Karen wandered into the kitchen and opened the door of her brand new American-style fridge. The light popped on like a ready-awaiting butler, keen to serve what she needed. Karen slid the milk from the door shelf and returned the remaining contents of the fridge into slumbering darkness. On her way to the kettle, Karen flicked on the light and, as if expecting her, said, 'Good evening!' to Tomorrow Karen sitting at the kitchen table. 'I really like the new kitchen!' she said in response. Karen made hot chocolate and sat down at the table with her friend. 'I have a sense that this is not all we are meant to be,' she announced, tentatively sipping the creamy hot drink. 'I have a bigger purpose than this, Karen, a bigger purpose than being a wife, mother and nurse! All of those roles are great, but not enough.' Tomorrow Karen agreed and, as they sat there, she reached into her handbag and pulled out her friend's perfume. The shiny black surface, with distinctive brand, cloaked the contents of the luxury scent. Tomorrow Karen sprayed the perfume into the air and its droplets of fragrance melted through the air like glitter on *a seasonal card, enveloping the two women it its loveliness. 'The aroma fills the air around us like an aura, an extension of us. Perfume can often leave a trace of someone having been in a room, or the whiff of someone coming. Your identity is like that aura; it goes beyond the constraints of your thoughts, beyond your physical identity and outwards into the world where it influences others. It is your aroma of "femininism" (my word, but I like it! It is a mix of feminist and feminine), who you truly are and it guides you towards your purpose.*

'Scent is also a warning, a message; animals catch the scent of impending danger in the air, the scent of a mate approaching, the scent of bad weather and the scent of water where none exists to the naked eye. Scent is therefore your intuition and your gut feel as well.'

Karen took the bottle of perfume and stroked the shiny black surface of its lid. It had been her favourite since she was very young, and whilst she had tried other brands, none of them really matched up to this one – this one was really her. As Karen pondered about whom she really was, that all too familiar spinning sensation began to rotate her downwards and into her bag. The bottle of Chanel No. 5 now towered above her, elegant in its stature and standing proudly by the contrasting deep orange lining of her autumn handbag. Karen stared at its glassy surface, looking up towards the band of gold and shiny black rooftop lid. She saw how the thick glass distorted her face and body like a circus hall of mirrors. 'Who am I really? What is my true purpose?' Karen asked as she stood there staring into the golden elixir within. As she did, the liquid swelled and swirled, bubbled and boiled. Droplets merged and foamed like 24-carat gold pennies. Tomorrow Karen asked, 'When you are living and working at your best, who do you become?' Karen, bewitched by the swirling mass of molten gold, felt the question splash through her, in time with the waves of gold in the cologne. Suddenly the waves of scent began to calm, the foam of gold surf receded and there, within the liquid, Karen knew that she was about to catch a glimpse of the woman that she is meant to be. She stared, her intuition excited as she took in every detail. Suddenly, there she was, clear and obvious in front of her and she knew what she must do next…

The Spiritual You

This is a tough area to explore, and for each of us it is likely to be different. For some of you, there may be no sense of any spiritual connection, for others a deep knowing. Wherever you are on the continuum, this is not about religion. Your religion or faith may be a part of spirituality, but it is not usually the complete picture. Whilst I may have been born and raised into a specific religion, I also have my own interpretations and truths in relation to what that is and also what my own spiritual truth is. These are my beliefs, and as we explored in the previous chapter, your values and beliefs form your identity – the woman you truly are. My beliefs have therefore created the different facets or faces of me. In a way, they are the notes or phrases of music that create the symphony of my dance of life. I believe, and that is just my belief, that I am part of something bigger. Whether I call that God, life force, energy, collective consciousness or Source is irrelevant. I believe that we are all part of Spirit and in this physical manifestation are here to create, develop and change. Those three things could be with love or they could be with fear. I believe that fear is the opposite of love and leads to hatred, exclusion, isolation, despair and a myriad of other outcomes. We see this at society levels where people fear others from different generations, races, colours and creeds. This leads to discrimination, exclusion and war. Just taking time to listen, explore, understand, empathise and share leads to inclusion, compassion, involvement, openness and love. What a wonderful world it would be if we lost the urge to judge others because of their physical qualities, geography or religion.

That is just a belief though, and some would say a utopian one! There is not tangible proof that we live on after death. There is no evidence to support that there is a heaven or hell, angels, witches, demons, fairies or any other spiritual being. What I am sure of is that my beliefs are mine, and yours are yours! Have you truly explored them? Are the beliefs that you have now the same as those you had when you were 12, or 21? Is our spiritual journey continually evolving just like our life journey? Do we have to live a few lives in order to learn all the lessons, or is there just one chance to get it right? Or are we all aspects of all possibilities?

One thing we can know for sure is that 100% of us will die. The bit in between should be significant and provides us with the opportunity to make a difference in our little corner of the world.

My good friend Jack Black who runs the organisation Mindstore describes spirituality as everything from religious beliefs to a moment of awe enjoying a great view, a sunset or the birth of a new child. It is that moment where you have a sense of being and not doing. It is a place of silence and awesomeness combined that not only makes you feel alive, but also makes you feel a part of a bigger mind, energy or system. A few nights ago, I was walking back from a friend's 50th birthday celebration with my daughter. We paused on the dark country lane down which we were walking to look at the stars in the summer sky. When she was little, she used to say that the stars were heaven shining through! We stared up at the vastness and the twinkling lights, like glitter on a seasonal card, and wondered if we were the only living beings on a planet, how long it would take us to get to the nearest and whether the most distant still existed at all. It was a beautiful sight, a peaceful and yet terrifying spectacle – truly awesome. As we came back to reality and the lane that we stood in, we looked to the left where the village graveyard lay sleeping, blanketed in darkness. We looked at the silhouettes of headstones aligned along the little pathways and marking each passed life like a granite milestone. These people were gone, many now gone for a very long time and the memory of their existence had faded just like their name on their headstone. There is no knowledge now of their life, their significance to others, what they did in their communities and the legacy each left. As my daughter and I observed the circle of life that summer evening, we both felt that we were part of a bigger thing that, one day, when we pass, we will know. However it is now that counts; it is how we behave towards each other, how we treat each other, what we do for our communities, businesses, environments and ourselves that matters. You have a few short years here on this planet; make every second count. I hope that there is something more afterwards, a spiritual realm where I go on to do and be more. I don't believe that there is some fearful bloke sitting on a throne passing out judgements to men and women for what they

did or did not do – who needs a control freak like that? However, I do believe that there is somewhere that we cannot see with our human eyes and that I will go there some day. I believe that it is a place of love – pure and simple. These, as you can read, are my beliefs and I have many more that I will not share openly, but would like to ask you to share yours with you. The following exercise should be done in a place of peace. For you, that may be at the top of a mountain, by the sea, by a riverbank, in a park, in your garden, in a church, synagogue, temple or mosque or maybe even under the stars on a warm summer night. It is entirely up to you, but choose a place where you will be inspired and feel the awe that I described.

Exercise – I Believe

To the statements below, provide your own answers and observations about each, then continue the exercise adding your own.

My thoughts about God.

I believe that God is...

_____

....

My thoughts about life after death.

I believe that when you die...

_____

_____

My thoughts about spirits like angels, guides, ghosts etc.

I believe...

_____

_____

My thoughts about religion.

I believe...

_____

_____

My thoughts about the meaning of life.

I believe that...

_____

_____

My thoughts about the female spirit.

I believe that...

_____

_____

My thoughts about my sense of being female.

I believe that...

_____

_____

My sense of femininism.

In relation to work, I believe...

_____

_____

I added the final three boxes to this exercise in order to ask you to truly explore your sense of feminine. I believe that the world is out of balance and there is a huge chunk of imbalance in our businesses at this time. Women come out of school with higher qualifications and emotional intelligence than most men, and yet do not thrive in our businesses, due in some part to business being masculine in their design. Now, I am not describing men per se, I am describing culture. Our cultures are masculine; they focus on results, targets, profits... hunting. They demand more for less – productivity, fitness, agility, leanness, speed, competitiveness... hunting. In these cultures, the customer and people are often secondary and people are often regarded as cost... hunting (hunting teams are small, agile and fast; too many people are a distraction from the goal). The female culture wants results and productivity too, but not at the expense of the customer or people. Her approach is the opposite. She says, 'Let's get the right people, with the right skills, behaviours and values to achieve our vision... nurture. Let's get people in the right roles, with the right tools to do the job, aligned to our customers' needs... collaboration. Let's build the right culture of support, coaching and mentoring to ensure that we deliver the vision... cultivation and development. Let's operate in a flat culture where everyone is valued for their personal strengths... nurture. When we have the right people, focused and developed to do the right thing, then we will achieve productivity... resourcing and organising. If we have the right people productive, then we can achieve results... outcome and legacy.' Female leaders balance the risk-taking, results-focused masculine with the collaborative and cultivating feminine. A balanced business is surely a successful one?

My strengths as a leader – the following questionnaire is taken from the Lipstick Leadership Research and will provide you with an indication of the leadership style that you use always or often, and what you avoid (seldom or never). Which strengths do you have that are feminine, and which are masculine? Many women who work in our masculine environments have become adapted. That means that they are wearing the masks of masculine and have lost their ability to use their feminine skills. The long-term outcome is often isolation for these women. Shedding the mask is the best option for adapted females. This can be done through coaching, mentoring, building alliances with other women and finding other female role models that do not use masculine styles to succeed. However, much needs to be done in the culture of these organisations as well, and that is the reason for the research and of course, my next book...

To complete the whole survey, visit: https://www.surveymonkey.com/s/LipstickLeadershipSurvey

My core strengths as a leader are:

	Always	Often	Sometimes	Seldom	Never
Creating and sharing vision					
Developing talent in others					
Coaching others for development and growth					
Organising and planning					
Process management					
Tenaciously achieving targets					
Collaborating with others					
Influencing others					
Sensing the needs in others					
Driving a focus on results					
Persuasiveness in order to get my needs met					
Empathising with the feelings and emotions of others					
Creating enthusiasm in others					
Having long-term focus					
Having short-term focus					
Building the strengths and talents in others					
Building relationships					
Valuing diversity					
Playing politics to get what I want					
Coaching others					
Taking ownership					
Paying attention to detail					
Other (please specify):					

Intuition

Intuition can probably be regarded as a gut feel – a knowing without actually knowing, present or future, or a sense of danger, threat and other unspoken emotion. It is linked to empathy and, when motivated to do so, women are better than men at intuition. When measured generally, women's and men's intuition is the same. It is suggested that women's intuitive instincts are often stronger than men's if empathy is her focus; in other words tuning into and feeling and empathising with the emotional state of another person. I don't know if there is a real gender difference, but what I do know for sure is that when either gender experiences it, it is worth listening to.

Gut feel – a knowing without a factual knowing, like knowing that the phone is going to ring and who will be on the other end, the knowing that you will find a car park space and the knowing that something is not quite right with your child.

For women, our focus is rarely car park spaces, and more a focus on empathy, or getting in tune with people. Becoming 'in tune' is something that women focus on in both work and life environments, and with teams or individuals. Have you ever walked into a room and sensed the mood? Have you ever been with someone and sensed his or her exact emotion? Empathy and intuition are good skills to have – not just in a family, but also in a work team – and should be valued more. Women can sense relationships, danger, mood changes and energy – let's be honest ladies, if we can train our menstrual periods to come at the same time as each others', emotions, gut feelings and sense of conflict or support in a team should be a piece of cake!

As part of my Lipstick Leadership Research, 100% of the women interviewed based the potential success or failure to achieve a vision or team success on their ability to sense and address two specific emotions – happiness and conflict. If the team were happy, then they worked well together (her need for collaboration) and more likely to be successful. If there was conflict that could potentially harm the long-term legacy of the team, she honed in on it, dealt with it and resolved the situation. She naturally balanced two sides of the same coin – happiness and conflict – and her antennae constantly scanned for both. One leader said to me, 'I could sense that there was conflict between Phil and the rest of the team. They were frustrated by the mistakes he kept making on the project.' She explained, 'So, I worked alongside him, mentoring him, training him, encouraging him and only when I felt as though he not only knew how to do the job, but was happy and confident to do it, did I walk away.' For women leaders, doing the task is not enough; being happy is an indicator of long-term success too. Just as a mother would in a family, her focus is to ensure the long-term survival of the family. A female leader does the same. In my opinion, we develop invisible antennae that sweep around a room, sensing mood and tuning into where empathy needs to be. By sensing mood we can sense relationship (family) health and potential survival of the family, so she will work alongside her children, mentoring them, showing them and helping them to be happy and confident to do it themselves. She also bolsters relationships in the team and between team members – how many mothers do you know that want their families to get on? Getting on with each other means keeping the family together because conflicts can cause splits and, at a basic level, death of the family. Therefore, I believe that these antennae sense empathy, collaboration and conflicts and know intuitively when and if something is going to go wrong. I remember a recent BBQ party that my husband and I were invited to where I said to him, having scanned the scene, 'Looks like John and Amy have had a row!' He looked at them, looked at me, looked back at them and in the gap between hunting down another sausage and looking for the beer tent, said in a bewildered way, 'How do you know that?' This is not to expose his inability to empathise, but only to show that my focus was relationship and his was hunting sausage! As it turned out, they had rowed, and although they were standing about 300 feet from me, I could still sense John's irritability and Amy's tearfulness.

But gut feel is not spooky stuff! It is scientific! Scientists have discovered that the gut (which is quite a few feet of stuff), contains neurons (of the brain variety) and most of the cells that manage our immune system. I am not a scientist, but common sense tells me that an organ that can

both think and is focused on keeping you healthy at the same time is going to warn you of danger, conflict or any other emotion! Listening to the thoughts of the gut could therefore be about our protection, but is it more than that? Is it linked with time as well and is it linked with a sort of internal guidance system?

A close friend was in London on the day of the 7th July London bombings. She was going to a client to deliver some work and, as usual, decided to use the Underground. Today was particularly busy and, as she stood there on the crowded platform, the preamble warm wind of the oncoming train blew across her face. She felt an overwhelming weight pulling her back, preventing her from getting on the train. Passengers, oblivious to the fact that she was rooted to the spot, pushed past her in their attempt to secure their place on the over-packed Tube train. The train doors closed, and it sped on its way leaving her alone on the platform with a strong urge to get outside, away from the feeling of dread within her. This was not normal for her. She had worked and even lived in London for years and used the Underground every day – and more than once! However, today she had to get out. Once back in the open air, and gulping lots of fresh air, she decided that she would not use any public transport at all and would walk the mile and a half to her client's premises instead. As she reached Hyde Park, sirens of police cars, ambulances and fire engines filled the air with their cacophony of panic. The rest we know. My friend's experience prevented her from being injured or killed on the Underground or indeed on one of the buses that were targeted for this aimless and desperate violence and hatred. Her intuition saved her.

Sleep on it

Before writing this chapter, I began to think about intuition and how I would research and write about it. I was distracted, I couldn't think what to write, I couldn't get into it. As I sat at my computer, I felt sleepy and could easily have nodded off, which can happen to me often! I walked round the garden searching for inspiration, I still felt sleepy and less than creative. I decided to take myself off to have a nap, and literally sleep on it! As I lay down on my bed, I picked up my iPad and began to read the latest version of my Oprah magazine, which I love to indulge in. I couldn't believe it! The main focus for this month's edition was, you've guessed it, intuition. Was my intuitive mind making me sleepy in order to show me this? Was I distracted because the answer was not in front of my nose but by my bedside? Either way, I was no longer sleepy, and the article on The Science of Intuition, by Annie Murphy Paul, Oprah, August 2011, was very insightful. However, in the context of this book, Annie's article provided me with a starting point for my research and how to support you to engage with your own invisible antennae.

Studies have shown that we are better at decision-making and problem-solving if we are not distracted, use our senses of smell, taste and sight and our gut. Intuition works when we are asleep to solve problems and make decisions about situations as well as when we are awake. It works better when asleep because the conscious chattering brain doesn't get in the way.

When I have a problem or challenge, I write my question on a piece of paper before going to bed, I read the words and then I literally sleep on it. Then, in the early hours of the morning, I awake with the answer. Sometimes, especially if it is a big problem or challenge, it can take a couple of days to find the answer, but if it is a small thing, like 'where did I leave my gold earrings?' then an overnight subconscious search is usually all that is needed! Over the last few weeks we have moved house, and as a result, I have misplaced a few things. I needed to send off my driver's licence to have the address updated, but could not find the paper counterfoil that matched the photo licence. I wrote the question 'where is my driver's licence?' on a notepad, read it and went to bed. What woke me the next morning was the flash of insight as to its location. It woke me with a start, and I smiled as I remembered 'ah yes, that's where I put it!'

The subconscious mind is a power-house and I use it all the time for problem-solving, manifesting and personal growth. The conscious mind, the one that you use when awake, is over-used and the unconscious or subconscious under-used and yet more powerful. By tapping into the unconscious mind you can achieve amazing things. You will do this in the

My Pen chapter to help you set goals for your work and life. Suffice it to say that much of your untapped potential lies in this part of who you are.

How will you explore your intuition?

Exercise: Dial In!

Read the following exercise through, and then with your eyes closed to remove distraction, do the exercise in an environment where you can have a few minutes' quiet time.

Imagine that you have invisible antennae that swoop around and can pick up the music, mood and sense of others. On your tummy you have a large tuning button; most of the time it can be tuned to your own emotions and playing your music, but sometimes you need to turn that big dial to tune into someone else's mood. Imagine that the person you are concerned about or that you want to engage with is standing in front of you. Turn the dial on your gut away from you, through the static and tune into them. Watch as the antennae sweep around them, spiralling their body, sensing their emotions. Begin to feel what they feel, sense what they sense. Amplify their emotions within you, feel it in your body where they feel it in theirs. What have you discovered? What are the emotions that you feel?

Then, turn the dial to tune back into you and your emotions, then open your eyes.

You can test this by approaching the person, tuning into them again and then reflecting their emotion or mood. 'John, you appear really hopeful today, is something good happening for you?' Or 'Alice, you seem irritable and confused at the moment, is there anything I can support you with?'

I have used this technique in sales meetings to say, 'I sense that there is one thing that I haven't been able to convey to you, what is that?' Or in a coaching situation, tuning into a client's state is very important to a successful outcome for them. Try it, have fun with it, tune in!

Identity

Imagine you were approached by a famous film director who wanted to make a film of your life; she suggests that the first step is for you to decide which actress you would choose to play the leading role that is you. Who would you choose and why? Take time to seriously consider this question and write your answer in the box below:

The actress that I would choose to play my life story is:

The reason that I have chosen this person is:

Now, imagine that the film is being made, the story of your life up to the present day is scripted and the actress is hired to play the role of you. She wants to play this role as closely and as authentically as she can for you. She has asked if she can interview you but has little time because of the busy schedule and can only ask three questions. She arrives at your home, you welcome her and invite her in. You are both alone, and while you chat for a few moments, you sense that she is keen to ask you the questions and get back to the film set. You ask her to begin, she pulls out a little note pad and pencil from her bag. You are curious about what she will ask, and she notices. 'I want to play this role to the best of my

ability and so it is important for me to gain a sense of who you truly are. Therefore, my first question for you is what are the key qualities about you that you want me to portray in this film of your life?' Write them in the box below:

'The second question is about the end of the film, I want to leave the audience with a clear and unequivocal idea of who you truly are. Therefore, I ask you this: when you are in the final scene of this film, who do you become?' Write the answer in the box below:

Before leaving, she turns to you, and with a curious look on her face, asks, 'If we decide to do a sequel, what would happen in the next part of your life?'

Write the answer in the box below:

The first question opposite is about your values and beliefs. How many of those do you share with your chosen actress? The second question is about your identity – who you truly are –and the final question is about your purpose. What insights have you discovered by doing this exercise?

If you now consider all three of these questions – your qualities, who you truly are and your purpose – please now project yourself to the end of your life. As you look back, and with those qualities, identity and purpose firmly in place, what have you achieved?

The answer to this question is your ultimate vision and goal, and is the input for the final chapter, My Pen.

BAG - My Action Plan

BAG stands for **B**in, **A**dd and **G**et

B	What will I **Bin** that no longer serves my life or goals and prevents me from dancing my best life?	_____ _____
A	What am I already doing, being or having that I could **Add** to or improve in order to dance my best life?	_____ _____
G	What will I **Get** that will serve me well and help me to dance my best life?	_____ _____

12 My Pen

This chapter provides you with the opportunity to explore goal setting and create compelling, exciting and action-focused goals.

Below are my top tips for setting goals, but the most important of all is your ability to 'feel' them; feel them as if you already have them manifested in your life. A thought is a thing but only becomes an intention when you can truly feel what it is like to have, be or do the thing that you are thinking.

Our story ...

Karen bounced out of bed at the crack of dawn, the interview was only hours away and she needed to get into the shower first before the rest of the family drained the last of the hot water from the tank. She stood under the cascading warm torrent as it rinsed away the remains of weariness from her body. She felt invigorated and, as she washed, she mentally rehearsed the day's events in the finest of detail. She saw herself walk into the room, shake hands confidently with the panel of interviewers, she looked smart, and her hair was perfect! Her silk blouse sat comfortably on her body and her suit looked crisp and professional

– she was dressed for the job she wanted. She heard conversations, watched smiles, allowed herself to be articulate and remembered to thank each person in turn before leaving. She saw herself returning confidently to the hospital and, as she walked out in time for home, heard her phone ring in her bag. It was the recruitment agency. 'Hi Karen! Good news, you got the job! They were very impressed!'

Karen rinsed the shampoo from her eyes, the smile rising within her as she imagined the outcome that she so wanted to happen. She could feel it in every cell of her body. As she rubbed herself dry, she still felt the tingling sparkle of excited emotion within her body; it was as if she had showered the inside too! She laughed and slipped on her dressing gown, cleaned her teeth and returned to the bedroom to dress. She felt good today and even though she was slightly anxious, she felt certain, positive and hopeful.

The walk to work would soon get rid of any would-be butterflies and the fresh air would help to clear her mind in time for the lunchtime interview at the RHS. As she walked, she soon became aware that her fully resourceful self was walking alongside. Karen turned to her, noticing that she was dressed exactly the same. In fact, she looked every bit the same as she did. It was with sudden realisation that Karen knew that the two of them had met in the middle of time and that this would be the last time she would see her fully resourceful self. 'Yes, we are one now, Karen, all apart from one final lesson, but as we walk towards that lesson, it is you who will lead.' Karen anticipated her meaning, and as the women strode forward purposefully they were for the final time inside Karen's handbag, making their way past all the items and towards her pen.

'The pen,' Karen announced 'is for me to write down my goals. To make decisions about our future where I can be fully resourceful and be the woman that I am born to be. I now have the environment, the behaviours, the capabilities, the beliefs and the true identity to achieve my purpose in life. Today, I will begin by getting the job of my dreams, *and within five years I will run my own business. The children and James are well and I am able to allow them to be who they are.' Karen continued to recite her goals while her fully resourceful self wrote each one down in turn. When finished, Karen read each one in turn and, as she did, she paused to consider how each made her feel. She felt inspired and energised.*

The two women hugged and, as they did, Karen's head began to spin. Familiar sights moved around her: James, the children, their home, friends. As she slowed, she realised that she was back in the restaurant by the sea. The dance floor was full of people, all dancing to the music. The disco ball above was spinning its fingers of light to capture and dance on the surface of the writhing mass. Karen looked around. Her fully resourceful self was no longer there, but she knew that, in a way, she was within – now and always part of Karen. As she observed the dancing, she recalled the journey to this moment, the learning, the need for balance, the need to be true to self. She felt content, sure, confident, ready to dance to her own music. As she looked down at her handbag, there, lying on top of all of its contents, was the list of goals. Karen slid the piece of paper out and read them once more. They made her feel good inside and the excitement and anticipation of achieving them welled in her stomach. As she slipped them back into her bag and zipped it securely, she drew in a deep breath, knowing that she was about to step back on to the dance floor of life, into a new and fully resourceful self, dancing to her own music.

She was ready to take those steps, to dance her best life.

Goal Setting that Works

Before detailing the process of goal setting that works, allow me to provide you with a Goal Setting Health Warning! Do not be tempted to set SMART goals! A SMART goal is self-limiting; it will keep you firmly entrenched in your comfort zone. Comfort zones are safe and predictable but they are rarely inspiring!

Inspirational goals come from your imagination and your imagination is located in the part of your brain that also houses your ability to dream, be creative, feel emotion and sense futures. It is this part of your brain that we spoke about in the My Perfume chapter, which works when you are asleep to solve problems. A goal is a future state of being, having and doing. If you set SMART goals, then you are setting specific, measurable, achievable, realistic, and timed goals. All of these are left-brain activities and therefore keep you in your comfort zone of known past experience that is achievable and realistic. If you want your future to be limited by your past, then SMART goals are for you, but do remember that no one ever bounced out of bed in the morning for a realistic and achievable goal! However, if you want your future to be different, exciting and inspiring, then the 7-P system detailed below may be more energising as it taps into the creative and imaginative right brain. Once you have set your goals, then SMART will help you to define objectives to achieve your goals. This is because SMART objectives are part of planning but they are certainly not part of visioning!

It has been proven time and again that people who set goals invariably achieve much more than those who just drift through life believing that 'life happens to them' and that they are not in charge of their own experiences. This lesson was taught to me a few years ago by my daughter. At the time, I was feeling particularly stressed, overworked and overwhelmed by a number of events happening in my work and life. This stress was particularly evident to my younger daughter, who at the time was aged seven. With wisdom beyond her years, she sat down with a little piece of parchment paper and a clutch of coloured pencils and wrote me (in rainbow text) a profound and life-changing message that has proved to be the single best piece of coaching that I have ever received. She sealed it in an envelope and handed it to me in a moment of perceived calm. I opened the little envelope expecting a picture and an 'I love you mummy xxx' note, which always melted my heart and resulted in cuddles and guilt-stricken critical voices that pointed out what was 'really important in life'! However, nothing could have prepared me for the message I actually read. The words washed through me like a torrent of water:

It read

'Life is a ship, steer it home.'

I was speechless. In one sentence, my seven-year-old child pointed out that not only had she recognised that I was in a storm, but that I wasn't in control. I was allowing it to throw me wherever it wanted, from one stressful situation to another! Those few words announced that I was both rudderless as well as directionless! They hit me like a tidal wave, splashing me in the face with their wake-up call. I had been afloat on the ocean waves of life not even realising that I was in a metaphorical ship, never mind that I could steer it! I know that I am not alone; many of us drift, believing

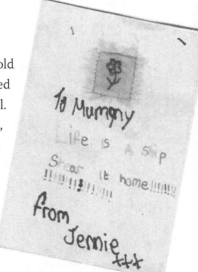

that 'life just happens' and there is nothing we can do about life's ups and downs. Bobbing around, buffeted by the storms of life and drifting aimlessly through the calms, directionless until we encounter another dark cloud on the horizon. My little girl taught me something different: not only was life a ship, but I could steer it! I was the Captain of my own life, I could take it in any direction that I wanted! From that day, I took hold of my wheel; I became Captain of my ship. I planned my direction and I navigated my way towards my own destination. Sometimes I still hit storms, but now they don't stop me from reaching the shores that I want to reach; I knuckle down, weather the storm and come out the other side still pointing the way I want to go. It may have knocked me sideways, but I am still voyaging towards my goal and I am steering my ship home. The calms allow me to refresh and rejuvenate the ship and me, which of course are one. The storms challenge me and create the most learning and I am always more resilient as a result.

I still have the little piece of parchment neatly tucked away for safekeeping and a copy of it pinned up in my office where I see its wise words every day. My goals are clear and the words guide me and keep me on track. One day when I have steered my ship home for the last time and moved into the next life, I intend to have the words etched on my gravestone so that they may inspire others who walk by, like ships that pass in the night.

Below, I have defined my tips for goal setting; use these alongside your Dance floor exercise from Chapter 1 to set your goals.

Dance Your Best Life

Begin by reviewing your Dance floor from Chapter 1 when you mapped the current reality of your work and life; it is now time to map how you would like it to be. For each aspect of your Dance floor, decide where you would like to be able to score it – if this is a 10 for each section that is fine, but you may prefer to score it at a different level. Once you have scored each, the next step is to answer 'What would achieving that score mean/get for me?' For example, if your current score for well-being is a 4, and your goal is to raise it to a score of 9, then ask yourself 'What would a score of 9 on well-being mean/get for me?' You may answer 'At a score of 9 I am a size 12! I am eating more healthily, I have cut sugar and bad fats from my diet, I am exercising more regularly and I have so much vitality.' You now have your goal. From your goal, you can begin to set SMART objectives for achieving your desired outcome, like 'Sign up for Pilates class at local leisure centre by Friday the 15th of May, and attend two classes per week for the next six months'. For each aspect of the Dance floor, score where you would like it to be and what that score would get for you. It is important at this first stage to focus on the 'what' of goal setting and not the 'how' you will achieve it. Remember, 'how' is a left-brained question and can often limit you or put you off even trying, especially as you consider the gap between your current reality and your desired state. 'What will I get?' forces you into a desired state and aspirational future that encourages the right brain to imagine. That is where you need to be!

A Time and a Place!

Think of a place that inspires you or where you feel relaxed – choose this as your setting for creating your goals. If you cannot find an inspiring place, then find a spot in your home or garden where you feel most comfortable. You need not be in the same place every time, the key thing is that you feel comfortable, relaxed and yet inspired.

Set aside some quiet time when you will not be disturbed. I usually set aside a couple of hours for my first sitting but will take a few more hours over the following weeks to finally settle on the specifics of each goal. You may want to play inspiring or relaxing music as you write your goals, but again this is not essential if you prefer peace and quiet.

According to scientists, and mentioned in Chapter 2, the afternoon is better than the morning for goal setting as our right brains are more alert – of course there is always that time during sleep where you can search for inspiration too. Therefore, try not to think of goals, or set goals, in the morning. Your left analytical and critical brain is too logical and may put you off!

The 7-P System

The 7 Ps of Goal Setting are: Positive, Personal, Present, Pleasurable, Proactive, Passionate and Purposeful:

1. *Positive* relates to the language, images, sounds and feelings that you will use to write or depict your goals. What you think about, you bring about! So, focus on what you want, not on what you don't want. For example, focus on wealth, not on debt. 'I am cash rich' is better than 'I am debt free!' If you focus on debt, you may create more debt…

2. *Personal* means that they are related to you directly and are about what you want to have, be or do. You cannot set goals for other people! Be careful what you wish for, be as specific as you can.

3. *Present* means that you write them in the present tense as if they are happening to you NOW. For example, 'I am enjoying the positive recognition that I am receiving now from my best-selling book.'

4. *Pleasurable* relates to the feelings that they invoke inside you as you read them – you've got to really want what they define! If you are not completely inspired by the defined goal, keep asking yourself the 'what' question above until you are inspired by what it will get for you.

5. **Proactive** means that they are taking you TOWARDS what you want to be, do or have and are inspiring action towards your goal. This means that you have a clear and compelling vision of what it will look like and that you have SMART objectives and action plans to achieve it. Even if you do not have clear plans, defining the direction and focusing on your goal will support you to develop clear actions over time.

6. **Passionate** relates to your determination, commitment and tenacity to hold on to your belief that you will achieve your goal. You may encounter setbacks on your journey towards achieving your goal. View these as tests and hurdles that you can work around, jump over or knock down. So many people give up at the sign of a small setback but those that are true winners never give up. They keep on keeping on and if one path doesn't work, they will try another. Many give up just before the goal would have been achieved.

7. **Purposeful** relates to the outcome of the outcome. What will it get for you? What will you become? What will others be doing? It is the future of the future and the result of achieving your goal. To just achieve it, with no sense of purpose as a result, can make achieving your goal feel empty. For example, if you have a goal to achieve a qualification in medicine, then the goal is empty if you do nothing with your new qualification. However, if your purpose is to use your qualification in medical research, then it has purpose. Ask yourself 'What will be the lasting legacy of achieving this goal?' Sometimes it is enough to just get a new job, or a new partner, or a new house, but it is the future beyond getting it that is important; getting something is one thing, keeping it is another. Think also of our exercise as part of the Perfume chapter where you explored your purpose. By thinking of your purpose 'already achieved' what goals would help you to get to that point? Ensuring that your goals serve your ultimate purpose means that you will be living the life you love, and loving the life you live.

Documenting your Goals

Vision Board or List? Either works, and so do many other methods. Depending if you are visual, auditory or kinaesthetic, and if you are right-

or left-brain dominant, you will intuitively know what will work for you. Below is a list of methods that I have come across; decide which inspires your own way of collecting and documenting your goals:

- **Vision Board** – *A large sheet of card, paper or board on which you can stick images, textures and words depicting exactly what you will be, do and have. These images, textures and words can be sourced online or from magazines, photographs, textiles, etc. Excite as many of the senses as possible – you're your vision board: texture, colour, fragrance, sound. Owners of vision boards usually pin the completed work on a wall where they can see it. This visual reminder programmes the subconscious mind through visual stimuli and emotional responses to achieve the goals therein. This method suits the visual and kinaesthetic person as the images, textures, words and colour invoke emotion and visual commitment to the goal.*

  Take the image of your Dance floor and place it right in the centre of a large piece of card, then get creative! Stick as many pictures, textures and colours as you can on the board. On my own board, I also have words that inspire me, like 'success', 'happiness' and 'freedom'. Go back to your values exercise in the My Keys chapter, the words that you identified there will be a good source of inspiration.

- **List** – *This can be a tabled list, a journalistic list, an alphabetic list, a calendar list or any other type of list you can imagine. Below, you will see a typical goal list tool, organised into seven goals for one year, three years and seven years. These could easily be any other time period to suit you as well! This type of goal setting suits the organised, planful and left-brain thinker and the auditory digital thinker who sometimes prefers defined factual lists.*

- **Letter to self** – *This method is often preferred by someone who is auditory or auditory-kinaesthetic, as they enjoy the sound of reading the letter to themselves as if it had come from another and, therefore, this invokes an emotional response and commitment to the goal.*

  To do this, simply write a letter to yourself with today's date at the top, and then simply write describing what it is you have done, received, become. Write it as if you have already achieved your goal and are now documenting how you feel and what you are doing as a result. The letter should include as much imagination and detail as possible. Include what others are saying, doing and feeling as a result of your achievement. Sign it as a commitment to your goal, put it in an envelope, address it to yourself, attach the appropriate postage stamp and then post it. When it arrives through your letterbox, don't be tempted to open it. Put it in a safe place – a drawer or secrets box – and leave it until after the date by which you wanted to achieve your goal.

I did this at the beginning of my coaching qualification course Our Course Director asked each student to write a letter to themselves documenting the outcome that we would achieve for ourselves. I wrote a letter to myself saying that I had been so successful, was top of the class and had completed all of the work set for me in a timely fashion and to a high standard. I had enjoyed the course immensely and my results allowed me to graduate quicker than others had done before. I sealed the letter and gave it to my Course Director, with his promise that he would give it back to me on graduation day. When I opened it, I could not believe the accuracy of the content. I had in fact forgotten all about the letter, so it was even more of a surprise when I read its promise – I had achieved every single thing in the letter!

A friend of mine wrote a letter to herself detailing all about the wonderful man that she had met and fallen in love with. She wrote so much detail, even his hair colour and the job he did! She put the letter in a shoebox in her wardrobe; it wasn't until some time much later when she and her new husband were moving house that she came across the letter that she had written before meeting her partner. 'It was so accurate,' she said 'even down to his height and what hobbies he enjoyed!'

▪ ***A voice recording*** *– Again, the auditory person will enjoy the chance to record their goals. This can be done in story form, a song, a news report, a documentary or just reading your list of goals. If you are going to record your goals, make sure it is your voice, because you will be able to record the passion, intonations and* *emphasis to suit your needs. It is also important to use your own voice as verbal commitment to your subconscious mind – after all, they are your goals, not someone else's. You may wish to use inspiring music in the background or music that will help to reinforce your goals. For example, if your goal were to run a marathon, then having music playing in the background that you associate with running would anchor the commitment to your goal. Alternatively you may wish to choose sounds associated with your achievement, like crowds cheering as you cross the finish line. The key is to be creative with this to invoke your right brain and your emotional commitment to the goal. This method suits the auditory goal setter and of course a visual recording would work well for the visual person.*

It's also about timing and type!

Each night as I go to bed, and each morning as I awake, I give thought to living the life of my dreams – all my goals for work and life achieved. The dreamy state just before you drop off to sleep, and again as you awake from sleep in the morning, is a good time to reinforce your goals. This is because the logical left and conscious brain that often limits our beliefs is not quite awake and therefore more silenced. This allows the subconscious and right brain to play with your goals and begin to explore the detailed outcomes and experiences of achieving them. It is often a time when ideas, insights and solutions to problems come to mind too that will help to project you towards achieving your goals.

The type of goals you set often falls into what you want to 'be', 'do' and 'have'. It doesn't mean that you need to define separate goals for each of these three as they are usually integrated. For example, if you want to HAVE a new car, BE - able to drive it well, and DO - drive to France to take time to enjoy holidays with family and friends.

Overcoming the Demons of Goal Setting

There are some things that will prevent goals being achieved, these are:

- **What you focus on, you get more of!** *Focusing on what you don't want instead of what you do want. For example, being 'debt free' is a focus on debt. How about 'cash rich' instead?*

- **Letting your head rule your heart.** *Using the left brain to set goals instead of the right brain – this is head over heart goal setting and often limits outcome. Remember, start with the heart for 'what' you want and then, later, move to the head for 'how' you will achieve it.*

- **Allowing war to break out between head and heart** *– this is about dilemma between what you truly want and your sense of deserving. Beware that the critical voice may say, 'HOW can someone like you achieve that?' That kind of 'how' question would not be allowed by your future self, she would de-clutter it from your handbag. The only 'how' question that you are allowed is 'How will I START to achieve this goal?' Go back to the Mirror chapter in the book and work on your self-limiting beliefs if they pop up whilst goal setting.*

- **Uninspiring goals** *– your goals are not challenging enough, or too challenging such that you are defeated by them before you get started. When you set a goal, ask yourself, 'Is there something bigger than this that I could achieve?' If there is and it is more inspiring, then go for that. You will know if it inspiring because it feels exciting and scary at the same time!*

- **Procrastinating** *– not getting started because you haven't got everything in place or perfect. Just get going! Remember the old saying 'A journey of a thousand miles begins with the first step'. I have a friend who is a millionaire, lives in a delicious home and has a fantastic business and a great lifestyle. I asked her, 'Faye, when you set goals to achieve something, how do you do it?' 'Simple,' she said, 'I decide what I want, then I just say to myself, 'I am going to do that! Or I am going to be that, or have that.' She never, ever says, 'I would like this' or 'I want that' or 'I need more of…' or 'I wish I were…' Her language is clear. Remember, if the subconscious mind hears that you 'need' something, it will create 'neediness' or 'want' or a head full of wishes! In the Bible, Christ said, 'Ask and it is given' – so be careful what you ask for! My friend Faye is clear; there is no wishing, needing or wanting in her life at all. Listen to the difference between 'I wish I was healthy' and 'I am going to be healthy'. In the second sentence, the affirmation is 'be healthy' and the action is 'going' towards it. Like all journeys, if you are heading in the right direction you are going to get there!*

🐚 **Substituting talk for action** – *many people spend all of their time talking about achieving their goal and they don't spend any time taking action towards it. Of course, this can be for many reasons including the fear of success or failure. Dealing with the fear, and taking risks towards achieving the first step, will help to overcome the lack of any action.*

How would you like it to be?

Now that you have an image of your current reality in front of you, and you have a clearer image of what has created this, the next step is to define how you would like it to be. In a different-coloured pen mark exactly

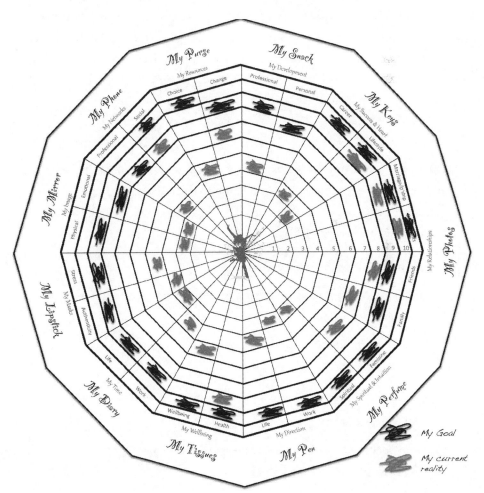

My Goal

My current reality

where you would like it to be. Continue to do this for every category on the whole Dance floor. The diagram below provides an example.

Now it is time to write down what it would be like if it were that score. Around the outside of the Dance floor there is lots of blank space for you to write what you are going to be, do or have for each category, or you can use the table provided as part of the Dance floor exercise that you can download from the member website. For example, if you scored your partnership as a priority area, write down what you would be doing if you were to achieve your goal score. For example, 'My partner and I spend more time together, we have weekends away, we enjoy intimacy and a good laugh together.' Then read it to yourself and think 'if it were truly like this, would it achieve the score I have given it?' If you have nothing else to add, then move on to the next one on your Dance floor. Use the following questions to really focus on each area in turn.

Useful Questions to Ask for Each Area on the Dance floor

Make sure that you don't rush this exercise. Take time alone to really reflect on the questions below in relation to each of the areas above, and make sure that you record your answers accurately. This will help you to define how you would like it to be.

- Which area dance am I focusing on?
- What challenges or problems is this causing in my work and life right now?
- What is the long-term impact of doing nothing about this imbalance?
- Am I investing more time in other areas in order to avoid this area?
- Is this causing the problem?
- What would my life be like if I had balance in this area? (Describe using all the senses.)

🐾 *Am I committed to achieving balance in this area? If so, what will need to change? If not, why not?*

🐾 *What would it look like if it was a 10?*

You will now have an image of all your goals – everything that you want to have, be or do in your life. Your right brain and its ability to communicate with intention will tend to focus on a vital few at any given time. That means that you will, consciously or otherwise, prioritise your goals. It is a true saying 'what you focus on, you will get more of' so if you are focused on a particular goal, then that is most likely to be manifested first. A word of caution: be careful about what you wish for. It is no good to wish for a brand new car if you don't also wish to see yourself enjoying having it for some time. So, when you focus on a goal, you must remember to do it in four stages:

1. **The past** – *What have things been like, what have you not had that you would like?*

2. **The present** – *What is the current situation, what is it like now, today, at this moment?*

3. **The future** – *What will it be like, feel like, look like, sound like etc.? (Use ALL your senses to really feel what it is like to have achieved your goal.)*

4. **The future impact** – *What will the impact or consequences be for you, others around you, the place where you live, the world? Whatever is appropriate. This is an important stage as you are looking at the future of the future. Many people forget this most essential step of goal setting.*

The next step is to reflect on all of the goals that you set on page eight, and document your TOP seven goals. Why seven? Well, seven is a number that we are used to and it appears regularly in our life – seven days in a week, seven chakras/meridians, etc. – but five may work for you, or ten or eight. You can decide.

One option is to consider the Chinese approach of calculating your birth number or Kua number. The Kua number will provide you with an auspicious number based on the year of your birth and, if studied in more detail, you could also find out the most auspicious area of your home to place the image of your goals. To calculate your Kua number, first of all write down your year of birth, e.g. 1971. Add the last two numbers together 7+1= 8. Then, if you are male deduct the number from 10; if you are female, add the number to 5. So, in this case, if you are male then your number is 10 - 8 = 2; however, if you are female, your number is 8 + 5 = 13, which should be reduced to a single number by adding the 1 and 3 to give 4. Always reduce the number to a single digit by adding them together. In this example, the optimum number of goals to focus on for men born in 1971 may be two and for women, four. On the next page, you will see three tables:

1. *Your top goals for this year*

2. *Your top goals for three years*

3. *Your top goals for seven years*

If you wish to take your goals further into the future than this, please copy the sheet. Be sure to write the goal in a way that documents steps 3 and 4 (future and future of future) and also write them as if you already have them. Finally, place it in an area of your home or office where you will see it every day. Some people carry their goals around with them in their organiser or handbag. This is a good idea too, as the right brain and the subconscious mind are being continually reminded of your intention every time you look at the goals. A colleague put the image of his desired home on the dashboard of his car. The image was reflected on to the windscreen and, of course, as he drove he was driving towards his goal for the whole journey.

Be creative with your ideas, but remember there are two key times in the day when you must focus on your goals and they are last thing at night before you sleep and first thing in the morning before you rise. Also, you may wish to set aside at least 15 minutes in the afternoon to focus on your goals. The right brain has a peak between 2:00 p.m. and 4:00 p.m., so take yourself off to a quiet space and focus on your goals; you can even do this on a ten-minute walk!

Year 1	Year 3	Year 7
1		
2		
3		
4		
5		
6		
7		

Thank You!

When you achieve your goals, it is always good to look back at how things used to be. This will help you to celebrate and be grateful for the fantastic changes that you've made. Gratitude is important, so take time to say thank you each day.

You are probably now beginning to have some idea about the dances that you want dance to, and what you need to do in the short term to free up either time or choice to make some immediate and positive changes in your life. Use this final BAG exercise to consider what you need to BIN, ADD and GET for you and your life so that you can achieve your goals and DANCE YOUR BEST LIFE!

Category	Sub-categories	B - Bin What do I need to stop doing/having or need to give up, bin or de-clutter from my life?	A - Add What do I currently have or do that I need to add to, continue doing or improve?	G - Get What do I need to start doing, believing or attracting into my life/work that I don;t have/believe at the moment?
Tissues	Health & Wellbeing			
Diary	Time - Work & Life			
Lipstick	Masks - Stress & Authenticity			
Mirror	Image - Physical & Emotional			
Phone	Networks - Social & Professional			
Purse	Resources - Choice & Change			
Snack	Development - Professional & Personal			
Keys	Success & Heart			
Photos	Relationships - Marriage/Partnerships, dependants, family & friends			
Perfume	Sensing Self - Spiritual & Feminine			
Pen	Goals - Professional & Life			

Additional Resources – Meditations for Goal Setting

This meditation is available on the website in audio format. The objective of this meditation is to harness the power of your subconscious mind to support you to set your goals. In the meditation, you will visit your Dance floor, meet with your future self, go into the handbag that is you, make the changes that you need to and return to the dance floor of life dancing to your own music.

As the tune of this book fades...

Barbara De Angelis was once noted to have said, 'The journey between who you once were and who you are now becoming is where the dance of life really takes place.' Remember always that you can go through this life dancing to the tunes of others and never becoming your fully resourceful self; that is your choice. However, you have a chance with the metaphors and exercises in this book to become the woman that you are meant to be. Promise yourself today that you will never look back on your life with the memories of not being the woman you could have been. Listen to the beat of the music within you and allow it to amplify. De-clutter all those things that make your handbag so heavy that it holds you back, then skip on to that dance floor of life with the belief that you deserve the best, you deserve happiness, you deserve the freedom to be you. Give yourself permission to be woman, and to release the feminine into this out of balance world. Go graciously and assertively, with manners, respect and dignity for self and others. Use your empathetic, nurturing, collaborative and relationship-focused self to make a difference in our world. Take your femaleness into your workplace, into the boardrooms of business and into the factories, shops, and public services that you deliver so that we, as women, begin to redress the balance of target-driven employers to ones that balance performance with engagement. Credit crunches, riots, long-hours cultures and stress-related illnesses are all the result of our world being too masculine in its culture. It is time for balance to occur. Take your female into your family to build and nurture relationships, develop your children, teach them right from wrong, a sense of dignity, manners, integrity, community and the love and respect of others. Take it

into your community to grow networks, build cultures focused on long-term well-being, sharing, and inclusion of all people. Being woman is so necessary at this time if we are to calm the tunes of masculinity that drive our societies and world. There is no peace when there is imbalance, and there is no balance where dominant music is played. Allow your feminine to rise so that we can balance our world – our men need this balance too, our children crave it and your music demands it. It doesn't serve women to be masculine; it serves everyone for all women to be female. Bring balance to the woman you truly are, give up the shackles of trying to be something that you are not. Live as your fully resourceful self and step now on to that dance floor of your life, lay down that new handbag that is you and dance like today is the beginning of who you truly are – a wonderful, fantastic, intelligent, empathetic, spiritual, resourceful, strong woman!

Lynne Copp

August 7th 2011

Summary and Ongoing Resources

As we draw this book to a close, I hope that I have given you some inspiration to dance your best life. Dancing your best life means recognising the dances that you are currently dancing to, identifying the imbalance, looking inside the handbag that is you, becoming aware of which aspect of you requires to be changed or enhanced, setting goals for that, de-cluttering old tunes and stepping back on the dance floor of life, dancing to your new music.

As you do, it is fair to say that the dance of life will take its twists and turns and these are my tips as you begin the dance of your best life:

- *Sometimes the speed of the dance will exhilarate you* – *enjoy the dance and be free, let yourself go and don't hold back.*

- *Sometimes the speed of the dance will trip you* – *when you fall down, decide not to stay down, pick yourself up, dust yourself down, tighten up your dance shoes and go again.*

- *Sometimes the speed of the dance will scare you* – *feel the fear inside, understand its cause, deal with it and, step by step, find the rhythm of truth.*

- *Sometimes the speed of the dance will be wrong for you* – *stop dancing to this tune, find new music.*

- 🎵 **Sometimes you will find it difficult to dance to the tune** – *decide if it is new dance shoes you need or a new way of dancing – never let the constraints of the past hold you back from the opportunities of the future.*

- 🎵 **Sometimes the speed of the dance slows** – *recognise this is time to rest, get your breath back, reflect, be in tune with you.*

- 🎵 **Sometimes the rhythm of the dance changes mid-way** – *embrace sudden changes in your life but always dance in the direction of your ultimate purpose.*

- 🎵 **Sometimes others drown out your tune with their own** – *you will come across those who would have you dance to another tune – be true to yourself, continually listen to the beat of your own drum!*

- 🎵 **Sometimes others will expect you to dance their way.** *Remember, Ginger Rogers once said, 'I do everything Fred Astaire does, only backwards and in high heels!' You have the power to do it your way.*

Sometimes it is tough for people to do this by themselves and they require the guidance and coaching of others to support them in their quest to be a great dancer. If this is the case for you, then Dancing 'round the Handbags® retreats, seminars, workshops and coaching are available for you to attend. The website lists all options and availability. You may also wish to stage an in-company event for your women; if so, details can be found on the website.

In addition, the website contains a number of resources and tools that you may wish to download or purchase to support your development. These include audio meditations and visualisations for each of the chapters as detailed below:

- 🎵 **The Dance floor Meditation** – *visit your dance floor, meet your future self and review the dances that you currently dance to.*

- 🎵 **My Tissues** – *with your future self, delve into the handbag that is you and visit the tissues in order to explore your health and well-being and how you might improve both.*

- 🎵 **My Diary** – *with your future self, delve into the handbag that is you and visit the diary to look at how you manage your time.*

- 🐚 *My Lipstick* – *with your future self, delve into the handbag that is you and visit the lipstick. In this meditation you will explore the masks you wear and your authentic self.*

- 🐚 *My Mirror* – *with your future self, delve into the handbag that is you and visit the mirror. Here you will take a look at your image – both internal and external.*

- 🐚 *My Phone* – *with your future self, delve into the handbag that is you and visit the phone. The phone is about your communication networks, both social and professional. You will discover how to improve both.*

- 🐚 *My Purse* – *with your future self, delve into the handbag that is you and visit the purse, which explores choice and change and how you deal with both.*

- 🐚 *My Snack* – *with your future self, delve into the handbag that is you and visit the snack. In this meditation you will discover your strengths, your development plan and the skills and capabilities you need for the future.*

- 🐚 *My Keys* – *with your future self, delve into the handbag that is you and visit the keys, which are symbols of the keys to your heart and the keys to your success. You will discover your needs in terms of the home, and your values and beliefs.*

- 🐚 *My Photos* – *with your future self, delve into the handbag that is you and visit the photos. Here you will reflect on your relationships and how they impact your balance and link to your sense of security.*

- 🐚 *My Perfume* – *with your future self, delve into the handbag that is you and visit the perfume. The perfume is your identity, your purpose and your sense of femaleness through spirituality and sense of community.*

- 🐚 *My Pen* – *with your future self, delve into the handbag that is you and visit the pen. This meditation is different from the rest as it not only delves into the handbag but also ends on the dance floor. In this final meditation of the book series, you will explore your goals and the vision for your life*

Lynne also writes a monthly blog that you can subscribe to at:

http://dancingroundthehandbags.wordpress.com/

Lynne Copp's 'Dancing Round the Handbags' book is a fantastic resource for women. It is packed full of amazing tools, exercises and wisdom that will help women all over the world to reach their potential as well as create balance between their work and life. I have known Lynne for many years and I know her passion for creating worklife balance, in our workplaces and communities. She cares deeply about helping people to create this balance, and also become the best they can as a result. This book is a gift of her generosity, expertise and insights, and if fully engaged in its metaphor, every reader will be compelled to make changes that will positively impact her life and the lives of others. Therefore I highly recommend that every woman who wants to change their life forever, read it, engage in its metaphors and make their life dance!

Jack Black, *Author and self Help Guru at Mindstore...*
www.mindstore.com

Forthcoming Publications:

The Rising of Yin
 – *A business parable that balances of masculine and feminine*

My Brand, My Career, My Way!
 – *A Lipstick Leadership Guide to Success*

Life is a Ship!
 – Worklife Balance, and individual's guide on how to achieve it

About the Author

Lynne is Managing Director of The Worklife Company, an organisation that she formed 14 years ago after leaving a senior role in HP, where she was Head of Marketing Communication. She is a leader with extensive experience in business coaching, organisational development, communication and culture change across a wide range of organisations and industries. She is passionate about achieving business success by releasing potential of people through effective leadership, communication, culture and inclusion.

Lynne is an internationally recognised expert in communication and diversity; an inspiring speaker and coach who not only creates motivation for change, but delivers solutions relevant to today's business, people and customer environments. She has worked with companies like Ernst & Young, Google, Microsoft, Hewlett Packard, IBM, Birmingham City Council, the Police and the Armed Forces.

She has appeared on the BBC Money programme, BBC Radio and is retained by many organisations as a regular speaker at international business events. Lynne's public speaking topics include: The Future of

Work, Worklife Balance & Wellbeing, career development for women and Women in Leadership.

Lynne has designed and run a number of Leadership development programmes including High Impact Communication and TimeOut.

Lynne is retained as an executive coach for a number of companies, and is an active member of The Association of Coaching, the International Coaching Federation, Association of NLP, The ILM and a Chartered Fellow of the CIPD. She has just completed her masters in Coaching and her Master Practioner in Neuro Linguistic Programming (NLP).

Lynne also writes for many publications and has recently published her own book 'I'm Glad I spent More Time at Work' and in October will launch 'Dancing Round the Handbags®', and next year plans to write a new leadership book for the 21st century Leaders.

www.theworklifecompany.com

lynne.copp@theworklifecompany.com

Brit Writers' Award Winner for non-fiction, 2011